Accidental Brothers

In March 2017 the four brothers (from left to right), Jorge, William, Carlos, and Wilber, gathered to celebrate Carlos's graduation. He received a certificate that declared him to be an *especialista en ciencias tributarias* (specialist in tax sciences).

Credit: Diana Carolina

Preface

―――――

Love and Luck

Call me a twin tracker—my boyfriend does. As a researcher I cannot resist hunting down nearly all the new and interesting twin and sibling cases I encounter. The latest result is *Accidental Brothers*, a moment-by-moment replay of a twin-tracking adventure like no other I have had. To call it a scientific thriller is neither bold nor boastful. I did not create the events described here; I only studied them.

I have been lucky to have a career I love. As a professor of psychology I have worked on dozens of exciting research projects involving twins, triplets, unrelated look-alikes, and other curious pairings. People in the United States and around the world send me all sorts of interesting stories involving multiples, and I appreciate their kindness. I answer every query I receive: Should twins be separated in school? Do genes influence sexual preference? Are twins *clones*? Are clones *twins*?[1] Then, every once in a while, a truly exceptional twin-related situation emerges from the long list of emails, so I dig deeper.

Just days after their birth, two sets of Colombian twins became unwitting subjects in an accidental study, twenty-five years in the future, because an identical twin baby from one pair was accidentally switched with an identical twin baby from another pair. The switch, probably the result of a momentary oversight, presumably by an overtaxed or inattentive nurse, created two reared-apart identical twin pairs *and* two unrelated sibling pairs who grew up believing they were fraternal twins. I saw their story as a rare opportunity to learn how the drastically different environments in which the separated twins were raised—big city versus remote township; university attendance versus fifth-grade education; father absence versus father presence—affected their abilities, outlooks, interests, and love lives. Aerial views of Bogotá and Vereda El Recreo (where the country-raised twins grew up) contrast high-density urban living and closely spaced neighborhoods with vast remote stretches of rural Colombia's green and brown earth.[2] *Vereda* means "path or sidewalk," an ironic name because Vereda El Recreo has none.

Both my colleagues who acknowledge twin study findings of genetic influence on behavior, and critics who question these findings, have been clamoring for such an extreme case of reared-apart twins, and the Bogotá brothers gave us not just one but two.[3] They also gave us a chance to see how alike two pairs of unrelated same-age siblings—what I call "virtual twins"—turned out to be. The effects of genetic and environmental influences on behavior have long been a matter of debate. The special legacy of the twins in Colombia is how four young men readjusted their lives—two after trading places—and what their experience means for our understanding of human behavior and personal development.

Accidental **Brothers**

———

The Story of
Twins Exchanged at Birth
and the Power of
Nature and Nurture

———

Nancy L. Segal
Yesika S. Montoya

St. Martin's Press  New York

ACCIDENTAL BROTHERS. Copyright © 2018 by Nancy L. Segal and Yesika S. Montoya. All rights reserved. Printed in the United States of America. For information, address St. Martin's Press, 175 Fifth Avenue, New York, NY 10010.

www.stmartins.com

Map of twins' birthplaces by Kelly Donovan

Design by Meryl Sussman Levavi

The Library of Congress Cataloging-in-Publication Data is available upon request.

ISBN 978-1-250-10190-7 (hardcover)
ISBN 978-1-250-10191-4 (ebook)

Our books may be purchased in bulk for promotional, educational, or business use. Please contact your local bookseller or the Macmillan Corporate and Premium Sales Department at 1-800-221-7945, extension 5442, or by email at MacmillanSpecialMarkets@macmillan.com.

First Edition: April 2018

1   3   5   7   9   10   8   6   4   2

In Memory of Irving I. Gottesman,
for insights and inspiration
—NLS

To My Family and Friends,
for your love and unconditional support
—YSM

There are really two kinds of life. There is . . . the one people believe you are living, and there is the other. It is this other which causes the trouble, this other we long to see.

J. Salter, *Light Years*

Contents

Conception of a Career

My career in twin research began in the preemie nursery of Boston Lying-In Hospital, when I exited my mother's womb six weeks ahead of schedule and seven minutes ahead of my fraternal twin sister, Anne. At three pounds, eleven ounces, I spent my first month alone in an incubator, where wires and monitors were my only distractions, while Anne, who weighed in at four pounds, seven ounces, was healthy enough to go home after a few days. No one would call us reared-apart twins, but after working with the Bogotá brothers and seven other switched-at-birth twin pairs, I think about our four-week separation more seriously now. I am grateful that I went home with the right parents and was raised with the right twin sister.

Twin research became my passion as an undergraduate student at Boston University. In my senior year I completed a psychology course project comparing the consequences of placing young twins in the same or separate classrooms when they first enter school. This was a topic to which I could relate personally—a story in itself—and I enjoyed researching it and writing it more than any other paper I had written. The following year I explored other aspects of twin studies for my master's thesis at the University of Chicago. My thesis adviser applauded my work but believed that my interests would change in time. However, they have only deepened: my doctoral dissertation was about twins' cooperation and competition, and I have undertaken many twin-related papers and projects since.[4]

I am drawn to unusual cases, especially those involving twins reared apart. I like peering into the alternative universes that these separated twins naturally create. Each genetically identical twin is a fresh take on what might have been—a rare glimpse of an alternate self experiencing life in a whole new way. When separated twins finally meet, they can see themselves packaged differently, keenly aware of what could have been had their families, neighborhoods, schools, and other life experiences been reversed. Brent Tremblay, an identical twin, grew up in Ottawa, Canada, not far from his genetic duplicate, George Holmes. Brent's adoptive mother maintained a beautiful *"House and Garden* style home," and while she loved her son deeply, she despaired at the constant messiness of his bedroom. She also denied his wish to have the puppy he craved. But when Brent and George finally met in their early twenties, following the unraveling of a case of confused identity, Brent found he was more comfortable in the more casual and relaxed home of George's family.[5] It turned out that Brent had been switched early on with an unrelated male baby who had taken his place as George's accidental fraternal twin brother. It made sense that Brent found comfort in George's home atmosphere, created by the couple who had given birth to him, too. Parents pass on genes as well as environments to their children—Brent was not raised in his biological parents' home, but his genetically based temperament was similar to theirs and to his twin's.

I have studied more than one hundred of the 137 separated twin sets who visited the University of Minnesota during my nine-year association with the Minnesota Study of Twins Reared Apart (MISTRA). Working on this groundbreaking and controversial project, which lasted from 1979 to 1999, was a dream job for a new investigator. The focus of the study was how differences in the separated twins' life histories were associated with current differences in their behavioral and medical characteristics.[6] The director of the project was Dr. Thomas J. Bouchard, Jr., a professor of psychology.

I interviewed identical female twins who were lively, fashionable, and adored animals, and identical male triplets who were outgoing, overbearing, and terrified of needles. And I also met fraternal twin men, one gay and one straight; fraternal twin women whose brittle hair refused to grow; and opposite-sex twins who seemed romantically attracted to one another. However, finding that behavioral similarities were greater among the identical than fraternal twins was not surprising because identical (monozygotic) twins share 100 percent of their genes, whereas fraternal (dizygotic) twins share 50 percent of their genes, on average.[7] All humans share some genes, such as those for developing a heart or growing bigger physically. But some genes differ from person to person, such as those affecting cardiac health and body size, and this is where fraternal twins can differ. For example, many different genes, each with a tiny effect, influence most complex human traits, such as height, and it would be unusual for fraternal twins to inherit the exact same gene combinations—it is estimated that fraternal twins' genetic commonality ranges from 37 to 62 percent for height.[8] And in 2017 researchers linked fifty-two different genes to general intelligence, with each making just a small contribution.[9] Thus it makes sense that fraternal twins are much less alike in their abilities, interests, and talents than identical twins.

Working closely with separated twins reunited as adults has allowed me to witness the similarities and dissimilarities tied to the identical and fraternal twins' degrees of genetic relatedness. This work also put me in a strong position from which to challenge twin research critics who insisted that identical twins are alike because of their similar treatment by others, not their similar genes, or felt that the data collection methods used in twin research are somehow flawed.[10]

I left Minnesota in 1991 for California State University, Fullerton, but I did not leave reared-apart twins far behind. In the years that followed I tracked the developmental progress of young Chinese twins separated as an indirect result of their nation's one-child policy. The Chinese government established the policy in

1979 in response to the need for population control; the policy limited urban families to one child and rural families to two.[11] This restriction on family size, coupled with China's preference for male children to continue the family lineage and contribute to family income, led to the abandonment of hundreds of thousands of baby girls, twins among them. Separating twins led to their adoption by families all over the world. I also studied adult twins raised in different countries because of unusual and extraordinary circumstances, such as family poverty in South Korea, emigration restrictions in Communist China, child tax exemption in Romania, and baby theft in Soviet Armenia.[12] The similarities that these separated identical twins display in intelligence, temperament, and even in how often they attend religious services are impressive. Even more compelling is the finding that the personalities of identical twins raised apart are more alike than those of fraternal twins raised together. This finding is difficult to explain without acknowledging the difference in their proportions of shared genes. However, identical twins are not perfect copies of one another, leaving plenty of room for environmental influences.[13]

In many ways the real identical twins in Colombia—Jorge and William, and Carlos and Wilber—aligned according to their genes. But while their similarities were striking, the parallel lines broke down in places, crisscrossing like streets on a Google road map. Tracing the origin and progress of these diverging paths was the challenge I shared with my collaborator, Yesika Montoya, who first told me about these twins in an email she sent to me in October 2014.

Beginnings: The Bogotá Twins

Yesika (pronounced Jessica) Montoya is an associate director of advising at Columbia University's School of Social Work in New York City. Born in Bogotá, Yesika came to the United States in

2001 to study English at Wheeling Jesuit University in Wheeling, West Virginia, before earning a master's degree in social work at New York's Fordham University in 2005. She is in her thirties and has long dark hair, a beautiful smile, and a penchant for earrings that dangle deliriously on each side of her head. I did not know Yesika until she reached out to me—she had read my 2011 book about an extraordinary case of accidentally switched identical twins in Gran Canaria, one of Spain's Canary Islands.[14] Yesika believed I would be interested in the Colombian pairs. Her own family history and childhood friendships included both fraternal and identical sets, which explains her fascination with twins and how scientists study them to address nature-nurture questions.

The idea of going to Bogotá to meet and study the twins began to germinate on Sunday evening, October 26, 2014. Yesika was in her Queens, New York, apartment, half listening to the program *Séptimo Día* (Seventh Day) on Caracol TV, Colombia's private national television network, on the Internet. At the end of the usual traffic and political news, a clip about two switched-at-birth twin pairs caught her attention. At first Yesika didn't believe what she was hearing—"a soap opera," she thought—but when she realized that what she had heard was not fiction, she found the link to the two-hour television program "Crossed Lives," and watched it from start to finish. It was riveting—as a social worker Yesika understood the research value and clinical significance of this unusual case.

On Thursday morning, October 30, I was alone in my office on the campus of California State University, Fullerton. This was unusual because panic about midsemester grades typically drives students to ask for my assistance or plead for more time to complete assignments. My office is like a small outpost of Amazon.com, with books stacked floor to ceiling, cabinets pushed into every conceivable corner, folders perched precariously on cabinets, pictures taped to all four walls, and a tiny thirty-five-year-old yellow refrigerator that works like new. I have accomplished some of my best work in this cluttered but comforting space, and it's where I wrote most of this book. In fact, photographers who film my Twin Studies Center invariably prefer this space to my well-appointed adjoining office and library. Yesika's message, which included the link to "Crossed Lives," interrupted the quiet productivity I was enjoying that day, but replaced it with thrill and energy. That first day we exchanged six emails with breathtaking speed. I finally announced that we should go to Colombia to meet the twins and she agreed. To paraphrase the famous line from the 1942 film *Casablanca*, it was the beginning of a beautiful working relationship.

Between our first-day emails, I Googled "Colombian twins" and "switched at birth 2014," but nothing came up. I was relieved that this news had not gone viral because I wanted to reach the twins before other researchers did. Abandoning my computer search, I hunted the halls of the foreign-language department for a Spanish-speaking faculty member who could translate the TV report. Finally, I peered into the office of a young Brazilian professor, Dr. André Zampaulo, who is fluent in both Spanish and Portuguese, introduced myself, and persuaded him to come to my office to watch the program. André was mesmerized by the story, but he had to leave after thirty minutes to teach a class. So I headed to the student lounge, where I convinced a Spanish-speaking undergraduate woman to translate the rest of the show.

An hour later, reeling from what I had learned about the discovery and its aftermath, I had the complete backstory except for three things: no one knew exactly how, where, or when the switch had occurred. Those details would have to wait. First, we had to be certain that the twins would be willing to undergo the weeklong series of interviews, inventories, and tests that I was starting to list in my head. Yesika was heading to Bogotá for the December holidays so we decided that she would approach the twins then. I was anxious, excited, and impatient, but the wait would give us time to reflect on what this incredible natural experiment could add to our understanding of personal development, family relationships, and sense of self—and what happens when these fundamental parts of our lives are severely threatened.

The Main Characters

William and Wilber's Family—La Paz

WILLIAM
Identical twin of Jorge and accidental brother of Wilber; born in Bogotá, raised in La Paz

WILBER
Identical twin of Carlos and accidental brother of William; born in Vélez, raised in La Paz

ANA DELINA
Biological mother of identical twins Carlos and Wilber; raised William and Wilber as fraternal twins

CARMELO
Biological father of identical twins Carlos and Wilber; raised William and Wilber as fraternal twins

ALCIRA
Older biological sister of Carlos and Wilber; accidental sister of William

EFRAIN
Older biological brother of Carlos and Wilber; accidental brother of William

ANCELMO (CHELMO)
Older biological brother of Carlos and Wilber; accidental brother of William

EDGAR
Older biological brother of Carlos and Wilber; accidental brother of William

Jorge and Carlos's Family—Bogotá

JORGE
Identical twin of William, accidental brother of Carlos; born and raised in Bogotá

CARLOS
Identical twin of Wilber, accidental brother of Jorge; born in Vélez, raised in Bogotá

LUZ MARINA
Biological mother of identical twins Jorge and William; raised Jorge and Carlos as fraternal twins

DIANA
Older biological sister of Jorge and William; accidental sister of Carlos

Other Main Characters

EDELMIRA
Biological aunt of Wilber and Carlos; accidental aunt of William; brought William instead of Carlos from Bogotá to La Paz

LAURA
Jorge's friend and coworker who mistook William for Jorge in the butcher shop in July 2013

YANETH
Laura's friend who witnessed Laura's mistaking of William for Jorge at the butcher shop

Landmarks and Landscapes

Map of Colombia showing the city and town where each pair of brothers grew up.
Illustration by Kelly Donovan. Photographs by N. L. Segal.

Accidental **Brothers**

Tales of Two Mothers

On December 22, 1988, forty-five-year-old Ana Delina Velasco Castillo hiked for three to four hours down a rugged muddy path from her home in the tiny district of Landázuri to the small municipality of La Paz in Colombia, South America. She was twenty-eight weeks pregnant with twins and in excruciating pain from a hernia. She found walking nearly impossible. As Ana passed by, men with machetes were clearing the path, which was narrow and treacherous. She hadn't wanted her husband, Carmelo, a farmer, to go with her because he didn't want to go—Carmelo was in the habit of getting other people to do things for him, leaving him free to do whatever he wanted. This left Ana's eldest son, Ancelmo ("Chelmo"), to walk alongside her on this part of the journey and hold her steady while Carmelo searched for drivers to take his wife from La Paz to the Hospital Regional de Vélez once they reached traversable roads. The entire trip would take eight hours.

A quick look at Ana suggests she could never survive the physical ordeal she was facing. She is about five feet tall and petite, with a dark straight ponytail that swings carelessly down her back, giving her a childlike appearance. Like many farmers' wives, she had aged beyond her years; her hard work at home and in the field had added lines and creases to her thin face and hands. But Ana had a toughness and determination, reflected in the strong line of her mouth and jaw and in the authoritative way she handled people and situations. She vowed to get through this latest ordeal successfully. Perhaps the thought of two new children—twins— after the death of an adult son years before tightened her resolve, although she didn't fully believe the alternative medicine doctor who had said she was carrying twins.

Carmelo was tall at nearly six feet and lean and tan from working hard outdoors. They had met as neighbors when she was sixteen and he was twenty, then married and started a family after he completed his military service. Carmelo lived in casual shirts, blue denim or khaki-colored jeans, a broad-rimmed hat, and high rubber boots to protect against the mud. Like his wife, his lined face and hands made him look older than he was. He seemed to always need a shave to smooth out his beard, as well as a dentist to replace several missing teeth. No doubt he also suffered bitterly from the death of their older child.

Ana's contractions had already started, so she was feeling desperate to reach the hospital in Vélez. The possibility that she was experiencing false labor—the kind in which contractions are irregular and spread out, rather than real labor in which contractions are regular and close together—did not cross her mind.[1] Still, something was going terribly wrong with this pregnancy, her seventh. Ana had delivered one girl and five boys. Most of her children had been born at home, as was customary for the women of her tiny district, because the hospital was far away and usually unnecessary for giving birth. But this time Ana had no choice because she had become increasingly ill since her fifth month. Even scarier was the real possibility that she was carrying twins, a high-risk pregnancy under any circumstances—too little womb space for two babies, as well as high maternal blood pressure, especially in women older than forty, can imperil such pregnancies. And twins are four times more likely to die from the hazards of delivery than nontwins.[2]

Ana's home, a simple wooden structure without electricity or running water, was about seventy miles from the modern hospital in Bucaramanga, the capital city of Santander, the Colombian department, or state, that includes La Paz.[3] She had successfully delivered five of her six older children at home, but its extreme isolation, lack of modern conveniences, and inaccessibility to urgent medical care made it no place for a difficult pregnancy and delivery. Her only option was to deliver her babies at the local hospital in Vélez, and the only way to make it through the first part of the journey to La Paz was on foot—people in her remote area were used to hiking long distances because there were no roads. From La Paz, Ana would need to get to Vélez, a long four-wheel drive across uneven terrain, rocky streams, and muddy corridors. She began her journey at six o'clock in the morning and arrived at the hospital at two in the afternoon.

Ana had only a vague idea that she was about to deliver identical twin sons, William and Wilber, her seventh and eighth children. That night, weak and exhausted from a caesarean section delivery, she caught only the slightest glimpse of her two premature babies, who were quickly taken from her for physical evaluation. The baby she named William was fragile, unable to digest or eliminate normally. He required more intensive treatment than the simple hospital in Vélez could offer.

"Do you have family in Bucaramanga?" her doctor wanted to know. He reasoned that relatives could bring the infant to the better-equipped medical facility there, stay with him, and return him to his parents when he recovered. But Ana had no relatives in Bucaramanga. "What about Bogotá, much farther away?" Yes, her younger sister Edelmira lived there. So the next day Ana's mother, seventy-six-year-old Eva Castillo, who lived in La Paz, made the 120-mile, six-hour journey to the Hospital Materno Infantil with baby William, riding a bus all the way on via Vélez Chipata. Subjecting a fragile, sickly newborn to potential infection from other riders and the uncertainties of public transportation was risky, but ambulances and medical vans were unavailable at such short notice.

The baby was wrapped in blankets, which made it hard to see his face. After bringing him to the hospital, where Aunt Edelmira was waiting, Eva returned to La Paz. The plan was for Edelmira to bring William home to Ana and Carmelo a week later by ambulance. For his return trip the baby was again completely concealed by blankets wrapped tightly around him. Tubes stuck out from everywhere. You couldn't see his face.

* * *

On December 21, 1988, two days before Ana Delina's baby William arrived in Bogotá, another mother, thirty-six-year-old Luz Marina Castro Chavez, gave birth to identical twin sons, Jorge and Carlos, at the city's Hospital Materno Infantil. Luz was forced to use this public facility because she had lost her health insurance. Four years earlier she had had health insurance as a seamstress employed by the Manhattan Company and she had delivered her older daughter, Diana Carolina, in one of Bogotá's preferred public clinics, the Clinica San Pedro Claver. But that job had ended when the company closed, and her children's father, Norman Enrique Bernal Triviño—who was still married to someone else—was rarely around and hardly supportive.

Luz was a slim beauty. A photo taken when she was twenty-four for her official identity card shows shoulder-length brown hair, dark eyebrows, and a flawless complexion. In her later years Luz cut her wavy hair short and put on several pounds, but retained her natural attractiveness. She was a hard worker, willing to do whatever it took to keep her growing family healthy and safe. Abandonment by her partner did not demoralize her—instead, Luz resolved to make the best of things as life progressed—but in photos taken in those years she never appears to be fully smiling. Several of her sisters lived with her and helped her raise her two sons and daughter, and some donated money for the boys' schooling. Luz had great respect for education and would encourage her children to achieve all that they could. She ruled with a velvet glove minus the steel fist, an approach that would cause her kids to laugh, not to cry.

Luz's babies were born somewhat early, at thirty-five weeks, which is about the average length of a twin pregnancy.[4] However, the twin baby she named Carlos was anemic and needed medicine and extra care. Luz saw her babies just briefly after they were delivered because they were immediately transported to incubators in the nursery. She remained in the hospital for five days to recover from her caesarean section delivery. Most twins delivered by planned C-section have better outcomes than those delivered by intended vaginal delivery; this was known in 1988, when the Colombian twins were born, and remains true today.[5]

Conditions in the nursery were chaotic. Luz's sons were two of the approximately ten to fifteen babies delivered at the hospital each day by the same physician and several physicians worked there. After they were born, a staff member attached adhesive tape with handwritten identifying information to the infant's wrist.

Premature babies like Jorge and Carlos (those born before thirty-seven weeks) were sometimes placed together on a large table.[6] Luz's older sister Maria Teresa recalls seeing one of the newborn twins with a small identification band wrapped around his tiny wrist. "Babies can rip these bands off by themselves," the nurse told Maria Teresa. And according to Maria Teresa, because the babies were born just days before the Christmas holidays, "the nurses were probably drunk—*seriously!*"

Of course, by the time Luz was well enough to spend extended time with her babies, someone had already mistakenly switched the twin she had named Carlos with Ana Delina's infant twin named William. Luz had no way of knowing this, nor did anybody else. Like all new mothers, Luz accepted the babies brought to her by the hospital staff and never thought that something was amiss. Why would she? Why would any new mother question whether the infants handed to her were hers? Even when babies do not resemble their biological parents, mothers find ways to justify their newborns' appearance, usually attributing any differences to their partner's side of the family—"dark-skinned like his grandfather" or "light-skinned like his uncle." That mothers generally attribute infants' unusual looks to paternal relatives is probably no accident. Because of women's hidden ovulation, internal fertilization, and continuous sexual receptivity, a man can never be certain that a child delivered by his partner is truly his. Evolutionary reasoning suggests that her attribution of differences to the father may actually help reassure a man that he is truly the father, but whether newborns actually resemble their fathers more than their mothers and the significance of father-child resemblance for childcare and investment are widely debated.[7]

Both Luz and Ana grew increasingly aware of their sons' lack of physical similarity to each other as they grew up. And the lack of resemblance of one boy to the rest of their family also became more evident. However, each mother decided that the whimsical ways of gene transmission, mostly on the father's side, were responsible. They had no idea that the minute Carlos arrived in Bogotá, a series of events had transpired to keep him there and send William to live in La Paz in his place. The twins' lives and the lives of their families had taken a drastic detour.

Jorge and his brother Carlos (who was really Ana's child) came home four days after their birth to a five-room house in Bogotá's working-class neighborhood of Quiroga. The twins were breast-fed one at a time by their mother while their aunt Blanca Cecilia held the other one.

Doctors had advised Luz to engage her twins in kangaroo care, the practice of daily skin-to-skin contact between mothers and newborns, especially preemies, to promote body warmth and psychological well-being.[8] The physicians Edgar Rey Sanabria and Héctor Martínez developed kangaroo care in Colombia in 1979. Luz used this method with Jorge while a cousin, Patricia, did the same for Carlos. Their division of labor suggests that Luz spent more time feeding, bathing, and playing with Jorge than Carlos; if so, this seems odd at first because Carlos was the sickly baby and needed more attention. However, mothers of extremely low birth-weight twins often favor their healthier infant.[9] Explanations include more favorable perceptions of the healthier twin and less positive feedback when mothers direct their attention to the less healthy twin. Of course, these differences are relative, may shift with family circumstances, and do not imply neglect or abuse of the less healthy twin. However, twin babies *are* more likely to be abused or maltreated than nontwins because of financial pressure and/or lack of support in some families. When only one twin is abused, it tends to be the less attractive or less healthy one.[10]

Jorge may also have looked and sounded more familiar to Luz.

As an infant Jorge looked a lot like his older sister, Diana, when she was born—even his ears stood away from his head at the same angle. And the cries of babies as young as two to five days old mimic the melodic patterns of their mothers' native tongues, sounds they heard while in the womb.[11] Both Luz and Ana spoke Spanish, but Luz's educated, soft-spoken speech contrasted sharply with Ana's fast country dialect. Perhaps Luz was unknowingly drawn to Jorge's more familiar baby noises.

* * *

Neither Ana Delina nor Luz Marina ever suspected that one of the twins they were raising was someone else's child. That is much less surprising than it seems. Questioning whether a baby is truly hers is *not* part of the human female psyche. During the course of human history women typically gave birth at home, attended by several relatives or friends, so they had no need for such concern. Today most babies in the United States are born in hospitals where room for error clearly exists, yet few women worry—an evolutionary legacy.[12] Ana Delina delivered all her older children at home except for Edgar, the child closest in age to the twins. Delivering Edgar in a hospital was a better plan at that time because Ana's mother was away and no one was available to assist in her delivery.

Human lives intertwine and intermingle in unexpected ways. We cross paths with hundreds of strangers, often on a daily basis, but only a fraction of these people become our friends. No one could have imagined that, twenty-five years later, two pairs of accidental brothers living 150 miles apart—William and Wilber in a tiny isolated rural community, and Jorge and Carlos in a lively metropolitan capital city—would learn that they were mismatched identical twins, not fraternal twins at all.

Accidental Brothers

Who we are and how we got that way partly reflect the social influences in our cultures and communities. But we are not blank slates upon which family, society, and other external influences leave a predictable or indelible mark—this outmoded thinking, which dominated American psychology from the 1920s through the 1970s, has been replaced with a more reasoned, balanced view, thanks to genetics-based research on behavior and disease. Except for identical twins, everyone has a unique set of about nineteen thousand genes, which interact with environmental events to shape our abilities, temperaments, and tastes.[13] Reunited identical twins are the privileged few who can see how their genes perform in places they have never been and with people they have never known. The rest of us can only imagine how things would have turned out had we lived in a different neighborhood, gone to a different school, or married a different person.

This book describes the exciting days that followed my learning about the Colombian twins, tempered by the knowledge that many lives were in disarray. I also experienced the thrill of starting a collaboration with a new colleague in Colombia, a place I had never been. I had seen and listened to the twins on TV and wanted to know more about them: Did they play sports and listen to rock music? Did they have romantic partners or were they unattached? What truly defined each of them? Most important, what were the switched twins, William and Carlos, doing and thinking when they learned that the lives they were living belonged to someone else? Also, the mysteries surrounding the exchange of the two babies were deepening, a perplexing and frightening, yet unanticipated prospect for all expectant parents. And central to this story is what my colleagues and I learned about the similarities and differences in the real twins' abilities, personalities, habits, and mind-sets during our memorable days in Bogotá and one extraordinary day in La Paz. Events from this first visit were captured in a *New York Times Magazine* article published several months later.[14]

Accidental Brothers tells the story of four young men—Jorge, Carlos, William, and Wilber—who found out that almost nothing about their lives was as it was supposed to be. We explored the lives they lived, the lives they lost, and the lives they gained, helping them and our colleagues make sense of the twins' similarities, their differences, their identities, and their futures. We followed their transition from fraternal to identical, from city to country, and from anonymity to celebrity. Their resilience impressed us as they became four brothers, not just two, which they did with grace and good humor.

The days in Bogotá brought surprises, expanding my thoughts about behavioral origins and outcomes. Because of these twins I grew wiser in many ways. My time spent with the accidental four was precious because of the insights I gained, not just from testing but from the comments, looks, and gestures the twins casually expressed while we snacked in local food shops, rode around Bogotá in taxis, or relaxed in my hotel lobby. More than twins, they were young men who were mulling over career plans, relationship issues, and other personal goals when their nightmarish circumstances began to unfold. I marveled more than ever at the parade of unexpected events that takes us from place to place. These visions are at the heart of *Accidental Brothers*.

Chapter 1

A Dubious Double

Brothers from La Paz

Some twins seem to belong together, but others don't. Abby and Becky Moore are fraternal twins, but you would never know it to look at them. Abby's long blonde hair and bangs border her round face and forehead, while Becky's short red hair accentuates her thin face and freckles. At age seven Abby towered nearly five inches over her sister and was eighteen pounds heavier. When the twins attended a birthday party, a friend's mother, who did not realize they were fraternal twins, actually introduced them to one another. But Becky looks *a lot* like her older brother, Adam.

No one would think that the Spooner-Durrant sisters are twins, but Lauren and Hayleigh are a fraternal pair. Lauren has the complexion of their fair-skinned mother, Alison, while Hayleigh resembles their dark-skinned dad. The twins' physical divergence is striking, but perhaps not surprising since many different genes working in concert significantly affect skin color.[1] Each twin apparently acquired different sets of those genes from each parent. In an unusual quirk of fate several years later, Alison delivered her second set of fraternal female twins, Leah and Miya, who show the same contrasting appearance as their older sisters. Bystanders seeing the family walk through a shopping mall or enjoying a Sunday brunch might easily assume that the different children were either adopted or brought together by their parents' second marriage, but they would be wrong: the children in both pairs are ordinary fraternal twins, conceived naturally like any other pair.

William and Wilber, and Jorge and Carlos, became unwitting members of an extremely rare group of "presumed twins." Such twins may, or may not, show the skin color contrasts of biracial twins like Hayleigh and Lauren, and Leah and Miya, but they hardly look related. In fact, these presumed twins are accidental brothers and sisters, brought together by a random act of fate—the inadvertent switching of two babies in a hospital nursery. But people *believed* that William and Wilber were fraternal twins—after all, their mother had a multiple pregnancy and two babies came home. People often tease presumed twins and their families because it is hard to imagine how the same couple could produce two such different children. However, most people know that fraternal twins inherit different genes from their parents, sharing an average of 50 percent of their biological relatedness, just like full siblings—and this bit of knowledge helps them reconcile the differences they see. Still, the extremely divergent looks and behaviors of these twins become a constant topic of conversation, more so as they grow older. That is because genetic influence on individual differences, known as heritability, becomes more important over time, emphasizing the twins' differences even more. This happens because as adults we move away from our families and gain greater control over our environment, so our choices are better reflections of our genetic predispositions. Genetic effects are amplified as we age.[2]

A great example of this phenomenon is religiosity (that is, religious interests and activities). Studies of religiosity using high school juniors living at home found that the similarity of identical and fraternal pairs was about the same. However, when studies used twins who were eighteen and older, genetic effects showed up—the identical pairs, whether reared apart or together, were more alike than the fraternal pairs.[3] Reared-apart identical twins Sharon and Debbie were raised in different faiths, Catholicism and Judaism, respectively. Both twins are heavily involved in religious activities today, although Sharon now identifies as an Evangelical Christian. Most important, both believe they would have fully embraced the other's faith had their adoptive families been reversed. Interestingly, neither of the adoptive siblings raised with them has shown the same high level of religious involvement.[4]

I also got to know reared-apart identical twin firefighters, Mark Newman and Jerry Levey, who grew up in different New Jersey cities about sixty miles apart. The two were occasionally confused with one another—Jerry's relatives were miffed when "Jerry" walked past them on the street without so much as a nod in their direction, and Mark's father was falsely informed that "Mark" had been playing hooky from school one afternoon. The twins finally met when they were thirty-one, after a friend of Mark's spotted Jerry at a volunteer firefighters' convention—he knew it wasn't Mark, but it was someone who looked a lot like him. At that time the twins differed in weight by about eighty pounds, but Mark's fellow firefighters could still see their friend in Jerry's slimmer version.

They had a lovefest at first as these big burly brothers slid effortlessly into a twin culture all their own. Both were six feet, four inches tall, with balding heads, bushy moustaches, wire-rimmed eyeglasses, and prominent noses. Both drank only Budweiser beer and in huge quantities, even positioning their little finger beneath the can for support in exactly the same manner. They craved Chinese takeout, ordered their steaks raw to rare, and showed zero tolerance for inept servers. Sadly, their bond weakened over the years after Jerry married and Mark moved to the Southwest. But they did have differences—Mark listened to rock 'n' roll, while Jerry liked country and western; Mark cheered on the Dallas Cowboys, while Jerry rooted for the Washington Redskins—however, both acknowledged that they liked each other's preferences. Both twins were raised in the Jewish faith and held their separate bar mitzvahs on nearly the same day; while neither twin is religious, both consider themselves Jewish.

Sports participation works exactly the same way as religiosity. Adolescent identical and fraternal twins from the Netherlands did not differ in how often they took part in physical activities. But adult identical twins were much more alike than their fraternal twin counterparts, evidence of genetic effects. Thus we can better understand why both reared-apart identical twins Lucky and Dianne rode and raised horses, Tom and Steve became bodybuilders, and Margaret and Caroline were great walkers—whereas Roger and Tony's preferred sport was eating. And during Olympic years we hear about identical twin competitors, such as the American skiers Phil and Steve Mahre (1984), Slovakian canoers and kayakers Peter and Pavol Hochschorner (2004), and Chinese synchronized swimmers Wenwen and Tingting Jiang (2008).[5]

Fraternal twins compete together less often, largely because of their different physical abilities and motivations. Notable exceptions are the US fraternal twin gymnasts Morgan and Paul Hamm—Paul won the overall gold medal at the 2004 Olympic Games, while each won a silver medal in the team competition. Another extraordinary exception is Dominique Moceanu, an elite Olympic gymnast and a member of the US Women's Gymnastics Team, the "Magnificent Seven," at the 1996 Atlanta Games. Although she is not a twin, she learned she had a similarly talented younger biological sister who had been adopted away at birth.

Amazingly, her sister, Jen, who was born without legs, became a champion tumbler and performer and had idolized Dominique long before she learned they were sisters.[6] As full siblings the two share the same genetic relationship as fraternal twins.

Twin research and reports such as these made it important to compare the religious leanings and sports interests of the four Colombian brothers. Would the real identical brothers be a greater match than the accidental brothers? As they transitioned from childhood to adolescence to adulthood, their differences were becoming increasingly obvious to everyone around them. Still, no one imagined that the two rather different children they knew, apparently born to a mother who had delivered twins, were biologically unrelated because one twin was accidentally exchanged with another twin in the nursery.

William and Wilber—Lads of La Paz

William and Wilber grew up in La Paz, in the north central part of Colombia, about 150 miles from the nation's capital city of Bogotá. La Paz is largely a farming region in the department, or state, of Santander. William and Wilber spent the first five years of their lives in the tiny area of Landázuri until their family moved to the equally tiny area of Vereda El Recreo.

People had marveled at the physical and temperamental differences between the two ever since they were born. William, slight and dark-complexioned, looks like no one in his family, although some people thought he resembled his paternal grandmother, Germina. In contrast Wilber, robust and light-skinned, looks a lot like his parents and some of his siblings. The brothers' temperaments are also at odds—William is warm and mild mannered, whereas Wilber is reserved and hot tempered. Tendencies toward explosive behavior are characteristic of Santandereans, who also speak at amazingly fast clips, making them hard for others to understand. William, however, speaks in a slower, more measured way than Wilber, even though they grew up together. This is not surprising because genes do partly shape our speech and language patterns.[7] I have seen (and actually heard) ample evidence of identical twins' matching speech. The "Jim twins"—Jim Lewis and Jim Springer—who were raised in different Ohio towns spoke in the same low, hurried, and hard-to-understand way when I studied them in Minnesota or listened to their interviews on TV. The religious twins Sharon and Debbie spoke quickly but clearly, and the voices and speech patterns of the famous firefighter twins were indistinguishable unless I was standing in front of them so I could see who was talking.

As of 2005, when William and Wilber were about seventeen and would have left for military service, La Paz counted a population of 773, although the greater area now counts about three thousand residents.[8] The population of La Paz is actually misleading. The brothers grew up in a farmhouse that stands alone amid the plants and wildlife—festivals and other goings-on are hours away and happen only occasionally. La Paz has several bars and pool halls to choose from, but nothing much changes from week to week— websites that list musical and cultural events in Bogotá do not exist for La Paz.

La Paz now has about one hundred small businesses, such as fruit and vegetable stands, shops for repairing farm equipment, and the bars and pool halls where teenagers like to hang out. The few restaurants, cafes, and markets are often family run and offer the same food, drink, and candy choices. People often lounge on benches at the entrances to these places—older women in long dresses with beautiful gold earrings and young men in high rubber boots and broad-rimmed hats. The bathrooms in these eating establishments are typically tiny, dark, and without toilet paper. Plumbing is uncertain—when we stopped for a bathroom break at perhaps the only shop open late on a Sunday night, the clerk sternly cautioned that we could urinate, nothing else.

To reach these businesses from the brothers' childhood home requires hiking several hours each way, riding a horse, or combining a one-hour walk with a one-hour ride in a four-wheel-drive vehicle. (Roads are finally under construction today, although many people still do not have cars and transportation.) Walking means navigating uneven terrain and either wading through muddy streams or risking a terrifying walk across an aging rope bridge. From an early age children walk these long distances to and from school—the trip to William and Wilber's simple, one-story schoolhouse required a one-hour hike each way. Getting there meant putting on high boots and negotiating long stretches of rough landscape. Paths are poorly defined, and anyone unfamiliar with the area can quickly get lost. Facilities at the school were sparse—a sports field looked more like an abandoned lot than a place to play. The school day lasted from 8:00 a.m. until 2:00 p.m., and when children returned home in the late afternoon they were expected to help tend crops, care for farm animals, and chop and carry wood.

Homes in the twins' tiny childhood district of Vereda El Recreo lack modern conveniences, such as running water, flush toilets, toilet paper, and electric lights. The twins' home did not even have an outhouse—instead, the bathroom was in the great outdoors, and bushes afforded (and still do) whatever privacy one can find. Their home from ages five to eighteen was an open, three-sided wooden structure with three rooms, or living areas, and a sort of patio out front, set within nine hectares (twenty-two acres) of land. The walls and floors show signs of age, and what looks like red paint on a crumbling wooden stove is actually blood from the cows and other animals that are slaughtered and prepared for meals. Missing planks let in rain, wind, and sun, so the family has little protection from the weather. William said the house was more rudimentary than others in the area, but Wilber (the native son) considered it about average. Thieves could gain easy access to these properties, but no one remembers any such crimes in a place where everyone knows their neighbors. However, guerillas, the terrorist rebels who fought the Colombian militia from 1964 until 2016, had no trouble demanding crops and supplies when they passed through La Paz and surroundings areas. The paramilitary, the peoples' defense against the guerillas, also came through some years later and would take cows or charge taxes for owning cows—the more cows, the higher the taxes.

Each family's relative isolation may partly explain the close relationships that developed among the siblings. William and Wilber have four older siblings. Ancelmo, called "Chelmo" for short, is Wilber and William's second-oldest brother. He is forty or forty-one and was born on March 30, but he is unsure of the year. Lack of attention to time is typical of residents in the Colombian countryside, especially among those with limited literacy. Like other individuals her age, Ana Delina, the mother of this brood, can barely read and write—she completed only the second grade. Their father, Carmelo, who attended school for less than a year and was just "fooling around" while he was there, can do neither. Ana claims to have been married on All Saints' Day, which falls on November 1, but that is debatable—her daughter, Alcira, claims that her parents were married on December 28. Regardless, Ana and Carmelo do not celebrate wedding anniversaries.

All the La Paz siblings left school between the ages of eight and eleven to work on the family farm, although all can read and write. But even William and Wilber have trouble listing the ages of their family members, and their responses often conflict. William says that Ana is seventy-eight, while Wilber says she is seventy—it turned out that Wilber is correct, because Ana was forty-five when she had her twins. And Alcira claims to be two years younger than she really is.

Birth dates are printed on drivers' licenses (*licencias de conduccion*, or *pases*), but the family never had any real need for a car because the area lacked roads. Of course, date of birth, as well as name, photograph, thumbprint, blood type, security holograms, and ID number are printed on Colombian government-issued identity cards *(cédulas)* that citizens must carry at all times. However, La Paz residents rarely use the card in their secluded town where everyone knows everyone else. No one has credit cards and crops often take the place of cash.

Set of Six: Three Brothers, One Sister, and So-Called Twins

Chelmo is Wilber's older biological brother and William's accidental one. Chelmo is lean and tan from laboring on the farm that he loves, growing cocoa and corn and raising cows. His short dark hair and imposing moustache are his most distinctive outward features. He wears the uniform of the town—a nondescript button-down shirt, faded blue jeans, brown belt, and brown work shoes. Chelmo looks older than forty (or forty-one), perhaps because of his hard work, constant sun exposure, and infrequent medical visits. He now lives in the house he grew up in along with his partner and children, including a nineteen-year-old son, Stevenson, and sixteen-year-old identical twin boys, Brian and Wilmer—the aging Ana and Carmelo no longer live there, having moved to a location that is closer to shops, but a three-hour walk from the house where they raised their family. Like all the brothers in the La Paz family, Chelmo is an avid football (fútbol) fan and supporter of the team Atlético Nacional. (Football in Colombia and other

Latin American countries is the same as soccer in the United States and some other western nations.) Like most rural inhabitants, he speaks quickly, sounding like an answering machine on fast-forward—people from Bogotá (*rolos*), who speak more slowly, have a hard time understanding him and other people from non-urban areas. The rolos inhabit a city rich with cultural and educational offerings that some have called the "Athens of South America."[9] Rolos are conscious of speech, dress, manners, family names, and other social conventions that define their urban life. On the rare occasions that they go to the city, Chelmo and his siblings feel like outsiders.

Chelmo doesn't smile often, but he becomes emotional when discussing anything to do with William. Chelmo broke down in tears when he and his family gathered for the first time with Carlos, Wilber's biological twin. They assured this newest addition to the family that they would never forsake him. William said he did not feel part of this scene, having learned that his biological parents had died several years earlier, so he would never meet them. But perhaps he had spent some precious time with his mother, Luz, in kangaroo care before entering the hospital's nursery. I hoped so because those moments with his mother would have been his last.

That both Ana and her son Chelmo had identical twins may not be coincidental. Researchers once thought that identical twinning was a random event, happening with equal chance across all families—after all, identical twins occur in only three or four of every one thousand births worldwide. But in the 1990s researchers found evidence that identical twinning may be a genetic trait in some families.[10] In fact, large multigeneration families teeming with identical twins have been located in parts of India, Iran, and Jordan. And in August 2017 I met identical Brazilian twins Marjorie and Mayara, who have twenty-four mostly identical female pairs across five family generations, probably the largest number reported in a single family. These twins and their family members come from Rio Grande do Sul, a region of southern Brazil known for its high rate of twinning, which appears to be genetically influenced. Being an older father also seems to increase the chances of twinning, but Chelmo was not an older father when his twins were born.[11]

Not all the La Paz siblings are married or have partners, so whether they will become parents of multiples remains to be seen. Edgar is closest in age to the twins—he was seven when they were born—and is now single and living with his parents in their new home. In both Colombian cities and countrysides, it is not unusual for family members to live together, even as children become adults, because of the financial and emotional benefits such arrangements offer. Nonetheless, Ana is concerned that most of her children are unmarried and childless.

Edgar turned thirty-four on February 18, but his year of birth escapes him too. Given the La Paz family members' relationship with time, it seems incongruous that they always carry their cell phones, even in the field, although reception is spotty. Edgar shares his siblings' joy in working on the farm, calling it "artwork in the country." He, too, is lean and tan. He favors the same casual clothing that Chelmo wears. And like his brother, Edgar is not much of a smiler. He seemed uncomfortably quiet unless answering a question posed directly to him, and when he met me in Bogotá for an interview he appeared ill at ease as we ate lunch at a local cafe or took pictures. His reserve may have been largely the result of feeling out of place in a noisy city surrounded by lots of people, traffic, and commotion. However, Edgar seemed more relaxed when his sister, Alcira, finally showed up. Ana and Carmelo's only daughter is more open and outgoing, and smiles somewhat more than her brothers.

The day we saw the twins' only sister, she was harried after a long trip in the middle of a strike by truck drivers that had made traveling to Bogotá from her home in Vélez treacherous. The traffic was heavy, even stalled in places, public transportation was operating only sporadically, and fires could be seen on the side of the roads. She also worried about getting home that night to tend to the small market that she owns and operates with her daughter. Alcira loves her work. She also prefers living in a small city to life in an isolated farm area, given the greater opportunities for employment. In fact, she had worked as a nanny in Bogotá when she was younger.

Alcira says she is fifty-four, but she is really fifty-six and the widowed mother of three. Dark-haired and light-skinned, Alcira inherited her father's prominent jaw and her mother's slim build. Like many Colombian women, she wears her lovely long dark hair pulled back tightly from her face, but the long dangling earrings favored by virtually all Colombian women are missing—eyeglasses are her only ornament. Alcira favors simple but attractive attire—black jacket, black slacks, black shoes, and a light-colored button-down shirt. She politely lets her wishes be known—she wanted lunch as soon as she arrived at the hotel and informed us that her time with us was limited.

Carmelo did not favor giving his only daughter an education; consequently, Alcira received less schooling than her other siblings, advancing only as far as the second grade, whereas most of her other siblings completed the fifth grade. She attended school between the ages of twelve and fourteen, later than the others, because her parents wouldn't let her take the hour's walk across the hills, streams, and mud alone when she was younger—so until that time she worked in the field, harvesting cocoa.

Farm life makes schooling less structured in rural Colombia than in the cities. A student's failure to show up, or a decision to drop out early, would not cause school officials to investigate, as in the United States, Canada, or Europe. In contrast to Alcira, the accidental twins William and Wilber started school at age seven, because they walked with their teacher, Domidti, who lived relatively close by. But the family could not afford to keep William in school—until 2012 school in Colombia was free only for the first five years.[12] This was a huge disappointment to William, who loved doing homework and did well at school. He was, of course, unaware that his true identical twin, Jorge, was a fairly serious student back in Bogotá and he would eventually attend college—living a life that they should have shared. Wilber, however, was not academically inclined and had to be nagged to complete his assignments. He was uninterested in going to school beyond the fifth grade, content to work on the family farm, then get a job on someone else's farm, and eventually join the military.

Wilber's attitude fit with Ana and Carmelo's view that the lessons children learn at home are more important than what they learn at school. But William thought much differently and set his sights far beyond the few years of education that La Paz could offer. The family sometimes wondered about the source of his motivations and dreams—they certainly did not arise from any encouragement at home. Ana would have allowed him to go to school, but the family simply had no money for this purpose.

Book Learning

The La Paz school was a one-room structure attended by children who hiked several miles each way to get there. Class size was about thirty-seven and might mix children of the same or different ages. Students frequently had the same teacher for more than one grade. The school had no kitchen or cafeteria, so William and Wilber carried their lunch from home, wrapped in a plantain leaf. Few students continued past the fifth grade because of money issues, work responsibilities, and family values (like Ana and Carmelo, some parents believed that going to school was not as important as working hard). As expected, both brothers left school when they were eleven to work full time on their family's farm. Many young boys eventually went to work on other properties to earn some money because working at home did not provide wages. Wilber worked on several nearby farms, but bouts of homesickness kept William close to home. Farm work did not come naturally to this sensitive, inquisitive boy who longed to go to school. Still, years of tending crops, lifting heavy equipment, and walking two hours each day to and from school added muscle and strength to his slight frame.

It was a hard life for both boys, but especially for William, who could not get the education he craved. This remains the greatest disappointment of his life, as it would be for anyone whose life circumstances prevent formal learning. But his regret is compounded many times over by the knowledge that a momentary oversight—an unfortunate mistake in the preemie nursery—cost him the education that would have been his. Nevertheless, William loved his La Paz family and accepted the fact that they could not afford to send him to school. His family did not have enough cash to even buy clothes—instead, they purchased cloth in town and paid a neighbor to make most of their clothing. Of course, they had to buy some things, such as overalls for heavy farm labor and high rubber boots for traversing the muddy hills. Costly shoes, dresses, and slacks were not necessities.

William and Wilber's brother Efrain is about four years older than Chelmo. Efrain is also a farmer and the father of two daughters, a one-year-old and an eleven-year-old; both live apart from him and have different mothers. Efrain is twenty years older than William and Wilber, so he was rarely at home after they were born, but he is close to them nonetheless. And Ana and Carmelo had two other older sons whose deaths left a lingering sadness in the family. Luis Angel died of an accidental self-inflicted gunshot wound when he was eighteen, and Israel died in the military when he was twenty-two. Some people in La Paz suspect Luis Angel's death was a suicide, although analysis and reconstruction of events on that day make suicide unlikely. Israel stayed in the military largely because his mother had encouraged him to do so, which compounded her grief with guilt and regret. The heartbreaking loss of two sons, especially given the public nature of Luis's accident, has made coping with their deaths extremely trying for Ana and Carmelo. William and Wilber are generally unaffected by these family tragedies because they never knew these brothers—the twins were only about four when Israel died and had not been born when Luis Angel passed away. But they visit their gravesites on occasion, wondering what these siblings might have been like. Surprisingly, neither twin mentioned how their siblings' deaths affected how their parents treated them. Perhaps Ana's special attention to William—sleeping with him until his early teenage years and allowing him to stay on the farm instead of taking a job with another farmer—was her way of making sure she wouldn't lose another son. Most family members attributed the relationship of Ana and William to his sensitive and caring nature, but there may have been more to it.

Brothers at Odds

Throughout their lives William and Wilber have looked and acted nothing alike. Their extreme differences have elicited the surprise and confusion, as well as teasing and taunting, to which twins who are markedly different become accustomed. Their dislike of each other's work attitudes, household habits, and relationships with girlfriends are at the center of their constant twin-on-twin combat. But despite their perpetual animosity, William and Wilber share a fierce family loyalty as brothers, a bond that was heightened, albeit briefly, during their dangerous stints in the military in 2008. They were in the same unit of ninety-two men and often at risk from guerilla attacks and the dangers of hidden landmines. As the soldier directing communications, William marched in position four, while Wilber stood fifteen or twenty places behind him. During these difficult times they stayed closely attuned to each other's safety and well-being because of the mortal threats they faced. Wilber often caught up to his brother so they could march together. Once, on a nighttime march in the jungle south of Bolívar, Colombia, William heard Wilber whisper in his ear, "Be careful—may God watch over you." William recalled: "You could see in Wilber's face the love he had for me, but then he forgot about it." Upon returning to civilian life they reverted instantly to their habitual bickering and badgering of one another.

Loyal feelings between accidental siblings, despite their clash of ideas and judgments, are not unusual. I also saw this in Gran Canaria, Spain, in 2010, in the case of the presumed fraternal twins Begoña and Beatriz. On an ordinary afternoon in December 2001 Begoña, a slim, dark-haired twenty-eight-year-old with a taste for fashion, entered the Las Arenas Shopping Mall in Las Palmas, the capital city of Gran Canaria. She wandered into Stradivarius, a popular clothing store chain for teenagers and young adults, and looked around for a while before purchasing a T-shirt. Suddenly, she was approached by a shop assistant who called her by the wrong name (Delia) and seemed puzzled when Begoña didn't recognize her. That night the shop assistant phoned her friend, Delia's mother, to complain that Delia had been rude to her and to find out why. But Delia hadn't been to the mall that afternoon.

Several days passed. Begoña returned to the store to exchange the T-shirt for a larger size, only this time Beatriz, her presumed fraternal twin, was with her. The shop assistant spotted them in the fitting room and wanted to know why "Delia" hadn't spoke to her the other day. Beatriz answered that her sister's name was *Begoña*, not Delia, and that she, Beatriz, was Begoña's twin sister. The assistant somewhat jokingly replied that Begoña had a real twin sister somewhere else. In fact, the resemblance of Begoña and Delia was so striking that the assistant arranged to have them meet later that day. She also observed that Beatriz looked a lot like one of Delia's younger sisters. Beatriz didn't know it at the time, but she and Delia had been switched at birth, so it made sense that Beatriz would resemble members of Delia's family, to whom she was really related.

The meeting took place in a coffee shop at the top of the Las Arenas Mall. Within minutes it was clear that Begoña and Delia were the real twins, because their similarities were so striking— hands, hair, nails, eating habits, and mannerisms. In fact, when Delia got her first glimpse of Begoña, she was shocked to see that they walked the same way, a gait that Delia describes as weird. The only major difference was that Delia had been diagnosed with leukemia when she was sixteen. Everyone grew increasingly uncomfortable as the truth became inescapable: Beatriz and Delia had been accidentally exchanged when all three were babies in the crowded preemie nursery of the Hospital Nuestra Señora el Pino (Our Lady of the Pine). Beatriz belonged to another family, which explained why she looked so different from her supposed twin, Begoña, and her other siblings. Delia also belonged to a different family, explaining why she looked like neither of her two sisters or anyone else in the family. Begoña was the only sister of the three who grew up where she belonged.

All three lives were about to change beyond recognition. Everyone knew it. Their personal and cultural identities were about to be shattered.[13]

One's identity includes one's goals, values, and beliefs in religious ideology, political leanings, family relationships, and friendship styles. The three young women experienced different, but drastic changes in how they viewed themselves and how others might see them. Suddenly, two were no longer twins and two had acquired a genetic duplicate. And two found themselves with a new set of parents and several new siblings. Cultural identity focuses on cultural values and practices and on how a person thinks about the group to which she or he belongs.[14] The switched sisters had been raised in rather different environments—Beatriz in a lively city with lots of opportunities and Delia in the quiet countryside with few. Who each one was and where she belonged suddenly were called into question. Their parents also suffered, knowing they had raised someone else's child.

Before everyone could fully accept what appeared to be true, DNA tests would have to confirm the genetic relatedness of Begoña and Delia, and the lack of relatedness of Begoña and Beatriz. Not surprisingly, Begoña and Delia proved to be genetically identical, whereas Beatriz was unrelated to both. All three finally understood why they had so little in common with their sibling's interests and aspirations, and why their discussions rarely ended in agreement. But the two who had grown up as fraternal twin sisters were highly protective of one another.[15] Begoña, the more extroverted and confident sister, protected and nurtured Beatriz, who suffered severely from learning that they were not really sisters—Beatriz also worried that their mother would reject her in favor of her real daughter, Delia. But Begoña made certain that their sisterly relationship did not change.

Studies show that the greater loyalty and allegiance we show toward close kin, relative to distant kin or nonkin, are most clearly revealed when something compromises their physical safety or threatens their life. People are more likely to assist close relatives in both ordinary situations (for example, when buying some items at a store) and life-or-death settings (such as saving a relative from a burning building), but the effect is especially strong when the life of a loved one is on the line. Researchers have offered different interpretations of this behavior that are not mutually exclusive. Developmental psychologists would attribute altruistic acts to immediate, everyday events and experiences, such as learned family kindness and devotion. Evolutionary researchers would additionally explain altruistic behavior with reference to such factors as promoting human functioning and survival. They would invoke the concept of inclusive fitness, the idea that because we share higher proportions of our genes with our parents, sisters, and brothers than with our nieces, nephews, and cousins, we are predisposed to benefit close family members whose survival gets our own genes into future generations. Of course, no one does genetic arithmetic in their heads when they act altruistically; they only behave as if they do. We tend to help people we have identified as close relatives, especially when we feel emotionally close to them. Helping close relatives, even at some cost to ourselves, brings us pleasure and happiness, feelings that most likely increase the probability of selfless acts.[16]

Two flights above Carnes Finas de Colombia (Fine Meats of Colombia), the butcher shop in Bogotá where William worked until recently and where Wilber still works, is the small apartment that they still share. The hometown friend who hired them owns the butcher shop and the building. Leaving La Paz, where employment opportunities were few, opened up new opportunities for the brothers who were then in their early twenties. Leadership is a hallmark of William's character, but he is mostly a clever, resourceful, and persistent mastermind. Moving to Bogotá also allowed William to enter a program for obtaining a high school equivalency diploma, the only one of his La Paz siblings to do so. He did this while working full time at the butcher shop, finishing the study program in November 2010, just before his twenty-second birthday.

Neither brother could know that accepting their friend's job offer began a strange series of events that would lead to the most life-changing event of their young lives. One can also ask: What if the brothers had turned down the offer? They would never have known the consequences of that choice because everyone's lives would have continued as before.

The brothers call their workplace a shop, but it is really a counter at the rear of La Gran Manzana (The Big Apple), a medium-size supermarket in the middle of a residential street packed with small businesses. To find it, you have to know the butcher shop is there because the big red apple over the bright green awning at the entrance overshadows the smaller picture of a cow that tells passersby that fresh meat is sold inside. The area behind the counter looks like a torture chamber with its collection of strange-looking metal machines for cutting up meat and bones. Sharp knives and electric blades are everywhere, intimidating to onlookers but handled expertly by the brothers clad in white aprons and surgical gloves. Dark blood stains are visible across the white-tiled walls and the floor.

The two would be unlikely business partners if they were not related, but working together and living together works for them. Like many people, they find it more comfortable to share their trade and home with a familiar, trusted sibling than a stranger or even a friend who is less well tested. This is true even when siblings' work practices and lifestyles clash, and this is especially the case for William and Wilber. William's relative lack of organization at home infuriates Wilber, who complains that William is always taking his things. Their cousin Brian, who worked in the shop part time while going to school, rolls his eyes when he describes the brother-brother conflicts that unfold on a continuous basis. Brian "often wondered how he could stand them—they fought every day for seven months." What William and Wilber see as their usual relationship seems fiercely contentious and quite unpleasant to many people around them. They argue about everything, but that is because there is a side of William that only Wilber sees.

William's childhood warmth and sensitivities became William's civic-mindedness as an adult. When he learned that the office of the governor of Santander was donating its old computers to schools, William stepped in and took them to schoolhouses throughout La Paz. In October 2015 he stood for election to the La Paz city council, but lost by six votes. Reflecting on this loss, he believes he was too laid-back during his campaign, confident that the support he received would be enough but it wasn't. Still, William will run for mayor one day to serve the people of his town. "What makes a politician is the will to work and the desire to help the people where you feel a sense of belonging," he told me. Until early 2016 he was working twelve-hour days, seven days a week, as manager of the Bogotá butcher shop in order to support his mother and the rest of his family. He was also saving money to buy an apartment—and then his unfulfilled dream of getting an education became a realistic goal.

He was convinced that a law degree would better position him as a candidate and public servant in the future. Finding the right law school wasn't easy, but with a high school equivalency certificate and some assistance he checked out various law schools and enrolled at Bogotá's Uniciencia in fall 2016. He was able to afford the tuition because he received financial assistance from La Paz's current mayor. None of this would have happened if William had not met his identical twin brother, Jorge, who inspired and supported him like no one else—and as a college student gave William a glimpse of the professional man he could become. William loves his legal studies and might not have found the right school if he and Carlos, Wilber's biological twin, had not formed their own relationship; in fact, Carlos accompanied William as he visited law schools. William's devotion and friendliness to the people of La Paz will never change, as demonstrated by his assisting the mayor in a project for building roads allowing easier access to the remote regions of his former home. He spoke excitedly about the tree-cutting and laying of pavement that have already taken place.

As the manager of the butcher shop, William made more money than Wilber, so William paid for Wilber's food and rent—Wilber was his employee and moonlighted at other butcher shops around town. Now, since his brother's enrollment in law school, Wilber is the new manager and has also become William's benefactor. Still, the brothers continue to clash over how to run the shop. William believes that serving customers and developing good relationships with them come first, but Wilber insists that maintaining equipment and cleaning up are higher priorities. Of course, these responsibilities are related, but each brother has different preferences. Now that Wilber is in charge, he runs things his way, but William voices lots of opposing opinions.

In fact, their people skills at work and at play are diametrically opposed. William is customer oriented, Wilber is task oriented; William is messy, Wilber is neat. William dates a few women seriously, reflecting his characteristically kind and caring nature. He is sensitive to the feelings and needs of others, and while he enjoys attention from young women, he does not exploit that attention to personal advantage. Wilber dates more women less seriously, and he is passionate about all things female. He is more playful and flirty and, like his true identical brother, Carlos, is not above telling little white lies to hide his tracks if he doesn't want to see a woman on a particular night. Had William and Wilber not ended up as accidental brothers, it is unlikely that they would ever have become friends. Yet, even as he complains, Wilber insists that he and William get along fine.

At twenty-six William has retained his sweet, sensitive nature. His small, slim build belies the sturdiness and strength he acquired from heavy farm labor during his childhood and adolescence. His short, dark hair scatters across his head in all directions, although several stray locks look carefully positioned over his forehead. His dark eyes, slightly bumpy nose, and even teeth are less distinctive than his ears, which angle sharply away from his head. His impish grin gives him an endearing, boyish quality, tempered by a goatee that adds a bit of maturity to his otherwise youngish face. William usually prefers to dress in casual shirts, shapeless sweatshirts, and pants. He remains a formidable opponent in arm-wrestling matches, bringing many able arms crashing to the surface in seconds. But when he was in school, he avoided the fights that sometimes erupted between classmates because he didn't think such combat was right.

Wilber is taller than William and has a more solid, athletic build. Like his real twin, Wilber looks like he should be stronger than his accidental brother, but he isn't—and he is less driven than

William, which may partly explain their difference in strength. The two also part ways when it comes to hair and clothing. Wilber is appearance conscious—he piles his dark hair fashionably high on his head and has always liked stylish clothes, including tapered shirts, tailored jeans, and leather jackets with lots of zippers. He regularly goes for manicures and eyebrow waxing, indulgences he sees as important and necessary. All this seems unusual for someone born and raised in a remote farming region. Around his neck Wilber wears a charm of the Virgen del Carmen, the patron saint of vehicles, because he likes the way it looks.

Wilber grew up in the right place with the right parents and siblings, but alongside the wrong twin. As a child he was never bothered by the greater affection his mother, Ana Delina, had for warm, sweet William, probably because Wilber was his father's favorite. In fact, Carmelo defended Wilber in twin-twin conflicts and other matters—Carmelo knew Wilber was bad tempered and did nothing to curb it. In part, Carmelo thought Wilber's hot-headed outbursts stemmed from being thrown from a horse as a child, because the fall changed the shape of a bone in his head, making it "curvy." So when Ana complained about Wilber's behavior, Carmelo would say, "Don't bother that kid—he's a little bit cuckoo, so to speak." Perhaps Carmelo felt responsible for not physically protecting his young son, and so stood by him in his adult years when he needed help. But a more likely explanation is that Carmelo saw parts of his own personality and beliefs in this son. Both become crabby, cross, and exceedingly annoyed when provoked, behavior that escalates easily. Neither father nor son has the affectionate, loving side that defines William, which he unfailingly showed to his mother. (William fell off the horse along with Wilber, but was not injured.)

When he was growing up, William supported Ana when his parents fought, whereas his brother took a more evenhanded approach. When Ana left Carmelo alone on the farm in the heat of an argument, William advised her to stay away and let Carmelo cook for himself. This sounds out of character for a normally mild-mannered child, but he was insightful—perhaps Ana's absence would make Carmelo's heart (if not his stomach) grow fonder and set their relationship back on a positive track. In contrast, Wilber believed it was better for both parents if Ana returned because his father's cooking skills were so questionable. Wilber chose an immediate, but short-term solution that favored his father at the expense of his mother.

The people of Santander have a reputation for being hot-headed. Although he generally is quiet and reserved, Wilber occasionally succumbs to sudden expressions of anger and irritation when tensions reach a certain threshold. William's constant teasing can unleash such behavior, but William does not back off. William's sweetness and sensitivity seem to vanish when it comes to Wilber, especially because William is aware of his brother's volatility.

> WILLIAM: When I'm not [in the store], I want him to be the one who is more responsible.
>
> WILBER: But he fights with me when everybody is there. . . . When I'm in charge of the business, everything is OK.
>
> WILLIAM: If I make jokes he immediately gets mad. And then I try to tease him or whatever and he's, like, OK, leave me alone. I say, OK, don't get mad about such a simple thing. And then I would tease him some more. Because he gets mad at such simple little things.
>
> WILBER: I don't like that when I'm working—they start joking

with me and teasing me. . . . I say, hey, cooperate and let's finish this [work] first. He starts to make jokes and makes fun of it. And that's what makes me mad.

William's pride and pleasure in getting along with others may reinforce Wilber's premium preference for privacy and independence. William's teasing may be partly an attempt to get his brother to become more open. Where William is quick to express friendly feelings toward others, Wilber is more likely to convey his love and devotion in extreme situations, such as a military march. During the time we spent with the twins, Wilber was less forthcoming than William about how he felt when he learned about the switch or how he reacted to meeting his identical twin. This does not mean that Wilber was not affected by these events, only that he is unwilling, uncomfortable, or unable to effectively describe his feelings to others.

Consistent with Wilber's preference for privacy is his refusal to use email, although he text-messages and maintains a Facebook page. This arrangement seems inconsistent—either you are part of social media or you are not—but it may be less complicated and less expensive to rely on texting than to also use email, and Facebook privacy settings can be controlled, preventing views from unknown visitors. Just for fun, Wilber chose "Wilbert Alberto" as his Facebook name; he was unaware that Alberto is the middle name of his real twin, Carlos. Food and women rank high among Wilber's recreational priorities. As a teenager living with his family or on a nearby farm, he made weekend hikes to La Paz in pursuit of women, frequenting its bars and pool halls—places his brother rarely visited. No such entertainment was available closer to home, and even neighbors had to travel considerable distances to share a drink or a meal.

The brothers *do* agree on one thing: both are devoted fans of Colombia's football team, Atlético Nacional, but only Wilber's bedroom is heavily decorated with banners displaying the team's distinctive crest. Both Wilber and William developed their taste for football when they were ten, hiking an hour up a mountain to their cousin's home to watch the sport on TV.

Although he prides himself on his maturity, Wilber bends to the will of others, walks away from confrontations, or erupts in bursts of emotion. And he doesn't give himself credit for his talents—for example, he is a natural dancer who is fun to watch, but complains that he isn't good enough. Not surprisingly, like his real twin, Carlos, Wilber moves freely and effortlessly—they are those lucky people whose bodies look good no matter what they do. Wilber performs the same beautiful undulating moves as Carlos, but does so with less abandon and confidence.

After fulfilling his obligations to the Colombian army, Wilber trained as a communications technician, installing Internet, telephone, and television systems. Never an eager student, he still has no interest in furthering his education—instead, he wants to own several businesses, although he is not specific about which ones or how or when he might accomplish these goals. He is task oriented and wants to get work done, but sees no need to add fun or zest to the job at hand. William is just the opposite, engaging friends, customers, and family (except for Wilber) with his charm.

Some people seem bigger physically than they really are, almost filling a room when you first meet them. Wilber is that way, but his quiet character and serious demeanor give way to William's lively personality and affectionate manner when the two are together. As a child Wilber did not fight back when his brother was quick to physically attack him, a curious difference from their adult behaviors. Perhaps Wilber felt threatened by

William's greater agility, but he can hold his own in their verbal battles.

While William is good at reading others people's thoughts and feelings, he is less understanding of Wilber, whereas other people, like Wilber's newly found twin, Carlos, understand him much better. The real reared-apart twins share an understanding without explanation, the finest kind there is. I have seen many examples of the immediate rapport that develops between reunited identical twins. One of the firefighter twins put it best when he said that meeting his twin was like coming back after a vacation—the basis for the relationship was there and he had only to fill in the details. Paula, a female twin in another reared-apart pair, approached her first meeting with her sister, Elyse, with some trepidation. "I wondered what we would talk about," she told me. Instead, they ended up sitting together in the Café Mogador in New York's Greenwich Village for several delightful hours, drinking a fruity Spanish wine from the vineyard Marqués de Riscal. They felt like they were seeing different versions of themselves, with their long fingers, delicate wrists, and similar faces that drew attention from a server. The sisters share a love of art films, especially *The Piano*, *Breaking the Waves*, and *Wings of Desire*. As they sat in a cab at the end of the evening, they held each other tightly, reluctant to let go.[17]

According to the psychologist Steven Pinker, researchers have largely neglected the role of chance in shaping the people we become.[18] In fact, chance played a huge role in the person William would become and is still becoming. Born in Bogotá, he was mistakenly taken to La Paz when he was just a week old—thus William became the accidental son of a farmer, Carmelo, and his wife, Ana Delina, as well as the accidental twin of Wilber. The boys' toys were cars and trucks made from sardine cans, and their wading ponds and swimming pools were local streams. William, Wilber, and their friends fought faux wars, taking sides as the Colombian militia versus the terrorist guerillas. Sticks, boxes, and even guava were their playthings. Their free time was a quick hour after dinner, just before bedtime—they had no television to watch or computer to use to surf the Internet. Neither William nor Wilber used a computer until his late teens, when both entered the military, but as young kids both learned to use guns for hunting and target practice.

William's life had changed a lot by July 2016 after the twins' true identities came to light. Meeting his twin and knowing that his personal destiny had taken an extraordinary detour answered many questions he'd had about why he always felt so different from those around him. This new knowledge was energizing, like taking a great vacation when one is feeling uninspired and overburdened. He enjoys his law school classes and has completed one semester with good grades. "I'm not among the best, but I'm not one of the worst, either," William said. "Even though I had not gone to school for such a long time, I picked up the pace slowly." The new apartment he bought with money he saved managing the butcher shop is still being built, but he is crafting plans for making money from it, such as by renting out space. He thinks of himself as knowledgeable about business, not shrewd but always alert to opportunities.

William gained a lot of weight after 2015 by working out regularly at the gym and consuming high-protein concoctions. He now wears more stylish, form-fitting clothes that show off his new physique, and he finds that women are more attracted to him. "I'm yummy now," he says. William is not a braggart, but his growing closeness to Jorge and more buff appearance may have given him a new kind of confidence.

William enjoys the spotlight, but he seems a little too trusting of people, perhaps because he grew up far from the city in a place where everyone knows everyone else. In fact, trust played a critical role in the first meeting of the real twins, William and Jorge. If not for them, Wilber and Carlos might never have met. "This is all God's doing," William said. "He made it perfect for me to be out there for twenty-five years and to make us meet again."

Manon Serrano, who was accidentally switched at birth with another infant girl in Grasse, France, says, "I tend to never leave anything to chance. Now I even try to anticipate the unthinkable."[19] Perhaps learning he was switched at birth will make William more vigilant in the future, especially when he is about to become a father. George Holmes, one of the switched-at-birth twins from Canada, insists that he will bring a video camera into the delivery room when he has his first child, and it would not be surprising if William does the same.[20] Some hospitals inform prospective parents about the procedures they follow to safeguard against accidental baby switching, but because such events are reported infrequently, many families may not take such possibilities seriously. Perhaps they should.

Twins Switched at Birth

Being called the wrong name by somebody you do not know—particularly by someone who is *certain* that he or she knows you—is sometimes more than a case of confusion. This may be especially true when you have lived your whole life as a fraternal twin. That was how Begoña and Beatriz, the fraternal twins from Gran Canaria, Spain, learned that they were not sisters at all.[21] Before meeting Begoña's look-alike at the shopping mall, neither sister was especially concerned about being confused for someone else, believing that the similarities the clerk saw in the two young women were simply coincidental. But thinking back, Begoña realized she had been confused twice before with someone named Delia—once by a young man at a bus stop who called her by the wrong name, and once by her neighbor who was certain she had seen Begoña at a coffee shop she had never been to. And Beatriz remembered that she was mistaken for someone else whenever she visited the northern area of the island—that person turned out to be Delia's sister, Gara.[22]

Of course, not all fraternal twins called by the wrong name turn out to have an identical brother or sister who was switched at birth. Alex, a somewhat olive-skinned, Latin-looking man in his forties, calls himself a "visibly very fraternal twin." His appearance contrasts sharply with that of his fair-complexioned, red-headed brother, Bob, so much so that the two were used to being teased about how different they look. But something happened to Alex at a tennis match that bothered him for nearly a decade, and he finally brought it to my attention in an email message, having read *Someone Else's Twin*, my book about the switched twins from Gran Canaria. As he was walking past the refreshment stand on his way to the restroom, a woman shouted out a name (not his), so Alex assumed she was calling out to someone else. Later he returned to the refreshment stand and heard the woman call out the same name once again. Realizing that she was speaking to him, the surprised and confused Alex turned around to face her. She said, "Hey, you're Steven!" He told her he was not Steven. Then she asked if he was a twin and he said he was. She also asked if he was from Kansas. Alex didn't live in Kansas at that time, but he had been born there. He saw the woman's expression grow strange— but she never apologized and, according to Alex, did not seem convinced by his replies to her questions. The encounter had upset him. Alex had been mistaken for other people before—could he have an identical twin, and could he have been switched with a nontwin infant in Kansas?

In such cases the recommended test compares the mitochondrial DNA (mtDNA) of two suspected twins or siblings. Mitochondrial DNA exists outside the cell nucleus and is involved in several cellular processes, such as energy production and cell division.[23] Because it is passed down intact from mothers to all their children, it is a way to determine whether twins or siblings *could* have the same mother. It turned out that Alex and Bob could have the same mother because their mtDNA samples matched, and their mother had delivered twin boys. However, this test does not prove shared maternity because first cousins related on their mother's side of the family could also have the same mtDNA. That is, children born to a woman and her sister would have the same mtDNA because the sisters would have inherited it from their common mother, making the children cousins.

Alex has fathered fraternal twin girls. As a father he can only imagine the pain that a parent might feel upon learning that a child you have loved and raised is not really yours and that someone else has been raising your child all along. He was relieved to have the mtDNA results in hand showing that he and his twin brother matched, mostly to spare his parents the emotional turmoil of finding out that one of their twin sons was not really theirs. It can be painful but can sometimes deepen the love.

Only nine cases of switched-at-birth twins, including the two Colombian pairs, are in the record books. But I am certain that more are out there because we learn only about the ones that are found. Moreover, independent findings from two medical companies specializing in infant products and services suggest that baby switches are more common than we realize. Those studies estimate that twenty to twenty-three thousand mother-baby mismatches occur each year in US hospitals (e.g., taking an infant to the wrong room), but are quickly discovered and corrected before the babies go home.[24] However, it is quite likely that some mistakes are never detected so we only think that baby switches are rare. In fact, every one of the documented switched-twin cases was uncovered because someone mistook one of the switched identical twins for the other. But if some switched infants are fraternal twins—and there must be some—they would be far less likely to be mistaken for one another because of their different looks, leaving their true identities forever unknown.

Switched singletons have even less of a chance of being discovered, although some are, like Manon Serrano. Two Russian mothers mistakenly received the wrong baby boy when the only nurse on duty mixed up the two children. The error wasn't uncovered until their sons turned two and one of the mothers, Zarema Taisumova, was looking through some baby memorabilia and noticed another mother's name on her baby's identification tag. Following a court ruling that the children must be returned to their biological families, both sets of parents struggled terribly with the unbearable task of giving up a child they loved and learning to love their new child all over again.[25]

I often marvel at the ordinary events that lead to the amazing discovery that one twin was switched for another. These events include enrolling a child in a different school, joining a college club, taking a youngster to a medical appointment, or walking into a shopping mall. Hundreds of people do these things every day without consequence. But every once in a while such ordinary acts become extraordinary, rewriting lives beyond recognition.

Seven of the nine switched-twin pairs involved an exchange of one identical twin and one unrelated singleton. I keep asking myself: What are the chances that an identical twin would be swapped *with another identical twin*, as happened in Bogotá? Identical twins comprise only a fraction of births worldwide, and preemie nurseries are the first home to scores of nontwin newborns. I couldn't begin to calculate the odds.

Carnes Finas de Colombia turned out to be the scene of the triggering event for William and Wilber. What happened in the butcher shop one day in summer 2013—"confusion at the counter"—also triggered a dramatic turn of events for another set of accidental brothers, Jorge and Carlos, who lived on the other side of Bogotá.

Chapter 2

Familiar Strangers

Brothers from Bogotá

C arlos had been repeating falsehoods all his life. He said that he was born in Bogotá on December 22, that his mother's name was Luz, and that he had an older sister named Diana and a fraternal twin brother named Jorge. He also told people that he had never been to Vélez, a city in Santander. But Carlos was not a liar—he was only telling the truth as he knew it. He had no way of knowing that his real twin brother, Wilber, was living the life both should have had in an isolated farm area with no modern amenities. And Wilber had no way of knowing he was growing up with an unrelated, accidental brother, the sensitive William, who had taken Carlos's place.

Luz, the mother of Jorge and Carlos, had delivered twins and brought two babies home. But sometime between the arrival of her twins and their discharge from the hospital, one of her twins changed places with another newborn. This twist of fate turned Carlos into Luz's accidental son, as well as Jorge's accidental twin and Diana's accidental little brother. The switch also transformed

Carlos into an unintended nephew, grandson, and cousin. He also became an accidental uncle to Jorge's young son, Santiago ("Santi"). Santi lives with his mother, Jorge's former girlfriend, and grandmother just down the street from the apartment Jorge and Carlos share, making it easy for father and uncle to see the boy often.

Jorge and Carlos grew up believing they were twins, but they inhabited separate interior worlds. Why? One of the great psychological insights of the late-twentieth century was that living with someone does not make you alike. My findings on virtual twins—individuals of the same age raised together from birth, but who are unrelated genetically—provide striking examples of how shared environments do not produce shared behaviors. Most of these pairs include two children adopted into the same family within the first year of life, while some pairs include one adopted child and one biological child born just before or just after a couple's decision to adopt.[1] Couples experiencing infertility can either adopt children or try to have biological children by one of several assisted reproductive technologies (ART). But adoption agencies sometimes have two children in need of a home, instantly transforming their clients into larger-than-expected families. Some couples try adoption *and* ART—and end up with one adoptee and one biological child. Parents without partners who decide to live and raise their kids together, adoption plus embryo donation, and adoption plus surrogacy have created other more exotic virtual twin pairs. Virtual twins generally turn out to be different in general intelligence, specific mental skills, peer networks, and body size, and they become less alike with time.[2]

When related family members are "chips off the old block"—meaning they are similar in some personality traits or personal habits—these similarities come about because they share genes, not because they share environments. As a young child the actor Skandar Keynes, the great-great-great grandson of Charles Darwin, looked a lot like the famous founder of modern evolutionary theory.[3] Different gene combinations that may or may not be passed down intact to future generations influence most physical features, such as jawline and nose shape. This explains why some grandparents and grandchildren vary in how much they look alike and in what ways.

Family resemblances are not limited to physical traits. Identical twins raised apart usually find that they were acting the same way and doing the same things in their parallel universes. The firefighter twins from New Jersey, Mark Newman and Jerry Levey, were fighting flames in different cities and flinging good-natured insults at their friends. Barbara and Daphne, the British reared-apart pair known as the "giggle twins," found humor in just about anything, laughing uncontrollably when they were together but with no one else. These identical twins showed little interest in politics; drank their coffee cold, black, and without sugar; and had suffered a miscarriage in their first pregnancy before each produced two boys and a girl. They were also the proud co-creators of Twin Sin, a drink made of vodka, blue curaçao, crème de cacao, and cream. Both Samantha Futerman and Anaïs Bordier, identical reared-apart Korean twins, were ignoring their lactose intolerance while they continued to consume cheese in their respective Los Angeles and Paris kitchens. Both twins were also scratching at hives and rashes.[4] These twins' similarities, expressed miles apart, were largely reflections of their common genes. All these twins exemplify "gene-environment interaction," or the expression of the same genes in different settings.

But, of course, genes aren't everything because not all the behaviors of these twins matched perfectly. Different environments can also interact with the same genes to produce different outcomes. Samantha was more outgoing than her twin sister, perhaps because she grew up in an ethnically diverse community that included people of Asian descent, whereas Anaïs was raised in a homogeneous Paris suburb where people would mistake her for a maid. Samantha also had two older brothers who adored and protected her, whereas Anaïs was an only child.[5]

The environments that set us apart from our family members in personality and outlook are those that we do not share with our relatives, such as taking an around-the-world voyage, having an influential professor, or taking up a challenging sport. Jorge and Carlos had many individual academic and athletic experiences that the other did not have because they preferred different things. Like all of us, their genes predisposed them to certain activities and events and away from others.

Jorge and Carlos were the second and third children of thirty-six-year-old Luz Marina Castro Chavez and forty-six-year-old Norman Enrique Bernal Triviño. Although Luz's doctor told her to expect identical twins, her sons were clearly not identical. Assuming they were a fraternal pair, Luz and everyone else figured that they had inherited different sets of genes. But the boys' differences in appearance and behavior had a simpler explanation—they were not genetically related, a truth that went undiscovered for twenty-five years. Meanwhile, Jorge and Carlos withstood the stares, jokes, and comments that inevitably surfaced when they told people that they were twins.

Jorge's and Carlos's interests diverged most dramatically during childhood. Carlos was the more serious and focused student, a mind-set that is still evident today as he pursues his professional career in accounting and finance. Bogotá's educational and cultural opportunities gave expression to Carlos's natural drive and inclinations to achieve in his chosen field. As such his unintended city proved to be a good match, allowing him to pursue his interests and talents at school and at work. In this respect he is quite different from Wilber, his identical twin, who has never been interested in continuing his education. It is impossible to know whether Wilber would have been more interested in education if he had been the twin who grew up in Bogotá—he has the same mathematical interests as his reared-apart twin, but never had the chance to explore his abilities to the fullest. It is also impossible to know whether Carlos, like his real brother, would have written off education had he grown up in the country, but it is certainly possible.

Different rearing environments seem to have had some varying influences on the true twins Jorge and William. Drive and desire are Jorge's hallmarks. In Bogotá he was pursuing a career in engineering while working part time in his field developing methods for gas and water transportation. Admittedly, he is often sidetracked by his love of football, which takes him to competitions across the country and around the world. However, events beyond his control, such as Colombia's plummeting oil prices, have also delayed his progress because he was laid off from his job.

William, his identical counterpart raised in La Paz, can also count drive and desire among his finer attributes, but the limited opportunities and financial constraints of his family meant he could not pursue his education, no matter how determined he was. He eventually was able to express these tendencies, which are partly genetically based, when he moved to Bogotá, and especially after he met his twin and received the assistance and support he clearly craved and required.

Reaching his goal of earning specialized credits and owning his own financial consulting business is within Carlos's reach. He is closer to fulfilling his goals than Jorge is to becoming an engineer.

Jorge, always a serious, but more casual, laid-back pupil, is progressing more slowly, not yet certain of the specific path he wants to pursue. He has not thought this through, partly because he follows his favorite football team, Atlético Nacional, wherever it plays, even traveling to Japan to watch the team compete for the 2016 World Cup. He cannot afford to do this, but he borrows money from close friends who trust him to pay them back. Jorge's love affair with football began in the seventh grade when a classmate introduced him to the game. His near obsession with this sport irks his brothers, but passion is a trait he shares with William, who has become a consummate weight trainer. The same genes inhabit the cells of these twins, but their different environments guided their expression.

In high school Jorge preferred rock to Carlos's taste for hip-hop and rap. Their clothing styles were also different. Jorge dressed in jeans and T-shirts, while Carlos wore the baggy pants and oversized tops of the hip-hop set—and both styles infuriated their mother, Luz. Their sister, Diana, recalls that Carlos looked funny in big clothes but "came to his senses" when he started studying accounting—then he chose more fashionable and traditional attire, paying particular attention to his hair, paralleling his twin's attention to fashion in La Paz. Jorge also thought about his hair, but he let it grow to his waist and pulled it together in a long ponytail, another point of contention with his mother. But to the relief of Luz and her sisters, neither Jorge nor Carlos used drugs or associated with classmates who used them. "They both have excellent values," observed their elegant aunt Leonor.

Growing up in Bogotá, with its many educational and recreational opportunities and events, allowed Jorge and Carlos to be themselves, doing what came naturally. "They were not typical twins," observed another of their five aunts, Maria Teresa. Hers was an astute—prescient, really—observation, because Jorge and Carlos weren't twins at all.

By the time Luz was pregnant with her twins, she had lost her job as a seamstress, so she couldn't afford an ultrasound, an important procedure for managing high-risk pregnancies. Once the twins were born, to make ends meet Luz cleaned houses, washed clothes, and ran errands to give her children the best future that she could. Their father, Norman, was variously employed in wood, carpentry, and machinery businesses; worked for a while in a restaurant; and drove a private car—"he was a man of all trades," according to Jorge. But Norman was rarely around and showed little interest in, or affection toward, the children he had had with Luz. Regardless, Jorge and Carlos were loved and well cared for. They were raised in an all-female household, where everyone doted on them. Their pretty sister, Diana Carolina, older by four years, adored them, jumping up and down when they finally arrived at the family's two-story home. They were also cherished by their grandmother, Leonor Chavez, and the two aunts, Maria Teresa and Blanca Cecilia, who lived with them; Blanca Cecilia considers herself their second mother. Maria Teresa's daughter, Gloria Andrea, lived with them as well—Gloria was the same age as Diana, but she played mostly with Carlos.

Luz had three other sisters—Leonor, Ana Rosa, and Maria Esther (Blanca Cecilia's fraternal twin)—who lived in Bogotá and were always around for the children's birthdays, communions, and graduations. Leonor, always bedecked in jewelry and wrapped in a stylish suit, acknowledged that Luz had had a difficult life and had worked hard to support three children on her own. Luz had insisted that they receive a good education so they could advance socioeconomically—she could read and write, but had gone only as far as the eighth grade. Luz's sister Ana Rosa had paid for her niece and nephews' high school education, but the assistance was never really enough. Jorge estimated that his mother's yearly earnings amounted to US$2,520, much less than what she had previously earned as a seamstress.

The family of eight lived in a modest five-bedroom house in a lower-middle-class area of Barrio Quiroga, far from the center of the city—housing costs and neighborhood quality generally dip as travel time to the heart of Bogotá increases. The house, now occupied by their aunt Maria Teresa and cousin Gloria, looks badly out of place on their quiet street—it is essentially a brown brick box dwarfed by two much larger structures on either side. A brick wall inlaid with white metalwork surrounds the entrance, but provides little security because even a child could easily hop over it. The house has a living room, kitchen, hallway, and bathroom on the ground floor. Stairs lead to the second floor, where Jorge, Carlos, and Diana had shared a large room for sleeping; other family members used other small spaces on that floor for bedrooms. The house sounds large but was cramped for four adults and four lively children, although it is similar in quality to most other homes in their working-class neighborhood. Jorge and Carlos lived there for the first nineteen years of their lives.

Their childhood home had a television, tape recorder, musical instruments, and a refrigerator. They played with store-bought toys and rode their bikes around the neighborhood. But the family was not wealthy—Jorge would have liked to have had a better bike, Carlos wished the family could have had a washing machine, and both would have enjoyed working with a computer. Their La Paz counterparts, William and Wilber, didn't have a refrigerator or a washing machine, but it never occurred to them to wish for these things. Both William and Wilber had wanted bicycles, but finding a place to ride them would have been difficult, if not impossible, because there were no roads nearby. Both brothers would also have liked to have had a TV, but virtually no one in their area had one because they also didn't have electricity. Indeed, neither brother listed electricity as something he would have wanted in their childhood home, perhaps because none of their friends had it.

Catholicism was important to Luz and she attended services frequently. "She always forced us to go to church," Jorge said. Neither brother was seriously religious when they were growing up, although both have turned toward religion in their own way since learning about their twins, probably because learning of the switch has made them think more deeply about who they are and why. Aside from Luz's insistence that her children attend church, she was a fairly lax disciplinarian. The children always exploded in laughter when she charged at them with a soft slipper. Luz scolded her sons on occasion but never really punished them, in the belief that reasoning with children has a greater influence on their behavior.

Although Jorge and Carlos were rather different children— Jorge was people-oriented and playful; Carlos was self-reliant and serious—they sometimes played together, usually in groups with other children. This is typical, because many fraternal twins and siblings are less inclined than identical twins to do things together in the absence of other children. (As a young fraternal twin I sometimes complained to my mother that I had "no one to play with," even when my sister was sitting in the next room.) Young Jorge and Carlos and their friends once had great fun walking along the main street of their neighborhood and throwing paper inside buses that had stopped. The kids did this for three days. When Luz learned what they were up to, she wanted to ground her sons but relented—too soon, apparently, because they continued to do this until one day a bus driver started to chase them. The children ran seven blocks to a park and hid, but then the driver, "this big guy," got out of the bus and came after them. When the driver tripped and hurt his arm, Carlos stopped running and the guy grabbed him, put him on the bus, and drove him home.

Luz was furious, scolded Carlos, and threatened to spank Jorge when he came home. But in the middle of her anger, Luz tripped and fell, and they all just laughed. Jorge admitted to his mother that when the driver lost his balance, he ran back and hid in a store. "Why did you run back?" Luz asked him. "You should have run forward so you wouldn't get caught." Her words seem surprising for a religious, conscientious mother who was determined to raise her children the right way—she was not into punishment, but she was into protection. Many incidents like these triggered the slipper attacks, but the children only pretended to cry, and when Luz left the room they would start laughing. This would bring her back and the fake crying would begin again.

Luz died of stomach cancer when she was fifty-seven, a terrible blow to her sons, her daughter, and her sisters. Jorge and Carlos never told their father that their mother had died because Norman's own health was poor, and they thought that the news might make him worse. In fact, Norman died of a heart attack about a year after Luz died. Carlos barely acknowledges the father who took so little interest in his family. He and Norman fought bitterly during the few times Norman did show up to visit; they mostly argued over Norman's failure to bring Luz some money. Unlike Jorge, who accepts people and situations as they are and who generally does what seems appropriate and expected, Carlos did not attend his father's funeral. He cannot always contain his extreme resentment of his father and uses angry expressions and impatient gestures when he speaks about him. Carlos believes that Norman had no influence on his life, but that remains to be seen—when Carlos becomes a parent, he may try especially hard to give his own children the fatherly love and attention he was denied. In contrast, his love for his mother was so great that it's hard for him to talk about her. If not for the love lavished on them by their aunts, Luz's children, then in their twenties, would have found losing her unbearable.

Some family members say that Jorge looks like Norman, which makes sense because he is Norman's biological son, but they say that Carlos also looks like Norman. I find this fascinating because, in nearly all the switched-twin cases I have known, mothers have commented on the resemblance of the switched child to relatives on the paternal side of the family. A father's own perceptions that a particular child looks nothing like him does not mean that the child is not his or that he will not care for the youngster. But fathers tend to invest more time and effort in children who look like them and whose mothers they see as trustworthy and faithful.[6] Of course, Carlos's family members did not offer these comments with questions of his paternity in mind— and, more important, they had no way of knowing that Carlos, the different-looking child, had no biological connection to Norman or to Luz. Perhaps Norman's failure to see any resemblance between himself and Carlos made their relationship especially contentious. Carlos too was hot tempered, which was different from Norman and Jorge, both of whom tended to remain calm. In reality Carlos shared his temperament with an identical twin he didn't know he had.

School Days

All three of Luz's children attended district schools, which are public and not as good as the costly private schools, but Luz saw to it that they went to the best ones in the area. She enrolled Jorge and Carlos in the school for boys and Diana in the school for girls. Kindergarten was an all-day affair, lasting from 7:00 a.m. to 4:00 p.m. Then, from the first grade through high school, the day began at 6:30 a.m. and ended at noon. The boys' high school was the relatively selective Colegio Restrepo Millan, housed in an imposing redbrick structure that has a large open area for assembly and recreation, a world away from the uninspiring field where the La Paz children played. The Colegio's current mission is to promote leadership in social and cultural projects, based on research and teaching in science and technology.[7] Gaining admission to Colegio Restrepo Millan was difficult, and the boys' older cousins had been forced to leave because they couldn't keep up. Some people doubted that Jorge and Carlos would succeed at such a school, but Luz disagreed. "You guys are the only ones who decide that," she told them. Both Carlos and Jorge graduated from the school, enrolled in college, and earned certificates in specialized topics, Carlos in finance and Jorge in mechanical engineering. They worked during the day and attended school at night, and were still doing this when we met them. Diana completed college with a major in social management, followed by one year of postgraduate study. She works as a public information officer for Colombia's national archives, advising people how to protect and preserve films and photographs. Diana is also her brothers' confidante and advice giver, a role that comes easily to her, especially since their mother's death.

Colombia is a country where people do not read for pleasure, but Diana is an avid reader. Neither Jorge nor Carlos reads much— Carlos follows city news on the Internet, but the last time Diana saw him with a book was two years ago. In fact, Diana does not recall having many books or newspapers around their childhood home, although a Spanish-English dictionary and world atlas were available. Once she started working and earning a salary, she ordered and paid for a newspaper subscription. "Maybe my profession draws people into reading," she suggested. I believe that the reverse is true, that people who enjoy reading and acquiring information are attracted to a job involving access to historical records and audiovisual materials of national significance.

Moving On

When Jorge and Carlos were nineteen, family squabbles prompted them, Diana, and their aunt Blanca Cecilia to move to a three-bedroom apartment in historic Candelaria. Candelaria is the charming colonial district of Bogotá known for its baroque and gothic churches, art museums, quaint hotels, educational institutions, and trendy restaurants. Candelaria draws hundreds of tourists year-round but especially during Holy Week, when a huge procession moves from Monserrate, the sacred mountain and iconic church that loom over Bogotá, to the streets below. But Candelaria is not just for tourists—Jorge and Carlos's family lived in one of the more residential, less upscale areas. Luz died two years later, in 2009. Deeply troubled by memories of their mother and sister, the foursome left Candelaria for a two-bedroom apartment in the somewhat nicer La Isabela neighborhood of Bogotá. They were joined for a while by Diana's boyfriend, Andres, but Diana and Andres eventually left, taking Blanca Cecilia with them. During this time Jorge lived intermittently with his girlfriend and her mother.

Soon it was clear that Jorge was not ready for marriage. But when he became a father, he and Carlos moved to an apartment in the working-class neighborhood of Barrio Bachué, just a block from Jorge's son, Santi. Jorge and Carlos still live there, along with their aunt Blanca Cecilia, in a duplex apartment that has two bedrooms, two bathrooms, a kitchen, and a living room. The furnishings are tasteful but a bit sparse. A table in the living room holds some amateur sports trophies that Jorge and Carlos won over the years, Jorge exclusively in football and Carlos mostly in basketball but also football. Among their proudest moments are Jorge's college championship in football, when he was eighteen and played for the team fielded by the SENA (Servicio Nacional de Aprendizaje, or National Learning Service); Carlos's district championship in basketball, when he was nineteen and played for the Kanguros (Kangaroos); and their childhood championship in football, when the twelve-year-olds played for Jaqu Mate (Checkmate) with other boys in their neighborhood.[8] Most striking to visitors is a photo of a smiling Santi with his arms around Jorge, whose long dark hair contrasts so sharply with his now closely cropped cut. He is wearing an old yellow Colombian football jersey with the word AGUILA (Eagle) emblazoned across the front over the words MI GUERRERO DE SANGRE (My Blood Warrior).

The brothers' apartment is on the second or third story of a big complex, reachable only by an outside stairway. A flat piece of ground separates it from an identical apartment building and provides a convenient play area for young children. It is a comfortable place to live, but hardly the somewhat upscale residence implied by the media once reporters learned of the twins' story. Nonetheless, Carlos and Jorge had choices that William and Wilber did not have or even know about.

Accidental Brothers of Bogotá

One brother in each accidental pair was born and raised where he belonged, and Jorge is one of them. He is the natural leader, the one who answers emails, does interviews about the twins' switch and reunion, and serves as general spokesman for the gang of four. To promote solidarity among his new band of brothers, he rules with a firm but tender touch. Jorge was the only one of the four twins who answered my initial inquiry, responding: *"Hola, Con mucho gusto eres bienvenida a Colombia y compartir todos una nueva experiencia."* (Hello, you are welcome in Colombia to share a new experience.) Jorge has a big personality and a big presence, captivating people with his charm, grace, and interest in who they are. He comes alive in the limelight, a role he enjoys but one that his more reserved accidental twin brother, Carlos, finds irritating. However, Jorge is firm in his belief that decisions affecting all four be made together.

Jorge is not big physically. He is slim and just under five feet, seven inches tall. His short dark wavy hair grows neatly and naturally away from his forehead, framing his dark brown eyes and slightly uneven nose. A recent picture shows Jorge and his identical twin brother, William, seated together at a wedding, heads cocked toward one another and touching slightly. It is impossible to tell them apart, especially because of their ears—ear shape and structure are, in fact, genetically influenced features.[9] In the photo Jorge is wearing a fancy dark suit and a purple tie—or is he the one sporting the black-and-white checkered tie?

This wedding scene hides how Jorge and William prefer to dress—both are oblivious to Bogotá's fashion trends, favoring loose T-shirts, jeans, and sweatshirts even as adults. (Even William's efforts to show off his new physique have not given him a style that matches that of Carlos and Wilber.) Jorge is clean-shaven except for a small goatee sprouting around his chin and accented by a small patch of hair just under his lower lip. When he smiles, he displays two rows of amazingly even white teeth. His boyish good looks have dazzled hundreds of young women who covered his Facebook page with love letters and friend requests once the twins' story became widely known.

Unalike and Unfamiliar

Some people are hawks (morning people) and some are owls (night people). Which one you are is not entirely a matter of how you were brought up; it's also a matter of your genes.[10] Of course, people can change depending on their assigned work schedules, but adjusting is harder and more unpleasant for some people than others. Jorge is not a morning person—he often breezes into appointments several hours after the agreed-upon time, conveniently blaming some football event or childcare issue for the delay. This tendency can be grating, especially for Carlos, who has deep respect for obligations. But like his reared-apart twin brother, William, Jorge's manner of smoothing tensions over with such complete sincerity means people never are angry for long. His friends allow him this slack because they see so much good in him.

Alongside his devotion to his favorite football team, Jorge has big goals and dreams, just like William, but Jorge's desires and plans to achieve them are not fully formed. He worked days at the Strycon Engineering company, designing gas and water lines until the company laid off employees in February 2016. He still takes night classes at the Fundación Universitaria Los Libertadores, where he is working toward a degree in mechanical engineering and is just starting his own construction company. As the only parent in the group, Jorge is closely involved in the care of Santi, who is now five. He gets Santi ready for kindergarten each day, plays with him on weekends, and "loves the kid to pieces." Jorge's strong devotion to his son surprised Diana. "I always knew he would be responsible, but I never thought he would be such a good parent," she told me. However, Diana doesn't approve of Jorge's travels to football matches—often sudden or unplanned—because it means leaving his small son behind, but "Santi brings Jorge back to earth."

Jorge's passion for football worries the people who know him, because he is a *fanatico* about Atlético Nacional. There are tense rivalries among fans with different team loyalties, and Jorge has been physically attacked at times just for wearing the wrong T-shirt—he claims he never starts these altercations. When I saw him last, he had an angry gash across his forehead, the result, he told me, of being knocked down by a strong wave at a Brazilian beach. But Carlos thinks a fan of a rival football team delivered a blow. They fail to see eye to eye on most things, from valuing privacy to respecting punctuality to washing the dishes. But like their La Paz counterparts, the two have often lived together, as many brothers and sisters do as they transition to adulthood, because as familiar figures in each other's lives, they can be themselves.

In fact, a growing trend in the United States is for young adult siblings to live together, despite the battles they may have fought as children. Benefits include safety (the presence of a companion), security (emotional support), and solvency (financial relief). The arrangement eliminates the gambling and guesswork involved in living with a friend or someone who answered an ad, because siblings know what they are getting into.[11]

At least one source of their brotherly tension was eliminated in the last year. Their aunt Blanca Cecilia now lives with them, cooking their meals, cleaning their house, and washing the dishes.

The accidental switching of Carlos and William turned each into an unwelcome reminder of their accidental lives once they met. Carlos was the baby who suffered from digestion and elimination problems and endured the six-hour bus ride from Vélez, where he and Wilber had been born, to the hospital in Bogotá for treatment.[12] He was in the Bogotá hospital's nursery when Jorge and William were there, and that was when the switch occurred. The baby named Carlos became William when he was sent home to the country, where farm labor was prized and education was not. And the baby named William became Carlos when he was sent home with Luz in Bogotá. Neither twin was responsible for what happened, but as adults William's initial resentment of Carlos for having the life that should have been William's was palpable and understandable. And Carlos saw William as embodying the life he should have led, and he found this difficult to accept. It would be a while before these two resolved their feelings.

Carlos's early life history had some significant consequences. He doesn't look like anyone in the family he grew up in. His looks clash sharply with those of Jorge, his accidental twin brother, no doubt explaining why friends and relatives sometimes teased both of them about not being real twins. He seems to tower over Jorge, but he is less than two inches taller—no doubt his solid build makes him appear larger than he is. Carlos's dark hair, which is straight and short, shows the start of an *entrada*, or receding hairline.[13] Male pattern baldness comes from the mother by way of a recessive gene on one of her two X chromosomes. Wilber also shows this trait.

Such X-linked traits seem to skip generations because they are not expressed in mothers whose other X chromosome generally has the dominant gene that does not code for baldness. However, X-linked traits are always expressed in sons because they have only a single X chromosome—their Y chromosome is much smaller and does not carry the same genes as the X. These sons can then transmit the gene to their daughters, who do not express it, but can transmit it to their own sons. That Carlos, but not Jorge, showed the beginning of baldness would not have caused anyone to suspect that Carlos had a different mother because women transmit just one of their two X chromosomes to their sons. In this case Carlos's X chromosome came from his biological mother, Ana Delina, and that chromosome carried the baldness gene.

Jorge also received an X chromosome from his biological mother, but it was from Luz and did not carry the baldness gene. This difference in hair growth would not have seemed unusual to anyone because everyone knows that fraternal twins do not have identical genes. Male fraternal twins and siblings each have a 50 percent chance of inheriting the same baldness gene from their mother. This means that in some twin and sibling pairs, both members will be bald, neither will be bald, or only one will be bald.[14]

Carlos's athletic build is enhanced by the stylish tapered shirts and the artfully ripped designer jeans he favors. He wears well-tailored suits to work, showing them off with plenty of dash and a touch of swagger. His nails are manicured and his eyebrows are waxed, part of the fastidious grooming regimen followed by many urban men. Wilber also indulges in manicures and eyebrow treatments, habits he acquired apart from his twin.

Born in the country but raised in the city, Carlos blossomed in Bogotá's cultural milieu. He easily acquired the urban sophistication, social skills, and self-confidence that allowed him to successfully navigate big-city life—work, school, dancing, music, sports, and women. Carlos worked as an accounts analyst while studying to be a certified public accountant, a credential he earned in May 2015. He is now a financial coordinator for the national education ministry and earned a certificate in tax sciences in February 2017. He prides himself on his individuality and independence, and he is careful about whom he trusts.

Like Wilber, Carlos prefers privacy to publicity and has been reluctant to do anything that brings public attention, but the other brothers' love of the limelight usually prevails, even though it bothers Carlos. Until recently Carlos had never visited his identical twin in the butcher shop where Wilber works, but when I returned to Bogotá in 2016, sixteen months after visiting in 2015, that was starting to change—lots of things were. Carlos was starting

to accept his biological family and place of birth. He was also setting aside his tensions with William, even planning a Mexican
vacation for just the two of them. Carlos's maturity and mind-set
were showing through, and the change was impressive. Meanwhile, ever since they had met, Jorge often visited the butcher shop
that William managed, working alongside his newfound identical
twin, and the two had taken several trips together.

Carlos hides many of his emotions. He wouldn't talk about
his breakup with a steady girlfriend but looks weepy when the
topic comes up. He has deep feelings for Jorge, but he expresses
them only when he's drunk. "I love you, brother," he has been
known to mumble, replaying Wilber's emotional outburst to William as they marched through the jungle. Reserve and reflection
can make Carlos appear callous at times. He barely acknowledges
the father who abandoned his family, and early on he maintained
long silences when anyone raised the topic of growing up in the
wrong family. When he did speak he referred to "the grandmother" who had brought him to Bogotá and "the aunt" who had
left him there. He had to confront the fact that he really belonged
in rural La Paz with a different mother, father, and twin, an existence far removed from the city life he thrives on. Chance kept him
in Bogotá—had his Aunt Edelmira brought the right baby back
to La Paz, Carlos would never have known the big-city ways that
define him.

During my first visit to Colombia, Carlos opened up just once
about the shock of learning of the switch, but when I saw him
again more than a year later, I got the complete story. What most
people took for coldness was a young man trying desperately to
come to terms with a life-changing event that caused him to question who he was and how he got that way. Carlos may be William's
unsettling shadow because Carlos enjoys the benefits of city life
that William should have had. But Wilber is Carlos's alter ego—

his identical reared-apart twin who is a version of who Carlos could have been.

Carlos has an uncanny ability to look back at himself with humor, revealing details that place him in silly or awkward positions. This behavior seems uncharacteristic of his generally detached demeanor, but is engaging when it appears. Several events from his past make him laugh, although they were awkward and uncomfortable at the time. Once he was sipping a Coke through a straw, picked up the bottle for some reason, tilted it, and ended up spilling the drink all over himself. As a teenager out on a date, his stomach revolted following consumption of a Cuban sandwich—a stack of ham, roasted pork, Swiss cheese, pickles, mustard, and sometimes salami and garlic sauce on bread. "I said "Bye' fast and started walking back to my house. I was in a cold sweat." Carlos has had second thoughts about consuming another Cuban ever since. His seriousness is balanced by this lighter comical streak and his willingness to laugh at himself publicly. Both stories seem funny to him now, and while they are entertaining, they are also somewhat self-deprecating. Carlos has admitted to losses of confidence at times.

Carlos does not have the spontaneous, adventuresome spirit that is central to the nature of Jorge and William. Visiting new places is not a high priority for Carlos, but it is for Jorge, who believes that travel opens one's mind and increases one's energy—he has no trouble taking credit for encouraging and helping Carlos buy plane tickets so he could finally see the sea. This is not surprising because scores of twin studies show genetic influences on openness to experience (curiosity and open-mindedness) and absorption (emotional responsiveness to sights and sounds). Genes account for about half of the differences among people in these two personality traits. Genetic effects are also responsible for about half the differences among individuals' social attitudes, such as tough-mindedness and conservatism, and vocational interests, such as adventurous and enterprising professions.[15] And genes explain between 72 and 85 percent of the differences in exercise behavior among older adolescent males.[16] Thus, the differences between these accidental brothers make sense because Carlos and Jorge have no common genes—whereas Jorge and William share them all—and agree that they disagree in many ways.

> CARLOS: Jorge believes he's always right, and he likes people to follow him. I don't like to follow anybody. I try to get people to respect what I think.
>
> JORGE: Although he follows me . . .
>
> CARLOS: I don't follow you. Jorge knows I support him in many things, but he knows there are many things I don't like about him. That's normal.
>
> JORGE: Yes, totally.

Carlos often seems to be on the periphery of events in which he is taking part. At such times he can be analytical, coming up with insights and observations that are important and meaningful. "When my identical twin, Wilber, teases Jorge, Jorge will take it only to a certain point. But Jorge and I, we can take the teasing longer because we've known each other our whole lives. Similarly, William should not assume he can tease me to the same degree." Siblings' shared social history can be a powerful influence, as it was, and is, in Carlos and Jorge's case. They tease and annoy each other on a daily basis, pushing each other to dangerous limits, but know they can rely on each other in times of crisis.

Carlos's reflective mind comes across in other ways. He showed the most interest and curiosity about what we would learn about him and his brothers, not just the physical traits that are obvious, but about their behaviors. Why, for example, was Carlos so terrified when a friend threw an insect at him, causing him to tear off all his clothes? And when they were children and a mouse disrupted their play, Carlos refused to kill the mouse because he was afraid of it. Where does fear of small nonhuman creatures come from?

> CARLOS: I said to Jorge, "You kill the mouse."
> JORGE: No, you said, "You kill it because you're the man of the family."
> CARLOS: I was scared and I just said, "You kill it, you kill it."
> JORGE: I know he remembers because we have talked about this many times.
> CARLOS: That's the point I want to make. He always has to be right.
> JORGE: I'm 80 percent sure of what happened.
> CARLOS: OK, I'll just say yes.

Fears and phobias among males are partly affected by genes, on the order of 37 percent for animal fears, such as fear of snakes, bugs, spiders, and mice, although experiences are more influential. Other fears, such as agoraphobia (fear of being trapped, helpless, or embarrassed in public places) and blood/injury phobia (fear of seeing blood or needles), are partly influenced by genes. These fears are largely irrational—Carlos had never had a previous encounter with a house mouse, yet his fear of this small mammal was real. He shared this fright with someone he had never met—his identical twin brother, Wilber, who had nearly killed another soldier who had chased him with a snake. It's strange to think that two strong, solidly built young men should be so afraid of things that might not bother others, but they are not alone. Reared-apart identical male triplets, Bob, Eddy, and Dave, met by chance when they were nineteen. Eddy had left a small college in upstate

New York, but when Bob enrolled at the same school for the next semester, students wanted to know why "Eddy" had returned. This case of confusion brought the two of them together, but they became a threesome after one of Dave's best friends saw a picture of Eddy and Bob in a newspaper. All three of these muscular, athletically built young men are terrified of needles, a fear we learned about when they visited our allergy-testing lab in Minnesota.[17]

In modern times wariness of mice, snakes, and sharp objects may seem groundless, but they posed serious threats to life in early human history. Our ancestors who feared them and took precautions survived and passed their genes on to subsequent generations, whereas those who were less concerned died off. Cultural changes occur more quickly than genetic ones.

At the end of their brotherly battle, Carlos seemed to give in to Jorge's version of the mouse incident, but I believe something else happened. Carlos was accepting Jorge for who he is while realizing that arguing about a mouse is a useless pursuit, a recognition typical of a thoughtful, reasoning person. Carlos also thought a lot about what it would have been like to grow up with his identical twin and decided that having an unrelated brother was more to his liking. Appreciation for individuality and diversity convinced him that being raised with Wilber, who is so much like him, would have been boring. It might also have robbed him of his unique identity. This perspective is understandable, but not tenable, because many reared-apart twins had similar concerns until they met, only to learn that they were not the photocopies they had feared. Investigators are also sensitive to twins' physical and behavioral variations—a fuller frame, a more even set of teeth, a more serious demeanor. (Only once did I confuse a sixty-two-year-old identical male triplet for another while waiting for one of the three to complete a medical appointment.) Most twins I have worked with found themselves celebrating their similarities and their differences, adding another unique layer to their sense of self—*us*—something only reunited twins can do. At the same time many what-if questions crowded their consciousness: What if their adoptive parents had been willing to take two children? What if the twin's adoptive parents had chosen the other child instead? Or, in some cases, why did the biological mother keep one twin and not the other? How did she choose? The twins' lives could have been dramatically different if their mother had made a different decision or had faced different circumstances.

The Minnesota researchers found it gratifying to see the twins' relationships evolving so effortlessly, especially among the identical pairs. We chuckled but also loved seeing some adult twins revert to being the twin children they never were, trying to trick us by switching places. Jorge and William, and Carlos and Wilber never knew the fun of fooling their friends by pretending to be the other brother—but, ironically, all four were accidental players in a somber and stressful game of switch.

Reflections

No other case of doubly exchanged adult identical twins has ever been recorded in the history of twin studies. From the first moment, I absolutely believed that the Colombian twins were at the center of the most extraordinary nature-nurture saga ever told. But would the four young men agree to undergo intelligence testing, provide saliva samples for DNA analysis, and reveal their thoughts and fears to two complete strangers? Would they be willing to do this during Colombia's Holy Week, which begins on Palm Sunday and ends eight days later? Holy Week—the time when Jesus entered Jerusalem and was received with palm leaves—is the most important celebration of the year for Colombia's predominantly Catholic population; they mark it with nationwide processions and ceremonies.[18] Most schools and businesses close, and many people leave town for vacations. I wondered whether the twins would forfeit their free time in exchange for what they might see as an unusual and risky venture. On the other hand, twins are generally fascinated with being twins and are eager to learn as much as possible about themselves.

Most twins also understand the critical role they play in scientific research and enjoy contributing to new findings. Sir Francis Galton of England, credited with founding the twin method in 1875, was actually approached by twins who volunteered to take part in his research. This is unusual because most behavioral science investigators have to work hard to attract a large enough number of participants to produce statistically valid studies. But, like Galton, I find that twins offer their time unsolicited and make efforts to take part in ongoing studies. In response to a twin-family questionnaire I sent by email, one identical female twin replied, "I would love to answer any other questions. Thanks so much." And after the airing of a television program discussing my work on reared-apart Chinese twins, a mother wrote, "My daughter, who is adopted from China, has a twin sister who was adopted at the same time to a different family. I just saw the show and many aspects resonated. Are you still doing twin research?"[19]

The greater resemblance of genetically identical than fraternal twins tells us that our genetic backgrounds influence particular behavioral, physical, or medical traits. It works that way with virtually every human characteristic, from verbal fluency to running speed to cholesterol level. It's a gorgeous natural experiment.

Chapter 3

Miles of Memories

Twins Past and Present

B ogotá, Colombia, is thirty-five hundred miles southwest of my
home near Los Angeles. Its name derives from the word *ba-
catá*, meaning "planted fields" in the Chibcha culture that pre-
dated Bogotá's founding. In 1538 the Spanish explorer Gonzalo
Jiménez became the first European to arrive in the Chibcha nation, where he founded the city of Santa Fé. Santa Fé became the
center of government for the territory, in the new kingdom of
Granada. The city was later called Santafé de Bogotá, but after
several more changes it officially became Bogotá, D.C. (Distrito
Capital), in 2000.

Some of my friends and colleagues were shocked when I said
I hoped to go to Colombia. They warned, "Be careful!" or joked,
"Don't mess with drug dealers!" Notorious for armed guerilla
attacks since the 1960s and for drug trafficking since the 1980s,
Colombia has been synonymous with crime for many years. The
crime has been concentrated in the metropolitan areas of Bogotá,
Cali, and Medellín but has also occurred in smaller cities. After

the 1993 death of Pablo Escobar, the head of Medellín's cocaine cartel, the drug trade lost its center. Colombian drug trafficking continues, but it is focused in other Latin American countries. Every Colombian with whom I spoke while I was there emphasized how safe Bogotá had become compared to previous years, and it is. Calling Bogotá a "role model of urban reinvention," the *New York Times* ranked Colombia twenty-sixth on its 2010 list of thirty-one places to visit.[1]

Unfortunately, the crime in Colombia has overshadowed the stunning accomplishments of its writers, such as the Nobel Prize winner Gabriel García Márquez, as well as its renowned artists, musicians, dancers, actors, scientists, and coffee growers. The sculptor and painter Fernando Botero is famous for renditions of voluptuous figures and objects, some controversial, that earned him the 2012 award from the International Sculpture Center for Lifetime Achievement in Contemporary Sculpture.[2] The pop singer and dancer Shakira is the highest-selling Colombian artist of all time, with recording sales reaching nearly US$10 million. Sofía Vergara is a well-known television and film actor, model, and producer. In the world of science Dr. Francisco Lopera is conducting stunning research on early-onset Alzheimer's disease in an extended family from the Colombian countryside of Antioquia. And everyone knows Juan Valdez, the fictional symbol of Colombia's National Federation of Coffee Growers, portrayed by the national folk hero Marco Fidel Torres. Colombia is the world's third-largest coffee producer and the biggest producer of Arabica coffee, a high-quality bean known for its intense flavor.[3]

Colombia remains a country in flux; its democratically elected government, headed by President Juan Manuel Santos Calderón, reached a peace agreement in October 2016 with the guerillas— the Revolutionary Armed Forces of Colombia, or FARC. Just five days after voters narrowly rejected the original agreement, Colombia's Congress modified and approved it, officially ending fifty-two years of brutal armed conflict. But terror continues in Colombia. Murders of, and attempts to murder, local community leaders occurred throughout November 2016, partly fueled by the uncertain future of the newly disarmed FARC members. And United Nations observers sent to Colombia to monitor the FARC were caught dancing with female guerillas on New Year's Eve, provoking sharp criticism from opponents of the peace deal and questions about the impartiality of the UN observers.[4] Struggles between rebel groups, such as the National Liberation Army (ELN), and the government have continued into 2017.[5]

The guerillas had preyed upon William and Wilber's family, as well as other rural families, for crops and farm animals. And Wilber had narrowly escaped capture by a guerilla unit when he was a young boy. Work on the farm continued against this backdrop of violence and terror.

I thought a lot about the four twins and how their reactions and feelings would compare with those of other switched-at-birth twins who have trusted me with their life stories. I also thought about some of the reared-apart twins with whom I had worked. Each pair came with distinctive features that made them memorable, making me wonder what unusual habits, quirks, or oddities would define the twins in Colombia.

Minnesota Days: Identical Twins Reared Apart

Sharon Poset of Nicholasville, Kentucky, and Debbie Mehlman of West Hartford, Connecticut, are petite identical blue-eyed twins who were reared apart.[6] Both wore their dark blonde hair at chin length and scattered their bangs across their foreheads.

They also shared the rare trick of rolling their eyes upward, leaving only the whites exposed, a skill they still love to show off because it horrifies other people. When they return their eyes to the normal position, both twins look pleased at their trick's intended effect.

When Debbie was forty-five, her mother summoned her for what Debbie presumed was an important discussion of family finances. Instead she received news that left her breathless: she had been adopted *and* she had a twin. Shocked but determined to find her sister, Debbie hired a private investigator, who located her but wisely contacted Sharon's parents first, which allowed them to gently share this life-changing news with their daughter. Sharon had been told that she was adopted, but no one in her adoptive family knew that she had a twin. Sharon's parents had traveled from their new home in New Jersey to Sharon's home in Kentucky to share this incredible news in person. Like Debbie, Sharon assumed that this sudden visit from her parents was for a talk about family finances.

The twins met for the first time at Bradley International Airport in Windsor Locks, Connecticut. They instantly fell into each other's arms and have been the closest of twin sisters ever since— loving and teasing, compassionate and supportive—and are very much alike in their tastes and temperaments. The only noticeable difference is their weight—studies of reared-apart twins have shown that in women genes account for 37 to 49 percent of influences on weight (whereas in men genes account for as much as 87 to 91 percent), perhaps because of women's greater sensitivity to hormonal influences, dietary changes, and/or exercise regimens.[7]

What makes both twins so notable is that they are extremely devoted to their different religions—one is Jewish and one Christian—demonstrating genetic influence on religious involvement and conviction. Religious beliefs, occupational interests, favorite school subjects, leisure pursuits, and values are more alike among identical twins than fraternal twins, whether reared apart or reared together, with genetic influence accounting for about 50 percent. It makes sense that many different genes affect a complex behavior like religiosity, expressed through various personality traits.[8] Some aspects of religiosity, such as the degree of influence of religion on one's life, are associated with some genetically influenced personality traits, such as traditionalism, but the association is modest and findings vary across studies.[9] However, religious affiliation, no matter the religion to which we subscribe, tends to come from our families and therefore is environmental in origin. Upon learning that her biological mother was not Jewish, identical reared-apart twin Debbie worried that she was not really of that faith because Jewish law defines Jewish children as those born to Jewish women. The solution was to undergo a formal religious conversion at her synagogue, then remarry her husband of twenty-three years. Her sister Sharon, who grew up in a Catholic home, had been growing frustrated with what she saw as the relaxation of religious rules and practices. She eventually decided to join the nondenominational Evangelical Christian Church because it promised her an appealing combination of faith, morality, grace, and forgiveness. However, both twins acknowledged that, had their adoptive homes been reversed, their shared spiritual nature would have absorbed the rituals and culture of their twin sister's faith.[10]

The religious lives of all identical reared-apart twins do not match at the same time or even at all. Both Mary and Elaine from Great Britain were raised in Catholic homes, but Mary's family was heavily involved in religious activities, whereas Elaine's family was far less active. The twins seemed to switch places in their later years—Mary turned away from her faith while her sister stayed connected. Family influences work in mysterious and unpredictable ways, either by instilling religious beliefs and practices in children, or prompting them to question formal religious practices, or leading them to choose some middle ground. However, Mary and Elaine agreed on one point: neither could accept that genetic factors influence a belief in God.[11]

Lively Laboratories

Twin research takes place at two levels, and both are lively, informative, and fun for the partnership that quickly evolves between twins and observers. Quantitative studies measure twins' personality characteristics, religious practices, and physical traits by asking them to respond to inventories and questionnaires, and to stand on scales or wear various recording devices. Researchers use these data to estimate genetic and environmental influences on behavior and physique by comparing the responses of identical and fraternal twins; greater resemblance between identical than fraternal twins demonstrates genetic influence on the trait(s) under study. Qualitative research identifies trends and patterns in people's behaviors and perceptions through structured and semi-structured interviews, surveys, and small group discussions. In Colombia, informal interviews and observations, such as those occurring during meals, travel, or at parties, when the twins were less guarded, also took place. These less formal sessions are often enormously revealing, allowing researchers not only to capture bits of behavior that they might otherwise miss, but also by allowing them to breathe life and meaning into the quantitative work.

The chance events that often lead to twin separations set up natural situations that cannot be duplicated because they would violate either ethical standards or respect for human dignity. The Colombian twins are a great example of such circumstances, but so are the reared-apart identical twins Jack Yufe and Oskar Stohr, who were born in 1933 in British-ruled Trinidad. Their Romanian father and German Catholic mother separated when the twins were six months old; Jack remained in Trinidad with their father, and Oskar went to Germany with their mother, so each one knew from an early age that he had a twin brother. Jack was raised Jewish, worked on an Israeli kibbutz, and entered the Israeli navy. Oskar was raised Catholic, joined the Hitler Youth, and labored in the coal mines of the Ruhr. After reuniting as adults—aside from their opposing political and historical views, which they variously argued about or ignored—the twins' abilities, personalities, and appearance were nearly indistinguishable.[12]

Most people with such conflicting backgrounds and beliefs could not imagine becoming friends, but identical twins are different. Jack and Oskar were captivated by their similarities and worked hard to develop their relationship as twins. Both wore identical light-blue epauletted shirts and wire-rimmed glasses when they arrived in Minnesota for the study at age forty-six, only the second time that they had met. Their intelligence test scores and personality profiles were nearly the same. The only obvious difference between them was the Jewish star that hung on a thick gold chain around Jack's neck. As they aged, their thinning reddish-brown hair, moustaches, and broadening bellies matched perfectly.

Jack and Oskar became famous in academic circles and in the press for their striking similarities: sneezing loudly in elevators, reading books back to front, flushing toilets before and after using them, draping rubber bands around their wrists, and shoving floral displays sideways if they blocked their view. All were behaviors each developed independently, without knowledge of what his twin brother was doing. Single genes do not code for these personal oddities, but broad personality dispositions influenced by many genes, each with small effects, may play a role.

Jack and Oskar's noisy sneezes may reflect a humorous streak with a touch of malice, whereas their toilet fixation may speak to an overall fearfulness that covers bugs, bacteria, and bathrooms.

I was mostly fascinated by Jack's acknowledgment that, had he been raised in his twin's home, he would have become pro-German and unsympathetic to the Jewish causes he enthusiastically supported. Likewise, Oskar acknowledged that, had he grown up in Trinidad, he would have become staunchly pro-Israel and anti-Germany. The crucial point is that the nature of the twins' attitudes matched and would have regardless of where they grew up—only the content differed. That is, both twins expressed fierce identification with their country and culture, one in an effort to hide his German roots in Trinidad, and the other in an attempt to hide his Jewish roots in Germany. Identical reared-apart twins can see many aspects of themselves in a life unlived, but the reflection isn't perfect because having a totally different mind-set and thinking totally different thoughts about important issues is difficult to imagine. I had no doubt that the switched Colombian twins, Carlos and William, would be informative and fascinating in this regard.

Not all identical reared-apart twins are as similar as Jack and Oskar, and Debbie and Sharon, but many are. Twin pairs like these, when compared with fraternal sets, show that genetic factors explain about 50 percent of the individual differences in most characteristics, although some traits, such as height, are more "hard-wired"—genetic factors explain nearly 90 percent—and others, such as job satisfaction, are more malleable, with genetic factors explaining 30 percent. Our genetic findings from reared-apart twins about intelligence hover between 73 and 77 percent, consistent with previous reared-apart twin studies in the United States, England, Denmark, and Sweden. Of course, genetic influence does not mean that people cannot change or improve with practice and training, although some behaviors are harder to alter than others, but it does mean that we cannot all be the same.[13]

It is mostly the reared-apart identical pairs who express the unusual idiosyncratic behaviors that the Minnesota investigators and other researchers have observed, such as eyeball rolling and rubber band wearing; this is less true for fraternal pairs, showing that genes partly affect even our odd habits and mannerisms. If you like your coffee warm (not hot), scratch your ear with a paper clip, or brush your teeth with Vademecum toothpaste—similarities observed in separated identical twins—it is likely that if you had an identical twin, she or he would be doing that too.

What Might Be

The story of Jack and Oskar brought my thoughts back to the Colombian twins, whose post-discovery lives were still new. I wondered how Carlos, raised by chance in Bogotá's rich cultural milieu, which he relished, thought about the life he would have had in La Paz's remote rural landscape. He would have known a loving father, rather than the one who deserted his family, and four older siblings. But he would not have gone to high school, attended college, or become an accountant. And he would not have participated in organized sports, grown up in a house with plumbing, or worn fine suits. Did Carlos realize this or did he deny it in the belief that he would become the same person no matter where he grew up? Was he horrified or relieved, angry or complacent, regretful or accepting of his circumstances? Carlos had only to look to Wilber, his identical twin, to see himself as he would have been with a limited education, a different accent, and a habit of commuting by horseback. But even identical twins would find it hard to *feel* like their twin because our identities are inside our head and are all that we know.

I wondered whether the reared-apart Colombian twins would, like Jack and Oskar, set aside their differences and celebrate their lives as twins. Colombia's citizens are highly conscious of regional and social differences. People living outside Bogotá tend to view its residents as arrogant and distant, while people from Bogotá generally regard rural people as unrefined and somewhat aggressive, qualities reflected largely in their speech.[14] The striking differences between the La Paz and Bogotá families were on display from the time they met, but especially during their first visit. The La Paz twins' childhood home was made of wood and open on one side, with an angled roof that reached out over a flat space resembling a patio. It stood alone with no other buildings in sight. The home of the Bogotá twins was a two-story brick structure with a large front door, two windows, a gate, and a house number over the entrance, and it was located in a densely populated residential district.

The other twins' stories also prompted me to think more about William, who was destined for life in the city but ended up in a rural environment. Was he bitter about his lost educational opportunities? Did he worry about rejection by the parents and siblings with whom he grew up? How did he break the news to his now accidental parents? And was he angry at Carlos for "taking" his place? I hoped to have answers to all these questions.

I did some research on La Paz because I was raised in the heart of New York City and wanted to have a better feel for the nature and quality of life in rural Colombia. Searching "La Paz Colombia" led me to TripAdvisor. As I hunted for hotels, I received the message, "We're sorry, La Paz doesn't have any hotels." I eventually found that the closest hotel was the Hotel Mayales Plaza located six and a half miles away in another town (Booking.com). Two people can stay there for US$38 per night, including a complimentary breakfast, Wi-Fi, shuttle service, and no advance payment. I later learned that there is one hotel in La Paz, the Hotel Karol, a property with no Internet connection. The list of things to do when visiting La Paz had just one entry, but it is a geological wonder.

The Hoyo del Aire (air hole), described by the Colombian lawyer, writer, and journalist Manuel Ancizar in 1850, is a land formation located on a mountain. It is believed to have resulted from a falling asteroid that created a hole with a diameter of about 394 feet and a variable depth of about 656 feet. It appeals to campers and hikers and is about an hour's walk from the road.[15]

I was sure that the La Paz brothers had visited the Hoyo del Aire at least once, but how often can people visit the same place for artistic, literary, or emotional fulfillment? I found no museums, monuments, libraries, theaters, concert halls, or sports stadiums listed for La Paz, and Bucaramanga, the capital of Colombia's state of Santander, is 270 miles away. Life in La Paz offered opportunities that had little in common with what the interested, motivated, and spirited William would have enjoyed had he not traded places with Carlos. I wanted to know about the prospects William had created, tried to create, or had hoped to create from the resources available to him. I imagined that social gatherings would assume greater importance in isolated areas than in populated areas, where more activities are available. Social gatherings can be rich repositories of certain types of information and enlightenment, although rural inhabitants may have to work harder to find them or to make them happen. In the process of doing so they form close relationships with the people around them, as did William and Wilber, who maintain many childhood friendships that will probably last a lifetime. It is also wrong to suppose that all city people are fully immersed in the educational and cultural activities around them; city living can be lonely and isolating if one is not a social mixer. Some people who live in apartments never know their neighbors. The Bogotá brothers had friends, but they could not know everyone in town.

The parents who raised William and Wilber were comfortable in the country, as they had lived there all their lives. Some of their older children had moved to or visited Bogotá for a while (it's a six- to eight-hour journey by car, not to mention getting to a car by hiking or horseback), but most had moved back after finding city life stressful and dangerous. Two older sons were still living and working on the farm they grew up on, and one brother still lived with his parents, who had moved to another house in the La Paz area, a three-hour walk from their farm but closer to neighbors.

William moved to Bogotá in his late teens. His motivation for doing so was the same motivation that drove him to join the military—it was a way out of La Paz. Becoming a soldier allowed William to escape his hard life on the farm and avoid the illicit drug crops and culture that were spreading across the region. But it did not provide him with the education that he desperately desired and that Colombia provides to qualified soldiers at no cost upon discharge.

Because he had not advanced beyond the fifth grade, he was ineligible for training as a military deputy, although a senior officer had recommended him for the course. In fact, William had been recognized as the best soldier in his platoon of ninety-two men at the Tolemaida military base. But having a high school diploma was an essential requirement for acceptance into this training program. Complicating William's situation was that near the end of his military service he contracted leishmaniasis, a parasitic disease found in parts of Mexico, Central America, and South America.[16] Leishmaniasis is treated with glucantime, a drug whose side effects can include weakness and muscle pain, as well as heart and kidney damage if used for extended periods.[17]

William recovered, but that would make little difference when it came to his goal of having a professional military career. Not knowing that, he persisted.

William moved to Bogotá and earned his high school credentials during the next eighteen months. He returned to the military base to apply for the noncommissioned officer course and to complete a second medical examination, but when it was discovered that he had had leishmaniasis, he was told that he did not qualify for further training. It was one of the saddest things that had ever happened to him. Refusing to give up easily, William remained in the barracks until he was thrown out, but a cousin helped him get back in, where he hid among the similarly attired two thousand soldiers stationed there. This final attempt lasted a week, until a colonel who was a personal friend made it clear that William had to leave. He was twenty-one.

When William lived in Bogotá, he sold *arepas*, a staple Colombian food made of ground maize dough or cooked flour. For the next year or so he and his cousin Brian operated their small business from a food court on a busy street. But when an old friend needed to fill a vacancy in his butcher shop, William took the job. A year later he became the manager of yet another butcher shop— Carnes Finas de Colombia, in the back corner of the La Gran Manzana market. This decision had the unforeseen consequence of adding his name to the short list of switched-at-birth reared-apart twin pairs.

Switched-at-Birth Twins: A Brief Chronology

Nine switched-at-birth twin pairs, in Switzerland, Canada, Gran Canaria (Spain), Poland, Puerto Rico, and now Colombia, are known to researchers, but there are probably more. Cases involving identical twins have a greater chance of discovery than those involving fraternal twins because of the confusion caused by mistaken identities. Fraternal twins do not look exactly alike, and some do not look at all alike, drastically lowering the odds that an exchange of nonidentical twins could be uncovered.

The first reported occurrence came from Fribourg, Switzerland, one of the largest medieval towns in that nation's western Üechtland region. The town is divided into French-speaking and German-speaking districts, known as the "twin towns" of Fribourg and Freiburg, respectively. On the night of July 4, 1941, Fribourg's Hopitale de la Miséricorde added three new babies to the nursery. Madeleine Joye delivered identical twin boys, Philippe and Paul, her first children, and another new mother, Berthe Vatter, gave birth to a son, Ernstli. The following morning Joye was told that Paul's birth weight had been incorrectly recorded but that the error had been rectified, reflected by a revised entry in the infant's chart. In reality the identification tags draped over the foot of each baby's crib had been accidentally switched.[18]

The five years that followed were a delight for both families. Joye celebrated the physical and behavioral differences of her fraternal twin sons, and Vatter bonded closely with Ernstli, whose gentleness and charm she found irresistible. Philippe and Paul, raised in Fribourg, spoke only French, while Ernstli, raised in Freiburg, spoke only German.

When the French-speaking brothers in Fribourg turned five, the Joyes enrolled them in one of Freiburg's German-speaking schools to broaden their language skills. Ernstli was a student at that school. Teachers and classmates immediately noticed Philippe's double, a source of great amusement even to the twins' parents. For fun Madeleine Joye insisted that her husband bring along a camera on the day the children would be marching in the Fête-Dieu, a celebration honoring those receiving first communion, and he agreed. But Monsieur Joye, startled by the two boys' physical likeness, instantly sought out Berthe Vatter and posed some hard questions: Was her boy born on July 4, 1941? Was he delivered at the Hopitale de la Miséricorde? And was he born sometime during the night? Her answers—yes, yes, and at 6:00 a.m.—told M. Joye what his wife refused to believe: A baby exchange had occurred. Even Madeleine Joye could not ignore the evidence for long because she noticed that Philippe, but not Paul, was missing two lower teeth because they had never developed. Approaching her son's look-alike, she examined his mouth and found that they shared this same rare dental anomaly, known as hypodontia.[19]

The three small boys were sent to Geneva's Cantonal Hospital for extensive medical testing to determine their relatedness to each other and to their parents. Blood group analyses were inconclusive, and modern DNA tests that compare twins across about fifteen DNA markers or sequences were not yet available, so the physicians performed a series of reciprocal skin grafts, an idea that was truly novel for the time and the first time the procedure was used to establish identity. Autografts involve the surgical removal of skin from one part of the body for placement on another part of the same body, as in the case of burn victims. Allografts involve the grafting of skin between individuals of the same species who are not genetically identical. Barring infection, autografts do not carry the risk of rejection because the skin donor and recipient are the same. However, medical treatment sometimes requires allografts, but these grafts usually last only seven to ten days because their genetic incompatibility causes the immune system to reject them.[20] Clearly, the idea of performing allografts among the three children to identify the real twins was a groundbreaking first. More recently, researchers have found that skin transplants between fraternal twins can work if their different blood groups were exchanged prenatally, an event called chimerism.[21]

Skin samples exchanged between the identical-looking boys (Philippe and Ernstli) healed perfectly, whereas those between the other pairs did not. Here was the solid proof that Philippe and Ernstli were identical twins, and Paul was really the child of Berthe Vatter.[22]

On June 19, 1948, a judge decided that Paul and Ernstli, by then nearly seven, should be returned to their biological families within two weeks. The emotional traumas experienced by the loving parents and contented children were heartbreaking— Madeleine Joye and her husband worked hard to make Ernstli feel happy and welcome in his new home.[23] Their task was daunting because Ernstli cried constantly, and no wonder. The young boy was confused about why he was there; he spoke a different language and wanted to return to his familiar home with his mother and big sister. And Berthe Vatter, forced to relinquish Ernstli, the unrelated son whom she adored, could feel no affection for her biological son Paul when he was returned. She left him in the care of foster homes and boarding schools.[24]

Missing from the picture was Philippe, the only child raised in the right place, the Joyes' home. Philippe's experience reminded me of the Colombian twins Jorge and Wilber, each of whom was raised where he was supposed to be. Strange as it may seem, Philippe, the twin boy raised where he belonged, suffered horribly from the exchange, feeling unloved and overlooked. His sadness was palpable, triggered by his jealousy at the attention his parents lavished on his new twin. The family's revised situation was beyond the comprehension of such a young child.[25] Twenty-five-year-olds like the Colombian twins can better understand that extreme circumstances can alter the behaviors and obligations of their loved ones, but they have insecurities too. Perhaps Jorge and Wilber, like Philippe, would feel dejected or depressed if family and friends directed disproportionate attention to their exchanged brother. Carlos and William were too old to be switched back, but they were not too old to become the new favorites of a mother or an aunt. Jorge and Wilber would also have to watch and see how their relatives reacted to their newly found identical brother.

A different set of worries consumed Carroll Tremblay and her husband, Jim, a Canadian couple who had raised two adopted sons, fourteen-year-old Wade and twenty-year-old Brent. Their story began in 1991 when Brent Tremblay, a student at Carlton University in Ottawa and a member of its Strategy Club, was mistaken for a fellow named George Holmes. George was not enrolled at Carlton, but his interests in cards, chess, and other board games attracted him to the same club. When a perplexed friend of George's brought the look-alikes together, Brent and George delighted in their shared tastes in music, film, and sports statistics. After they'd been close friends for about a year, one conversation turned to their birth.[26]

It seemed more than coincidental that Brent and George had shared the same foster home for two months, placed there by the Children's Aid Society of Ottawa on behalf of their parents. Their unwed mother and father had left them there temporarily until they could marry and manage a home suitable for raising two newborns. The twins shared their foster home with a third newborn named Marcus, who was destined for adoption. But when the elderly couple in charge found it too strenuous to care for three babies at once, they moved the twins to a different home but sent the wrong pair by mistake, separating the twins. As a result Brent was adopted by the Tremblays in place of Marcus.

DNA testing performed when the young men were twenty-two confirmed that a switch had occurred and that Brent and George were the true twins. Brent's mother, Carroll Tremblay, was grief stricken because, rather than gaining a son, she felt she had lost one. Her adopted son, Brent, was instantly at ease in his twin's more relaxed, slightly disorganized home, so different from the regimented, perfectly ordered household that the Tremblays maintained.[27] I wondered to what extent William would embrace Jorge's lifestyle and if William would leave behind his life in La Paz. And would Carlos opt to spend more time with his biological parents in the countryside? How would their families feel if this were to happen? Abandoned? Accepting? I sensed that both William and Carlos would slowly insert themselves into their new families, never forsaking the ones that raised them, and I couldn't wait to find out if I was right. I thought about other twin sets to gain insight.

Lech Kaczyński, the former president of Poland (2005–2010), and his identical twin brother, Jarosław Kaczyński, the prime minister (2006–2007) are the only known identical twins to have held their nation's top governing positions, and at the same time. But these twins were famous long before the twenty-first century, as childhood stars of the 1962 film *The Two Who Stole the Moon*, a fantasy tale of twin troublemakers who try to make money by stealing the moon and selling it. Their twinship came to a sudden and tragic end when Lech was killed in a plane crash in Russia in 2010, and the cause of the crash has never been determined. The plane was carrying a large number of Polish government officials and military personnel.[28]

Poland has other twins of interest, most recently the fraternal twins George Skrzynecky and Lucian Poznanski, who met for the first time in 2015, when they were sixty-nine. Their mother, who had been in a forced labor camp during World War II, gave birth to them in Germany after she was liberated but was too weak to care for them. They were taken to Poland by the Polish Red Cross, which arranged for their separate adoptions. George knew he had a twin and in the 1960s had asked the Red Cross to find his brother, but it could not; Lucian had no idea he had a twin brother. The Red Cross Restoring Family Links Program brought them together in a poignant taped reunion that went viral in 2015. Embracing just moments after meeting, one twin gently cradled his brother's head, holding him close. Life histories cannot be rewritten, but the twins say that the best part of everything that happened to them is that they found each other after so many years.[29]

Another case of reunited Polish twins seemed to go well at first but ended sadly. I never met Kasia and Edyta, the switched Polish twins who met in June 2000 when they were seventeen, after a friend of Kasia's encountered her spitting image on the far side of Warsaw. However, I interviewed three of their four parents when I visited Poland in October 2011. Their story adds a new twist to how and why one identical twin could be replaced by a nontwin, sending two babies home with the wrong family.[30]

Both families brought the right children home from the different hospitals in which they had been born. But two weeks later all three babies were referred to the Saskiej Kępie Clinic for treatment of lung infections. No one knows exactly when the switch took place, but in the early 1980s hospital procedures were lax. Nurses removed the babies' identification tags for bathing, the newborn nursery was overcrowded, and all four parents could only peek at their babies through a small glass window. Communist policies strongly discouraged people from asking questions, so no one did, even after the twins' mother learned that the club foot of one of her twins had miraculously disappeared, and the other mother became newly aware of this defect in her baby. One infant twin had been released two weeks ahead of the nontwin.

The exchange was uncovered after Kasia's friend thought she saw her on the opposite side of Warsaw from her home, but in fact the friend had seen Edyta. This was not the first time people had confused the twins—earlier that year a young man Edyta didn't know had approached her at a concert and planted a friendly kiss on her cheek. The twins met for the first time at Zygmunt's Column, a famous landmark in Warsaw's Castle Square. When Kasia told her parents about meeting her identical twin, her father dismissed the news as the notions of a crazy teenager. But when Kasia invited Edyta to her home, Kasia's parents were stunned by the girls' identical looks and realized what undoubtedly had happened. Their mother grew deeply depressed and required medication, while their father was furious with the physicians, brought a lawsuit against the hospital, and won.

At first Edyta seemed to enjoy her biological parents and twin, celebrating her birthday with both families when the twins turned eighteen. In actuality she was severely traumatized by knowing that she had grown up with the wrong parents. No one knows why she distanced herself from her family, her friends, and her twin sister, and to this day no one knows where or how she is living. Friends of the twins' mother disparaged her because she had not known who her baby was, but she should not be faulted: studies have shown that newborn recognition is not built into the behavioral repertoire of human mothers. Based on even limited exposure to a baby's smell, touch, sound, and sight, most women can pick out their own infants from two or three other infants in research laboratories. However, like Ana and Luz, mothers rarely question the identity of an infant brought to them by nursing staff.[31]

Based on the information I had, I did not anticipate that the Colombian twins or their families would register negative reactions. According to Ray Williams, professor of Hispanic studies at the University of California, the pervasiveness in Colombian culture of *convivencia* (variously translated as "tolerance," "togetherness," "coexistence," and "cohabitation") may have softened the twins' and their families' attitudes and eased acceptance of their revised relationships.[32] Williams also observes that in Colombia "family raises family," largely replacing social services. But some of the Bogotá twins' personal struggles could affect their relationships with their accidental twins, either now or in the future. Perhaps one would blame the other for living the life he should have led, even though his twin was not responsible. Maybe one twin would resent the closeness developing between his accidental brother and the brother's newfound twin. Or maybe some or all the twins would turn against the aunt who had brought the wrong baby back to La Paz. These relationships, in turn, might affect how these young men would get along with their real twins and with both sets of their relatives.

Since I learned about the Bogotá twins, I have thought about chance encounters a lot. Whenever I walk into a clothing store in a mall, I recall the switched twins, Begoña and Delia, and Begoña's unrelated "twin" sister, Beatriz, in Gran Canaria.[33]

All of us have made choices that have led to chance encounters, unexpected wealth, personal harm, or other life-changing moments. We pick one restaurant over another and happily run into a long-lost friend. Or we accept one job offer over another and find interesting opportunities we had not anticipated. These decisions usually do not seem to change our lives significantly, but we really cannot know. If Begoña's T-shirt had fit her well, she would not have returned to the store to exchange it and might never have known of Delia's existence. Under these alternative scenarios, everyone's lives might have gone on as before. Think about that the next time someone calls you by the wrong name.

Chapter 4

The Friends Investigate

Mysteries Deepen

Walking into a butcher shop to order meat for a summer barbeque is usually a pretty uneventful transaction. Millions of people do this every year when the weather is warm and the sky is light. If your guest list is long, you want to get the best deal you can and that takes connections.[1]

Carnes Finas de Colombia, where William and Wilber worked, is tucked at the back of La Gran Manzana, a small market in the densely populated, low-income Kennedy district of Bogotá, named in honor of the late US president John F. Kennedy. Large crates of oranges, bananas, guavas, papayas, and other glorious tropical produce surround the entrance to the market, giving it the appearance of a fruitarian paradise. But Laura Vega Garzón, an attractive mechanical engineering student in her midtwenties, knew that it also sold quality beef and chicken because her best friend, Yaneth Páez, was dating a student named Brian who worked part time at the shop. Laura had never visited this particular market, which is far from the city's center, but this hot Saturday afternoon in July 2013 was an exception. Laura was hosting a barbeque at her home the next day and hoped to get a good deal on some meat.

Laura and Yaneth sauntered past the fruit stands and headed toward the back of the store. As they approached the counter, Laura was stunned to see a familiar figure on the other side. "Huh?" she asked herself. Then, in a flash of recognition, she turned to Yaneth and shouted, "It's Jorge! He works in my office at Strycon, in mechanical engineering."[2] But even as she said this, her mind started sprinting at record speeds—what was Jorge doing here, far from the Bogotá neighborhoods where he lived and worked? Her first thought was that he was moonlighting as a butcher to pick up extra money—she reasoned that he was embarrassed to be seen cutting up meat and poultry and, therefore, chose a place far from his usual haunts. Fully convinced that this young man was her coworker, Laura gave him a friendly wave, but he did not react. As the young man came over to greet them, Laura expected a hug and a kiss, but none came. Instead, Yaneth was the one who received these gestures of affection.

Turning to Laura and thinking she was crazy, Yaneth explained, "This is William, my boyfriend's cousin. He works here." Then Laura and Yaneth went back and forth—he's Jorge, no, William; he's Jorge, no, William—and started giggling. Their half-hilarious, half-serious repartee ended when William confirmed that he was, in fact, Brian's cousin William Cañas Velasco, the manager of Carnes Finas. When he said he had never worked at Strycon or even heard of it, Laura couldn't believe it.

By the time Laura left the butcher shop, she had secured a good deal on meat for her barbeque but was puzzling over a mystery that would take more than a year to solve. The strange encounter with the young man who had sold her the meat haunted her. Who was this person if not Jorge? Was it possible that two people could look so much alike? Her mistaking of William for Jorge would begin a *CSI*-like mission of inquiry, uncertainty, heartache, and ultimate resolution that would occupy her and her friend Yaneth for the next fourteen months. Laura was determined that, come Monday, she would jokingly tell Jorge that he has a brother who looks exactly like him.

WhatsApp?

Laura and Yaneth's verbal back-and-forth on that 2013 summer day in the butcher shop eventually turned them from confused onlookers into single-minded detectives desperate to identify the source of the confusion. At first their joint venture was fun and exciting as they shared new bits of information and determined their next steps. They began with basic facts, such as the brothers' dates and places of birth, then turned to more specific information, such as Facebook photographs and blood types. One set of clues led to another as pieces of the story fell into place. It was a heady feeling, a world that they concealed from everyone but their closest partners, and it was addictive. New findings sometimes made them fearful about where their efforts might lead, but they couldn't stop as their curiosity, combined with coincidence, gave way to obsession and certainty. Ultimately, they would have to reveal the hard truth that they had learned.

A strange aspect of this story is that the critical events occurred at two specific points, within the first few days after Laura mistook William for Jorge and again a full fourteen months later. The complete record of Laura and Yaneth's investigation is preserved in their lively WhatsApp exchanges, beginning on September 9, 2013, and ending on September 12, 2014. Their greetings, questions, comments, and exclamations are sprinkled liberally with *hahahas, LOLs, OMGs, jajajas, noooos,* and various emoticons. Collectively, their messages read like a spy novel, but one that goes beyond pure entertainment. Embedded within the lines is an informed, well-reasoned dialog between two people as they piece together information and decide where to look next (see appendix B for excerpts of their WhatsApp exchanges).

Chance Encounters

Laura could not forget about William's likeness to Jorge. The following Monday morning, as planned, she approached Jorge in his office at Strycon. "You have a twin brother!" she announced, at once jokingly, seriously, and hesitantly, as though testing his reaction. To her surprise he said he did have a twin, adding that his brother, Carlos, didn't look anything like him. Laura insisted that the person she had met looked a lot like him and described the strange encounter. He asked her exactly where she saw this person, and she said that it was at a butcher shop in Bogotá's Kennedy district, about ten miles from the apartment Jorge and his brother shared in the popular middle-class Barrio Bachué. Jorge rarely went there, not just because the trip takes thirty minutes by car (which the brothers didn't own) and even longer during the city's frequent rush hours, but mostly because that neighborhood had nothing special to offer. At any rate, Laura now knew that her coworker was not the closet butcher she had suspected he was, but an explanation for the incredible likeness of the two young men eluded her.

Jorge's mind was churning. Perhaps his father had had a child with a woman other than his mother—after all, he'd heard rumors that his largely absent biological father, Norman Enrique, was already married when he met Jorge's mother. But in the end Jorge decided that Laura had merely had a chance encounter with someone who looked a lot like him, so the topic faded from their conversation, except that she sometimes teased him about his strange doppelgänger.

If Jorge had taken the story more seriously, the twins might have met sooner. Two years before, a security guard who worked in Jorge's office building bought some meat from William at his butcher shop. William recalled, "He asked me if I had a brother named Jorge, and I told him, 'No, sir,' and that was all." Jorge continued, "The next day the guard said something like, 'Hey, Jorge, I saw a guy exactly like you! I swear I think he is your brother.' Well, we just laughed, changed the subject, and forgot about it."

There was another close call. A woman who cleaned the common areas in Jorge and Carlos's apartment building had babysat for William and Wilber in La Paz. The two young men she occasionally walked past probably looked quite different from the two small children she had known, but had she stopped by the meat counter, she would have noticed the resemblance of at least two of them. A casual conversation about who they were and where they were from might have led to the truth.

A month after Laura and Jorge spoke briefly about her encounter in the butcher shop, and in an odd course of events, Yaneth took a job at Strycon, the company where Laura and Jorge worked part time. Yaneth soon ran into Jorge, a chance meeting that reminded her of his stunning physical resemblance to William. At the same time she knew that he was *not* William. Yaneth had socialized with William on many occasions, such as birthdays, holidays, and family get-togethers. But now that she had a chance to see Jorge, she gave more thought to the confusion at the meat counter: *"Oh, my God, they look exactly alike—even the way that they walk is the same!"* The two never spoke, but each time

Yaneth saw Jorge at work, she was surprised, awed, and perplexed. Teasingly, she told her boyfriend that she sometimes saw "William's twin brother" at work.

At first Yaneth didn't question why the two looked so much alike and didn't act on it; sometimes she wondered whether she had even gotten a really good look at "the double." Perhaps she was mistaken about their similarity because unrelated look-alikes can appear more alike when they are apart and the comparison isn't one on one. The same is true of identical twins because any differences in body height, body weight, or facial markings may go unnoticed when they are apart unless the differences are extreme. Regardless, Yaneth thought the whole situation seemed surreal, which explains why it became an occasional inside joke between her and Laura. Just as Laura teased Jorge about having a physical duplicate, Yaneth teased William, telling him that she worked at Strycon with his "identical twin."

Several other events occurred at this time, and in hindsight they were significant. Yaneth downloaded pictures of Jorge from the Internet to share with William's godparents, Ana Liria Hernandez Velasco and her husband, Luis Hernando Mateus Orduña. Yaneth didn't do this for fun, but to find out whether people who knew William well would think it was he when they actually were looking at a picture of Jorge. If others couldn't tell the two apart, Yaneth and Laura would know they were not the only ones to see the striking resemblance. The Velascos had known William his entire life, so they were excellent candidates for this test—in fact, Ana Liria had helped her aunt, William's mother, Ana Delina, care for her twins when they were babies. When he was older, William often visited his godparents in Bogotá and had even lived with them for a while; as a result Ana Liria considered him her son.

Both she and her husband were certain that the young man in the photo was William. William also saw those pictures, as did some other people he knew, and everyone was surprised, then amused, at seeing his look-alike. Sharing a beer with the guy in the photo seemed like a cool idea to him at the time.

Like Jorge, William had apparently forgotten about the security guard who had come to the store to buy meat and told him about "this guy" who looked just like him.

Digging Deeper

For the next six months no one said or did much about the Jorge-William confusion. Everyone was concentrating on their own lives. Yaneth left her job at Strycon in February 2014. Then, while communicating with Laura on WhatsApp on the afternoon of September 9, 2014, Yaneth made an offhand remark and asked a question that made them return to the mystery and set their brief, but intense, investigation into overdrive. For some unknown reason Yaneth recalled Jorge and William's incredible similarity and asked Laura where Jorge was from, whether he might have grown up around La Paz where William had grown up. She also wondered, "What if they got exchanged in the hospital after they were born? Let's plan a reunion." It's hard to judge how serious she was on this particular point, but she was thinking big. Laura agreed to cooperate by finding out where Jorge was born and asking Yaneth for a picture of William so she could show it to Jorge.

With picture in hand, Laura told Jorge to sit down at his desk at Strycon because he would be shocked. He was, because the face staring back at him in the photograph was his—only the picture was of someone else. He called a coworker to come over and asked, "How do I look in the picture?" "Good," was the reply. When

Jorge told him that the person in the photo was someone else, the coworker refused to believe it, and others in the office had the same reaction. Finally, Laura got around to asking Jorge where he was from, and he said Bogotá, denying that he had relatives in or around La Paz. Jorge was growing increasingly curious, nervous, and fearful, to the point that he didn't know what to do, and for the next several days got nothing done at work. When something gets into Jorge's head, he focuses completely on the issue or problem at hand.

People who knew Jorge at work grew curious about his double, and their curiosity turned what had been a game into a more serious investigation because his resemblance to the young man in the picture was so striking. A friend and coworker named Diana started downloading pictures of William from his Facebook page. By now William's two family names—Cañas Velasco—were known, so Jorge's coworkers could surf websites and download information from the Internet. Diana, too, was startled by the remarkable similarity of the two young men. She knew that Jorge had a twin brother who looked nothing like him and decided to send a picture of Jorge and Carlos to Yaneth. Meanwhile, Yaneth had downloaded a picture of William with his twin brother, Wilber, and sent it to Diana. Both photos showing the two sets of accidental brothers appeared on Yaneth's cell phone at the same time. This was a pivotal moment—the emergence of a crucial piece of evidence that strongly suggested that a mistake had been made years earlier. Yaneth no longer had any doubts because Jorge looked exactly like William, and Carlos looked exactly like Wilber, meaning that one twin in each pair had been exchanged. It was scary, and figuring out how it had happened was Yaneth and Laura's next big challenge. They had to proceed cautiously.

Meanwhile, Jorge was the only one of the four twins to see the two pictures. He was stunned, anxious, and confused to see someone who looked like him in places he had never been, wearing clothes that he didn't own. More baffling was that, seated next to his likeness in the photo, was an exact replica of Carlos, the twin brother with whom he had grown up. The caption read, "Thank God, one more happy year of life together—brothers forever." Jorge grew quiet and pale, actually aging before Laura's eyes. A terrible truth, unthinkable but possible, was taking shape in his mind—he must have an identical twin who had been switched at birth. Most likely out of fear and shock, he uncharacteristically felt powerless and allowed his friends to investigate for him.

While all this was happening, Jorge managed to call his sister, Diana Carolina, to tell her to look at some photos online. Diana was making a bank payment when the call came through, so she didn't pay much attention to her brother, who had a tendency to be annoying. He was being especially annoying this time, phoning her about every half hour. Later that afternoon she called him back and turned to the Facebook photos he had told her about. She was unmoved at the sight of William despite his strong resemblance to her brother Jorge who insisted that she keep looking. But even when she saw Wilber, a nearly identical copy of her other brother, she thought nothing of it. Jorge pleaded with her to pay more attention, adding that he had just learned that their birthdays were only one day apart, but Diana still thought it was all a coincidence.

Later that night Jorge returned to the apartment he shared with Carlos. He found his brother talking on his cell phone and told him to hang up because he needed to tell him something. Jorge began by teasing Carlos, asking if he believed soap operas were true stories, then asked how he would feel if it turned out that they were not really brothers after all. Jorge then started to laugh. At this point Carlos wanted to know what was wrong, and

Jorge said he thought he had learned something. As per their usual bantering and bickering, Carlos told him to stop joking, but Jorge continued to laugh as he turned on the computer to locate the telltale pictures. Carlos was relaxed at this point, waiting to find out what was making Jorge act so strangely, but as the shots of William and Wilber popped up on the screen, his expression grew pensive, then grim, and, according to Jorge, he "freaked out." He wanted to know who these people were, then shut down the computer and raced off to his room. He told Jorge not to bother him anymore about it, warning, "You don't know what kind of people they are." But Jorge would not be dissuaded—he wanted the four of them to meet, although he kept asking Laura what kind of people "they" were.

Yaneth did not send William the photos of Jorge and Carlos until the following day, September 10, when she had more revealing information to give him: each twin's birth date and blood type.

Discoveries

The first key question that had to be settled was whether William and Jorge had been born on the same day. Laura recalled that Jorge's birthday was December 21, while Yaneth remembered that William was born in December, but at first she didn't know exactly which day it was. Slowly, she reasoned that he must also have been born on December 21 because her boyfriend, Brian, did not attend a novena—the nine days of devotional prayers that last from December 16 to December 24—held at her home on that day because of William's birthday. She was certain of that because it was a Saturday. But William's official birthday is December 22, not December 21, so Yaneth was off by one day; perhaps William celebrated a day early that year. When the two friends realized that there was only a day of difference, they decided it was close enough.

In fact, Ana had given birth to her twins on December 22, just a day after Luz had delivered her twins. Because of the switch William and Carlos traded birthdays (and names), making William's birthday December 21 and Carlos's December 22. These incorrect dates of birth appear on their identity cards, or *cédulas*, and their other official documents. Jorge had learned about this one-day difference in birth dates just as he was phoning his sister to tell her about the probable exchange, and he found it chilling.

Satisfied that William and Jorge shared their actual date of birth and believing that so many similarities could not be mere coincidence, Laura and Yaneth tried to figure out which of the twins might have been switched. It was conceivable that Jorge, not William, had been exchanged and belonged to a different family. If so, this would mean that Wilber, not Carlos, had grown up in the wrong family. The likelihood that a baby exchange had occurred was now less in dispute than how it had come about. At this point Laura and Yaneth didn't know that Carlos did not resemble anyone in his family; they knew only that he and Jorge did not look alike. They also had to find out how much William and Wilber looked like other members of their family.

Jorge and Carlos's parents were deceased, and their only other sibling was female. So the best way for Laura and Yaneth to get the answers they needed was to compare the physical resemblance of William and Wilber to that of their three older brothers and older sister still living around La Paz. A good person to consult about this was Yaneth's boyfriend, Brian, who, as the brothers' first cousin, knew everyone in the La Paz family. It seemed that all three brothers, and the sister to some extent, looked like Wilber, with the same compact build and angular facial features, but none looked like William—in fact, William didn't look like any of his relatives. Thus, it seemed clear that William and Carlos were the twins who had been switched, but this did not explain how one got to La Paz and the other got to Bogotá.

Aware that they needed more definitive evidence to confirm the switch, Laura and Yaneth inquired about the blood types and birth histories of both sets of twins. Their blood types were available from their national identity cards, which they are required to carry at all times. The Bogotá brothers did not have matching blood types—Jorge's was Type A-positive and Carlos's was Type O-positive. Laura pressed Yaneth hard to find out the blood types of the other two. The La Paz brothers also didn't match—William was Type A-positive and Wilber was Type O-positive. Most telling was that the identical look-alikes, the young men suspected of being real twins, *did* match. That was when Laura and Yaneth started to feel really scared because they could not dismiss hard biological data.

In fact, this bit of information was not definitive.[3] Identical twins always have matching blood types, and if the blood types of the look-alikes had not matched, Yaneth and Laura might have given up the hunt. However, that they did match did not necessarily mean that Jorge and William, and Carlos and Wilber, were identical twins or that they were even biologically related: fraternal twins, full siblings, and unrelated individuals can have the same major group blood types. In the case of fraternal twins and siblings, parents transmit one gene from each of their tens of thousands of gene pairs to each child, so each gene has a 50-50 chance of being passed on.[4]

An important reason for caution regarding the young men's blood types is that 78.75 percent of Colombia's population has the gene for Type O blood, so any two people randomly chosen from that population could have matching blood groups by chance alone. However, when blood types are relatively less common in a population, the probability increases that two people suspected of being related actually are. The gene for Type A occurs much less frequently than the gene for Type O among Colombians— only 15.55 percent are Type A, but the match between Jorge and William could still have happened by chance.[5] Clearly, confirming the biological relatedness of two people requires much more genetic information.

Most current researchers classify twins as identical or fraternal by means of extensive DNA testing. The four in Colombia did not undergo this procedure until early October 2014, several weeks after they first met. Until then, the two twins suspected of having been switched—William and Carlos—could hope that somehow the DNA findings might show that the uncanny resemblances were pure coincidence and that they would awaken from the nightmare that was profoundly shaking their identity.

The blood type information that Laura and Yaneth uncovered was a small, but nevertheless consistent, addition to their accumulating evidence. In their minds the only remaining mystery was how the switch had come about—how did two babies born one day and 150 miles apart change places? With her usual prescience Yaneth wondered whether the La Paz twins had been brought to Bogotá as newborns for some unknown reason. And, indeed, they learned that one of the La Paz twins *had* been brought to Bogotá *"at seven months"* for medical care at a modern hospital. But Laura was confused—she was the mother of a young son and knew that parents can distinguish their own seven-month-old baby from other seven-month-old babies. If Carlos had been exchanged with another infant, his parents would have known it the instant he came home. But Laura had misunderstood—Carlos and Wilber were *born prematurely at seven months*, just twenty-eight weeks into Ana's pregnancy, and that was when Carlos was brought to the Bogotá hospital. Twins are four or five times more likely to be born prematurely than nontwins or singletons.[6]

Jorge and William were also born somewhat early, in Luz's thirty-fifth week of pregnancy. They were delivered on December 21, two days before Carlos arrived for treatment—this was easy to deduce because he was just one day old when his grandmother brought him to the hospital in Bogotá. But was Carlos treated at the same hospital where Jorge and William were born? That was the next question Laura and Yaneth needed to answer.

At first they had trouble determining the name and location of the hospital. Yaneth heard from William that one baby from La Paz was taken to a clinic in the northern part of Bogotá, but Laura and Yaneth later confirmed that he was brought to the Hospital Materno Infantil in the eastern Santa Fe district. Now Laura needed to ask Jorge where he was born, but he had left for lunch. When Jorge returned an hour later, Yaneth and Laura had their answer: Jorge was born at the Hospital Materno Infantil in Bogotá. Then Laura told him about the matching blood types. He put his hand to his head and said, "Oh, my God, not something else."

Yaneth and Laura now were convinced that the newborn exchange happened early in the twins' lives, in the crowded preemie nursery in Bogotá.

At about this time Laura's husband, Cristian, begged her to stop searching for clues. He worried that any suggestion that the brothers who grew up together were not really twins would badly damage two families. Cristian believed that if destiny wanted the real twins to meet, it would happen naturally. Laura's response was that she was part of that destiny.

Terrible Truths

While Laura and Yaneth waited for Jorge to return from lunch, Brian was at the butcher shop with William. The two were laughing together, trying to ease the tense situation, but in truth William's anxiety was escalating and he was growing increasingly depressed. Then the photographs arrived, the ones showing both unrelated pairs of brothers, and he became "superconcerned." He screamed at the sight of them, uncertain whether to laugh or weep.

At about 2:00 p.m. William was feeling hungry and left for lunch, climbing the two flights of stairs from the store to the apartment he shared with his brother. Yaneth phoned him just after he got there, and by the end of their conversation he knew that Carlos, the baby from La Paz, had been brought to the same hospital where Jorge, and presumably he, William, had been born. This, then, was the indisputable evidence that William had feared would prove that the parents who had raised him were not his parents, his twin brother was not his twin, and his three older brothers and older sister were someone else's siblings. Even his cousin Brian, with whom he had been so close for so many years, was not his cousin. Brian recalled William's expression as he descended the stairs: "Dead serious." When Brian asked what had happened, William was silent except to say that there was nothing left to confirm, then sat down, held his head in his hand, and cried.

After a short time William called his then girlfriend, Alejandra, who arrived to hug him and try to console him, but he just "cried and cried and cried." Suddenly he stood up, said there was nothing more to be done, and reminded everyone that there was plenty of work to do. The butcher shop was serving customers for another six hours, until 8:00 p.m. that evening. But he *had* to meet Jorge, the guy who looked so much like him in pictures.

Reunion

Laura gave Jorge's cell phone number to William so the two could arrange to meet that night since Jorge said he felt weird about sending him the phone number himself. Who was William, anyway? Was he a good person? Laura said he was, but she had only met him once, fourteen months earlier, at the butcher shop.

Jorge was attending a night class at the Universidad Las Libertadores when the call came through. Seeing William's name pop up on his cell phone screen made him anxious—seeing photos of his look-alike was one thing, but meeting him in person gave the situation a reality that it didn't have before. Meeting this stranger could change his life and his brother's life in ways that he could not begin to imagine or comprehend, and it scared Jorge.

Jorge suggested that they meet at 9:30 that evening at the Lourdes Plaza, a large square surrounding the Church of Our Lady of Lourdes (Iglesia de Nuestra Señora de Lourdes). The church, an impressive neogothic structure completed in 1875, is a popular attraction and meeting place for Bogotá's tourists and residents. His other reason for choosing that location was that a police station is located there and could provide a safe haven if something untoward happened at their meeting. Both Jorge and William originally intended to go alone, but William called Jorge back to say he was bringing Yaneth, Brian, and Carlos's look-alike. No doubt, William was feeling the same last-minute anxiety that was taking hold of Jorge. Hearing that William would not be alone, Jorge felt even more grateful for the police presence, and when he ran into a college friend on the way to the meeting, he convinced him to come along.

En route, Jorge kept reminding himself that William was a good person. And he had been impressed with the humility and deference William had shown toward him during their brief phone conversation. His use of "yes, sir" and "no, sir" signaled respect for others and is characteristic of people raised in Colombia's rural regions.

Earlier that day Jorge had asked Laura how he would recognize William when he got to the plaza. "Silly boy!" she said. Most people meeting for the first time agree not only on a time and place but also share details about their appearance, such as their height, hair color, or what they will be wearing so they will be more easily recognized. But identical reared-apart twins need only find someone with their own face. When the separated identical Chinese twins Sarah Heath and Celena Kopinski first met in their late twenties at a New York restaurant, they laughed about how easy it was to find each other.[7]

The look-alike pictures Carlos had seen on the Internet had upset him so much that he refused to come to the meeting at the church plaza, saying he had a date with a girlfriend. Whether the date was really an excuse is uncertain, but it was clear that he wanted nothing to do with the situation or anyone involved.

Across town a similar scenario was playing out for Wilber, Carlos's identical other. He knew nothing of the communications between his brother and everyone else during the previous forty-eight hours. It seems astonishing that William shared his incredible news with some family members but kept it from his brother, who might be more directly and more seriously affected than the others. Although William wanted to gather all the facts before involving Wilber, social distance and detachment were typical of their relationship. William finally phoned Wilber and told him to come home early on the pretext that they needed to run some errands together. When his brother arrived and saw the photographs, he reacted almost exactly like Carlos had—he didn't want to pursue it. And true to his hot-tempered Santanderean nature, Wilber became angry, actually furious. Leaving things alone was best, he argued, because, even if there had been a switch twenty-five years before, nothing could be done about it now. "We drank from the same breast," he told William, meaning that they were, and would always be, brothers. Later, Wilber did not remember saying these words, suggesting that William only believed he had said them. But he conceded that people say things in the moment that they fail to recall.

In the end Wilber agreed to attend the meeting, probably because he was secure knowing that he had been raised in the right home, enabling him to act on his curiosity without fear. Carlos did not have these luxuries; although his initial urge to leave the situation alone was similar to Wilber's, his reaction had different and terrifying roots.

When Jorge and his friend arrived at Lourdes Plaza, they didn't see William at first because it was dark and the plaza was packed with visitors. Then William called Jorge's phone and said they were there. Suddenly Jorge's friend spotted them and announced that "you" are coming toward us. The friend had seen William, and he looked and walked exactly like Jorge. The two look-alikes studied each other intensely for a bit before exchanging a few words. They laughed nervously, then Jorge hid his face in his hands as though to ease the intensity of the moment.

I have witnessed such reactions between separated identical twins who are meeting for the first time. They show a mix of emotions, including disbelief, elation, amazement, relief, surprise, and regret, and Jorge and William displayed all but one. They were not elated because elation is outside the switched-at-birth twins' reunion experience—none of the other switched twins I have known took pleasure in learning that they were part of another pair and another family. This is understandable because the members of this unique class of reared-apart twins turn into accidental brothers and sisters, separated because of a careless act that edited their life stories beyond recognition.

Jorge, too, was overwhelmed at the sight and sound of Wilber, who looked and laughed so much like his brother. Their only significant difference was the way they wore their hair—Wilber's was longer and more styled, whereas Carlos's was cut close to his head. But they had the same dark eyes, shaped eyebrows, and full lips, and Wilber swayed slightly side to side as he walked, just like Carlos. "You are the same," he said to Wilber, and they burst out laughing. *"Marica!"* he then shouted to Wilber; the word literally means "sissy" but also an effeminate male or a gay man. Jorge said it in a joking and familiar way, like he did with his brother and his close friends, probably because he felt that he already knew this young man. Friends' and siblings' shared understanding frees them to say such things in the ways that they do.

They all spent the next hour at a nearby coffee shop. Jorge and William continued to talk, feeling a kind of personal chemistry percolating between them, one they did not share with the brothers with whom they were raised. William learned that their mother, now deceased, had been a fighter who had raised her sons and daughter well as a single parent. And he learned about their father, also deceased, who had abandoned his family. William said that his parents were good people, farmers living to the north in the Colombian countryside. Jorge talked about his studies at the university, and William described his job at the butcher shop. Everyone talked about the apparent switch, wondering how it had happened. Then, taking the leadership role he would continue in the future, Jorge decided that all four twins should meet that night and called his brother to say that they would be coming to the apartment shortly. The three twins got into a cab.

* * *

Carlos wouldn't open the door at first, perhaps because the dark reality that he dreaded waited on the other side. When he finally undid the lock, Jorge entered first, followed by William, and their resemblance shocked him. Wilber came in last and that was when Carlos wanted to hold his head and curse because this mirror image reinforced what seemed so clear: that he belonged with another twin in another family. But like other twins meeting for the first time, the two stared at one another, laughed in the same nervous way, then turned their backs toward each other as though their resemblance was too hard to handle. Most reunited twins search for similarities as a way of affirming and celebrating their newfound relationship, but Carlos looked for differences, reasoning that if he found some, perhaps he and Wilber weren't twins after all. Wilber's hands were much rougher than Carlos's, but that was easy to explain—Wilber had labored on his family's farm for many years and was now using his hands to clean, cut, and lift large racks of meat, as well as move equipment. In contrast Carlos had always gone to school or worked in offices, mostly using his hands to write and type—the most arduous use of his hands involved tossing a basketball. He was running out of differences.

William looked longingly at the framed photo of Luz Marina on a table in the living room, visibly saddened and shaken by the sight of the biological mother he would never know. He could see his own facial contours, dark eyes, and wavy hair captured in her image. Mother and son had spent less than a day together, nearly twenty-six years earlier, but he would visit her grave when he could. As agonizing as this was, it was not the only heartache that lay ahead: William would have to tell his parents, Ana and Carmelo, that he was not their son, and he would have to tell his older siblings that he was not related to them, not a natural member of their close-knit family. How he would manage to convey these terrible truths while assuring them that he loved them, would always love them, and would always be their son and brother was not immediately apparent, but he was determined to find a way.

Aftermath

It was getting late and everyone had to be at work or school the next day. William and Wilber waited for a taxi to take them back to their apartment. The brothers' first meeting was over, but their separate lives were just starting to converge. They took their first group photograph together.

The experience of that night, while shared by the four brothers, affected each of them profoundly but in different ways. Everyone was changed, some more than others, and some of those changes would not be known for some time. But for the moment Jorge and William saw the conclusion to a long mystery that had begun as a joke. Ever the optimist, Jorge didn't cry that night but identified a bright side to the situation—everyone had gained a twin without losing a brother. Most likely, being raised in the right home, albeit with the wrong twin, afforded him the luxury of staying positive. He slept well.

Carlos couldn't sleep at all. He cried all night, tortured by the now unavoidable reality that nearly everything about his life was untrue. His beloved mother, Luz, had not given birth to him, Diana was not his older sister, and Jorge was not his twin brother. The large company of aunts who had helped raised him and loved him so deeply should have nurtured another nephew. The opportunity to climb the professional ladder belonged to another young man, while he, Carlos, had been destined for a life of farm labor in the remote Colombian countryside. As if to salvage a part of his unraveling sense of self, he reasoned that with his interests and drive, he would have become the financial analyst he was, even in La Paz. But that was unrealistic thinking because he had never been to that region and did not yet know the insurmountable hardships and struggles he would have faced. In fact, he might not have known what a financial analyst was. Perhaps the only real solace he could derive from this total rewriting of his life was that Norman, the father who had abandoned his family, turned out not to be his father at all. As he dragged himself out of bed the next morning, his eyes were puffy and surrounded by dark circles. "I want to be your brother," he told Jorge, who assured him that he always would be. It was a rare exchange of affection between these two brothers, who were usually at each other's throats.

Not long after that Jorge asked Carlos for a picture of himself, a request that struck Carlos as odd and unexpected, but the reason eventually became clear. Several weeks later, as a profound act of brotherly loyalty, Jorge had the picture tattooed on his chest next to the one of their mother. The words MI SAGRADA FAMILIA (My Holy Family) appear beneath them. Tattoos mean a great deal to Jorge, something Carlos knew well, and tattoos are permanent. This gesture came at the perfect time, in the early stages of everyone's attempts to cope with the shock of the switch and its ramifications. In the future some decisions made by one of the twins might reverberate throughout the group, so they would have to be made collectively. But above all, the tattoo that adorned Jorge's chest would be a constant reminder that family ties go beyond just blood, born largely of the shared time and investment that shape our common memories.

Wilber was raised in the right place with the right parents and siblings, except for his actual twin. Aside from his initial shock and anger, he took a relatively laid-back view. "If they [their families] changed us, they changed us" captured his feelings well. Perhaps he would have felt differently if his brother had rejected him after twenty-five years, but he knew that was not in William's nature.

In fact, when Wilber finally learned about the emails, phone calls, and WhatsApp discussions that had been flying around, he focused more on meeting his look-alike, "the other one," than on William's not being his twin brother.

William didn't sleep well the night before that first reunion or for the next several nights. He hardly ate, resisting his favorite dish, *mute Santandereano*, a soup made with pork, corn, and vegetables, that his godmother, Ana Liria, thoughtfully prepared for him. She and her husband were in utter disbelief when they examined the photos of the two pairs of accidental brothers, so different within sets, but so identical between them. Their reaction this time was a huge departure from their previous amusement at seeing their godson's look-alike alone in a single frame. But Ana Liria had no intention of abandoning the godchild she loved, and making his favorite meal was her way to show this.

The job in the butcher shop kept William's mind occupied for the next ten days, and for that he was grateful, but his unhappy state lasted longer than that, as some family members later acknowledged. William believed his ability to cope with this personal disaster attested to his inner strength, and he was right—children and parents who are less grounded have succumbed to alcohol, drugs, or depression when they learn of a baby exchange. In Gran Canaria the isolation and depression of the unrelated "twin" Beatriz led her to resume an old smoking habit. And now in his seventies, Philippe Joye, the Swiss twin raised in the right home, still feels the intense anger, grief, and loss that the return of his switched-twin brother caused his family.[8]

William, focused on being upbeat, uploaded the photo of the four brothers to his Facebook page within twenty-four hours of their first meeting. He wrote, "God knows how to do his stuff—

after twenty-five years, we found the true identical twins." Ever the optimist, just like his identical twin.

Many of us have been told that we look "just like" someone else, but, like the Colombian brothers, we tend to joke about it and dismiss the topic. But what fraction of these seemingly random encounters involves unsuspecting twins, brothers or sisters waiting to be discovered? We will never know for sure. Some people act on these curious confusions, while others leave them alone.

Several chance factors played key roles in the eventual meeting of the four Colombian brothers. Jorge had cut his long hair short just before the incident in the butcher shop—from the age of thirteen his hair had reached nearly to his waist. He had actually cut his hair twice, the first time to appease his mother and the second time to placate his clients, just one short month before Laura walked into the butcher shop. Had he not cut it the second time, she may not have mistaken William for Jorge; in fact, Jorge's other friends hadn't recognized him at first without his long ponytail. And what if the twins mistaken for each other had been Carlos and Wilber instead of Jorge and William? Both Carlos and Wilber were reluctant to explore the unusual situation further, raising the not unlikely possibility that the separated twins may never have met.

There was also Yaneth's casual comment and question that rekindled the friends' interest in the striking resemblance between William and Jorge, a topic that had been dormant during the previous six months. And one more thing: had Laura heeded her husband's warnings to drop the investigation entirely, her mistaking of a butcher for a coworker would have become nothing more than a joke, one that would have eventually lost its punch. "A good lesson: do *not* listen to your husband," she said.

Chapter 5

Revelations

Telling Their Families

A new reality was taking over. Sitting in their little apartment over the butcher shop, the La Paz brothers faced the daunting task before them: telling their four older siblings that William was not their younger brother and that Wilber had an identical twin living someplace else. They also had to tell their parents that William wasn't their son and that another woman had raised their natural-born child.

The parents of Jorge and Carlos were deceased, but several aunts had helped raise them and they remained close. These two young men had to think of the best way to tell them that one of their beloved nephews belonged to another family. They also had to persuade their older sister that her real brother wasn't Carlos but a young man named William, a task that would require some convincing since Diana had dismissed the matching photos as mere coincidence. Diana is a reality-based person, so the idea that one of her brothers of twenty-five years had been switched with another baby was preposterous. When her boyfriend looked at the photographs, he insisted that an exchange had occurred, but she still denied it. Because she didn't believe it, she claimed that she wasn't even curious, but her encouraging Jorge to meet his look-alike and tell her about it suggests otherwise.

The morning after the twins met, Jorge told Diana that William was like their mother, Luz, in how he thought and expressed ideas and that Wilber talked and laughed exactly like Carlos. This information did not change her mind—only a DNA test would convince her.

Finally, what of the friends who had teased Carlos and Jorge, and William and Wilber, about not looking like twins? Would these friends take the news seriously or think it was just one of Jorge's usual pranks? Would others take it as a tall tale that William intended as a jab at his brother? DNA tests had not yet been performed, but the Facebook photos, birth dates, birth histories, and blood types foretold a compelling story of baby switching, one that seemed impossible to explain away, especially after all four had met at Jorge and Carlos's home and the physical and behavioral similarities of the reared-apart twins grew stronger in full view. They were still twins but not fraternal as they had thought, so all their friends would be seeing them in a whole new way. Being an identical twin has that power because it is a relatively rare human relationship—only one-third of naturally conceived twins are identical—so when separated identical twins meet, they become objects of utter fascination, challenging cherished beliefs about human uniqueness and individuality. Of course, identical twins are never exactly alike, but they are as close as any two people can come. The four brothers had to relay their incredible news to friends and family members while trying to cope with how they would now see themselves. It was all still raw and new.

Siblings from La Paz

The media, and researchers to some extent, often overlook the thoughts, feelings, and impressions of the siblings of switched twins. Because these brothers and sisters grew up where they belonged and outside the twinship, it is easy to assume that their lives are untouched by the revelation of a switch, but that is hardly the case. These siblings have front-row seats that allow them to variously watch, take part in, and react to family dynamics as they unfold, making most siblings more astute observers and interpreters of events than their parents—after all, siblings share secrets and memories to which parents are never privy. So it was with the older brothers Chelmo, Efrain, and Edgar, and older sister, Alcira, in La Paz.

Chelmo was out in the fields working with his cousin in September 2014, when an ordinary morning became a horrific afternoon of dread and dismay after his cousin's brother called. The cousin at the farm took the call, then stared intensely at Chelmo. When Chelmo heard him mention William, he grabbed the phone, worried that something had happened to his youngest brother. After listening quietly for a few moments, Chelmo said, "Promise me on your mother's life that what you say is true." The caller promised. The thought that William was *not* his brother and had been exchanged an as infant with his real brother was too much for this loving, gentle man to bear. The news came out of nowhere—and, if true, what would it mean for the future of his family? Things like baby switching just did not happen.

Chelmo headed home immediately, afraid that William was lost to him. Chelmo phoned William several times to learn what he had to say, but William was evasive—William wanted more facts, the same reason he had delayed telling Wilber what he had learned. But William quickly called Chelmo back to ask, "How are you, man?" and to say, "I'm here—God and the Virgin Mary will give us strength." Then he summarized the events of the past several days.

Chelmo is emotional because his family means a great deal to him, and this made the next several days especially difficult. He worried that William would find a better temperamental fit with his newly discovered twin and family, but mostly Chelmo was in shock at learning that this "elegant boy" was not his real brother. This brother's demeanor had set him apart from his siblings, but by elegance Chelmo did not mean that William was stylish or fashionable. What he meant was that, as a child, William had created things by pulling ideas out of his head, building objects using knives and mud, once nearly severing an index finger in the process. During their play times at home, the brothers and sisters would call William *papito*, or little daddy, and jokingly ask him why he was so appealing. His candid answer was that he was a modest and respectful little boy.

More important questions needed answers now. Chelmo assured William that they would be brothers until parted by death—and William assured Chelmo that things would never change between them. But their tears continued.

Their brother Edgar, born seven years before the twins, learned about the twin switch in a phone call from another brother, Efrain, who had heard it from William. Efrain is about twenty years older than the twins and had moved away when they were born, but he had returned home when they entered the military because of escalating warfare in his area. Although he grew up apart from his two youngest brothers, his sudden fear of losing William was powerful and kept Efrain largely silent on this subject.

Edgar had never suspected that William was not part of their family and didn't believe what Efrain told him. Only when his parents said they believed it could he accept the truth, crying along with his family, especially his mother. That he had watched his young twin brothers grow from babies to children to young men made the news especially hard to hear. It was heartbreaking to realize that a brother he adored was part of his family only because of a terrible mistake. The chaotic days to come were made worse by the uncertainty of it all—would his younger brother sever ties with the family that had raised him?

Bereavement studies highlight the tragedy of loss among surviving family members and have found that the grief following the loss of an identical twin is more intense than for the loss of any other relative.[1] A bereaved seventeen-year-old twin tried to fill the void by reaching out to others, but hardly anyone understood what she was going through. "Our relationship was so wonderful and close. I lost the person I loved the most and even though I appear happy and strong, I'm absolutely devastated and my inner self is in shatters."[2] Even identical reared-apart twins who have known each other a short time feel the loss intensely. And in an unusual case of three separated sisters originally from Sri Lanka, two, Sita and Sharon, met for the first time when they were thirty-one and thirty-four, respectively.[3] But when Sita learned that she had a twin named Charlotte, she began an extensive search. Her sadness at separation was deepened by the shock and disbelief of learning that her twin had ended her life the year before; DNA samples confirmed their genetic identity. Perhaps if she had found her sister sooner, they would be together today because twins are 25 percent less likely to commit suicide than nontwins—identical twins' close relationship generally provides a high level of emotional support that sustains them through trying times.[4] Such a promising relationship left unfulfilled is a tragic loss and difficult to overcome.

I have also known twins whose twin cut them off socially, as a result of disagreements or misunderstandings, leaving them isolated and alone. Their squabbles are variously caused by differences in lifestyles, religious beliefs, or choice of partner. The inability to regain or maintain the trust and affection of a living loved one is painful and perplexing—Edgar and his family wondered whether that would be their fate. Growing up, Edgar was often the twins' surrogate parent, constantly breaking up twin-on-twin combat. Typically, William attacked his brother by hitting him, pulling his hair, and scratching him. Wilber didn't hit back because William was smaller, although he was physically stronger. "You couldn't put the two of them together," Edgar recalled, but he still loved them both.

Alcira, the La Paz brothers' oldest sibling and only sister, was away from home while they were growing up. She was sixteen when she left La Paz before they were born, to be a domestic servant for a family in Bogotá, and she stayed there eight years. When she returned to La Paz, she met her future spouse, married, and moved to Vélez, the small city twelve miles from her family's farm where the twins had been born. But she remained part of the same tight-knit family, and news of the switch brought extreme shock and sadness.

It took three people to convince Alcira that the life-changing family event had actually happened. First, William called her and told her to look at some photos online. But the photos had little impact because she didn't know what to look for and hadn't been told about a possible switch. The same thing happened when Alcira's youngest daughter Natalie showed her mother a different set of photos and asked if she recognized anyone. She thought they were her brothers, William and Wilber. Even after Natalie told her to look more closely, the photos made no impression. In fact, Alcira had seen shots of William and Wilber *and* Jorge and Carlos, but she assumed that she was looking at her brothers in every picture. It is unclear why no one explained the situation to her, but perhaps William wanted her to figure it out as he had, or maybe he and Natalie felt that allowing her to figure it out herself would soften the blow. But Alcira had to be told.

The next day Alcira's brother Efrain showed her more pictures, telling her plainly that one of the twins had been switched and that William was not their real brother. This time she believed it was true. Alcira recalled the intensity of those early days—feelings of sadness at losing a brother, and joy at gaining one, mixed with lots of tears. But she dreaded telling her mother that her favorite son belonged to another family—Alcira still grows emotional when this subject comes up.

William was the special child, the only one of his siblings who looked after their parents and the only one to phone Alcira on her birthday and on Mother's Day. Alcira found it ironic that someone who was not a blood relative treated her better than someone who was. Her observation raises the question of sibling identification—how do people know who their siblings are? Genetic relatedness cannot be seen directly, and people do not typically take DNA tests to confirm the identity of their brothers and sisters. Moreover, DNA testing is a recent technology, devised in 1984 by Sir Alec Jeffreys at the University of Leicester, and therefore was unavailable through nearly all of human history. Nevertheless, distinguishing relatives from nonrelatives, acknowledging maternal and paternal family lines, and differentiating close genetic relationships from distant ones have been universal organizing themes within all families and cultures.

Evolutionary psychologists suggest that humans possess "detection mechanisms" for assessing kinship. These mechanisms involve perceiving cues relevant to genetic relatedness, plus a kind of "built-in algorithm" that allows people to process this information and decide who is, and who is not, a relative. Researchers have described two key cues for sibling recognition: one is maternal perinatal association, or seeing a newborn in a lasting and caring relationship with one's mother. It is perfectly reasonable to assume that a baby breast-fed and cuddled by one's mother is part of the same family. The other cue is duration of coresidence, or continuity of the particular mother-child association, until the child reaches adolescence.[5] Virtually all parents nurture their children until they reach their late teens, at which time they leave home for school or work. Therefore, it makes sense that other children who remain in the home from infancy on are one's bona fide brothers and sisters. Even when some children leave home earlier for boarding schools or extended vacations, their parents attend to them through phone calls, emails, and texts, unambiguously affirming their membership in the family.

William and Wilber's older siblings were always in physical and social proximity to their mother—in fact, both twins were breast-fed and everyone could see that. The older siblings could also see that they and the twins lived with the same parents, although this cue has proven to be less salient than maternal perinatal association. Researchers also have proposed phenotypic matching—comparing someone's features, such as voice quality or skin tone—with a learned standard that represents that same trait in yourself or in other relatives as a way to distinguish kin from nonkin. Research suggests that, under certain circumstances, people are sensitive to such cues regarding genetic relatedness.[6] However, these cues are not essential to kin recognition or the development of close social relations. An interesting question becomes: Would identical twins or other close relatives recognize each other if their paths crossed by chance? The answer is a tentative yes, and here is why, based on several revealing anecdotes.

The identical reared-apart twins Caroline and Margaret Shand of Scotland met for the first time when they were sixty-four.

Each knew she had a twin sister, but they had never met—they were raised by different families and told never to ask questions. One day Caroline, who worked in a church, heard a strange noise and went outside to investigate. She noticed two women standing by a gravesite and wandered over. She recognized herself in one of them, and realizing it was her twin, they hugged each other and cried. Neither twin had married, so they decided to move in together and become a family.[7] Had they not known they were twins, they might not have responded to one another as they did, but we cannot be sure of that. There are, however, other separated siblings and twins who became close friends before they knew they were related, including several sets of male-female twins who became a couple because of their strong attraction to one another. Shared habits and behaviors are probably the social glue that drew them together and kept them close. (Spouses generally resemble each other in age and ethnicity, but especially in behaviors such as attitudes and values.) Furthermore, these coupled twins did not develop the incest taboo or sexual aversion to one another that evolves among relatives living together. Such aversion most likely evolved to prevent the production of genetically defective children, which is more likely to arise from mating by close kin because they carry common detrimental genes in recessive form.[8]

William looked and behaved quite differently from his other siblings—everyone said so. Why didn't William's older siblings question his relatedness to them, which happened in an extraordinary case of switched nontwin infants in Japan? In November 2013 Japanese newspapers carried the story of an unnamed sixty-year-old factory worker, born into wealth and privilege, who was inadvertently exchanged with a male infant from an impoverished single-parent home. Desperate for an education but financially responsible for his putative mother and brothers, the man worked days and studied nights. Eventually he became employed as a driver for a transportation service. His switched counterpart received private tutorials, attended university, and eventually headed a successful real estate company.[9]

The misplacement of these two nontwin male babies was not revealed by mistaken identity, as happened with William and Jorge. Instead, the three biological brothers from the wealthy family strongly suspected that their oldest brother came from a different family because they believed that his appearance was so different from theirs that it went beyond what biological connectedness would allow. The three never raised the possibility that their mother had had an extramarital affair, probably because a baby switch seemed more likely—when a nurse returned the newborn to his mother after his first bath, she had noticed that he was wearing different clothing.[10] However, the mother never questioned the nurse about the change in clothing, which might have suggested that a switch had occurred. This case was closely guarded, with little information seeping outside the courtroom where the case was successfully tried against Tokyo's San-Ikukai Hospital. When I met with the brothers' attorney, Yoshiko Oshima, in Tokyo in 2015, she provided few new facts.

The three brothers reviewed hospital records that showed which babies were born on which days, and DNA tests were performed on likely candidates. When presented with the difficult truth, the impoverished exchanged brother sadly replied, "I might have had a different life. . . . I want the hospital to roll back the clock to the day I was born."

This story of the Japanese brothers has a quasi-happy ending. The three wealthy brothers have embraced their older biological brother, and the four have continued to bond over beers. Oshima had no knowledge of the actions and reactions of the initially disadvantaged baby who became wealthy just because a nurse gave him a bath.

As I left Oshima's office, my thoughts focused on that oldest brother, who was hardly mentioned in the newspaper coverage. Perhaps he drew little sympathy because he had slipped into a life rich with opportunity. We cannot know the mental anguish he may have suffered from feeling out of place, surrounded by his three brothers' suspicions that he belonged elsewhere. Their collective efforts to confirm his outsider status must have hurt. Carlos, the switched twin who accidentally grew up with Jorge in Bogotá, comes to mind—his place in his family was never questioned, but perhaps he felt adrift from his assumed twin, his sister Diana, and their mother. And what about William, raised with Wilber in La Paz where he didn't belong? Did he, like the sixty-year-old Japanese factory worker, want to turn back the clock?

The three younger Japanese brothers seriously doubted and actively challenged whether their oldest brother was biologically related to the rest of the family. Perhaps the differences between them were too great to be explained away by different genes, or maybe the three also worried about the family fortune their brother would inherit—however, the few studies conducted on primogeniture in Japan show that just 40 percent of city dwellers believe that the eldest son should receive a larger share than his siblings.[11] It is also possible that they recalled their mother telling them about the baby being returned to her in unfamiliar clothing. A final possibility is that the particular personalities of the Japanese brothers led them to ask questions when things did not seem quite right, whereas the La Paz brothers were more accepting.

I suspect that William's position as "co-youngest" in the family took him out of any real contention for inheriting resources such as the family farm, which ultimately went to Chelmo; therefore, William was not a threat to his older siblings. William was also a warm, generous, and studious child, making it easy to love him—his sibling conflicts were mostly with Wilber. In contrast, the wealthy Japanese brothers may have worried that a large portion of their parents' assets would pass to their oldest brother, leaving them relatively empty-handed. Little information about the relationships among the Japanese siblings is available, but the enduring doubts of the youngest three and their intensive search for their biological brother suggest they were not close to their putative older sibling.

As an infant, youngster, and young teenager, William shared a bed with his mother, while Wilber, Edgar, and their father slept nearby. Ana cried when William left for the military, but she didn't cry when Wilber joined four months later. It seems reasonable that her increased focus on William was connected to her knowledge of his poor health as a baby—the twin who was taken to Bogotá for treatment. However, mothers of extremely low birth-weight twins generally favor the healthier baby, who usually is the one who comes home first from the hospital.[12] This could have been true early on, but as the years passed it was William's sensitive nature and kind spirit that Ana found so endearing—although William may have actually been the healthier baby because he was born at thirty-five weeks, whereas Wilber was born much earlier, at twenty-eight weeks. William was also the twin preferred by Ana's mother, Eva Castillo, who loved telling the story of how she brought him to Bogotá bundled in a blanket. Later, when William visited his childhood home, Eva doted on him. She died in about 2005 and never learned that the baby she brought to Bogotá was not the one who came back. Wilber felt no jealousy at his mother's and grandmother's preference for William, because Wilber believed he was his father's favorite twin son.

Mothers have no reason to doubt that the babies they deliver are their genetic children, and maternal grandmothers have no reason to doubt that the babies their daughters deliver are their genetic grandchildren. The much longer history of having babies in intimate settings, rather than impersonal hospitals, explains why few question whether the baby handed to them is theirs, a postpartum response that has been preserved across generations. Thus the term *maternity uncertainty* is nowhere to be found in the scientific literature. Certainly, Ana Delina never suspected that she was raising someone else's son—nor did Luz Marina, who was in exactly the same situation in Bogotá.

Ana and Carmelo: Breaking the Silence

Ana and her husband, Carmelo, were past seventy when these events unfolded. William, Wilber, and their four older siblings were justifiably worried that revealing what had happened would be such a big shock that their aging parents might be physically and emotionally overwhelmed. So William and Wilber crafted a plan to break the story gently and gradually to Ana and Carmelo. But in so doing they inadvertently raised their mother's hopes that they had some good news to share.

William and Wilber agreed that they could best prepare their parents by casually tossing out suggestive questions and comments. This task, strung out over two weeks, was assigned to Alcira, their older sister, who enjoys a close relationship with their mother. In fact, Alcira was among the first to learn that her mother became pregnant for the seventh time and that a local natural medicine doctor had said she was having twins. She recalls that her mother didn't believe the doctor until she delivered her twins after that tortured journey to the hospital in Vélez.

Ana may have been unaware that in developed countries older women, especially those aged thirty-five to thirty-nine, have a greater chance of conceiving fraternal twins than younger women. Releasing two eggs at once is actually a reproductive "error" because human females are built to carry just one baby. It is also true that as women approach the end of their reproductive years, their chances of conceiving a child with a genetic defect such as Down syndrome increase. Evolutionary psychologists have, therefore, speculated that some women's bodies go through a kind of cost-benefit analysis—that is, bearing fraternal twins could be a final effort for them to transmit their genes to the next generation, but with the dual gambles of a high-risk pregnancy and delivery of one or two children with a genetic liability.[13]

Ana was about forty-five when she had her twins, an age by which twinning is on the decline, and her twins were identical, not fraternal, so another explanation is needed for why this older mother conceived an identical pair. Some scientists have wondered whether an aging egg might lack some nutritional and energy sources, leading to developmental delay and programming errors in the developing cells, creating identical twins in the process. It is also possible that, in older women, the membrane surrounding the early fertilized egg fractures, causing it to divide. I remember the reaction of a fortysomething mother whose identical twin daughters took part in one of my studies—she was in utter shock and disbelief at being pregnant, especially with twins. Studies in the United States and Israel have demonstrated that men past the age of forty, like Carmelo, are more likely to father twins than younger men, although the "older parent" effect for having multiple births is stronger in females.[14] How older fathers contribute to twin conceptions is unknown, but could be partly linked to some men's higher levels of an insulin growth factor called IGF-2, which is involved in cell growth and division; however, IGF-2 could affect twinning in both older and younger men, so there must be something more to this story. Many men like to think that their exceptional virility explains why their partner conceived two babies rather than one, but it's just not so.

Alcira began by asking her mother how she would feel if one of her sons was not really hers. Since people had joked about this for years, Alcira's remarks never aroused Ana's suspicions—but she grew impatient with her daughter, whose questions seemed vague and insensitive. Instead, Ana was excited when William and Wilber invited her and Carmelo to Bogotá for an important visit—she was certain that Wilber was about to be married.

The days passed. Ana eventually learned that Wilber was not getting married—instead, the excuse was that she and Carmelo were needed in Bogotá to sign papers related to their son Israel's death while he was in the military. Only one of her six children, Alcira, had married (and was widowed), so Ana was disappointed to learn Wilber was not engaged, but there were plenty of grandchildren. Alcira had six children, three boys and three girls. Chelmo had lived with two different women and fathered a boy with one and identical twin boys with the other. And Efrain had two daughters who lived with their different mothers.

The La Paz parents made the all-day journey to Bogotá several weeks after their children knew the truth. The family gathered in the modest apartment that William and Wilber shared over the butcher shop. Wilber had to work at the store, leaving to William the difficult task of telling his parents how he had been mistaken for someone who looks exactly like him and how the switch was discovered. It was easy for Wilber to walk away at this point—as the twin raised in the right place, he was angry but not emotionally distraught the way his brother was. And William was better suited to break the news gently and to assure his parents that he would always be their son. He was the boy she cherished for his kind, sweet manner.

Yet another odd twist had intervened in this already strange story—Ana already knew! Just minutes before she arrived at the apartment, someone in Bogotá told her the truth and swore Ana to secrecy—and Ana has never revealed the identity of this woman. More than once we asked her who it was, but Ana refused to say, leaving us to speculate. A likely candidate was Ana's sister Edelmira, the twins' aunt who had taken William back to La Paz a week after his grandmother had brought Carlos to Bogotá. Edelmira learned about the switch from one of her nieces. "I fixed my eyes on the baby—only it was the wrong one," she said. An ambulance had carried Edelmira and the baby back to La Paz, but the baby was concealed in blankets and tubes sprouted across his entire body, making him hard to see. Like everyone else, Edelmira was shocked and horrified by the news, but she never felt guilty because she had focused intensely on the baby each day and had immediately notified the nurse when his wristband was missing— that happened one afternoon at about 3:00 p.m., but it was in place when she returned the next day. Edelmira had read the baby's tag on both days and they matched. Thus, it is likely that the switch happened before Edelmira first saw him.

Another potential whistle-blower was William's godmother, Ana Liria, who nurtured William throughout this ordeal. Another was William and Wilber's housemaid, Marlen Rodriguez, who cleaned their apartment and was privy to some private conversations—maids in Colombia are plentiful and inexpensive, even for people on limited budgets. But we will never know who told Ana. That may not matter now, although it may have mattered at the time. Learning life-changing news from someone outside the immediate family can be particularly devastating, because his or her intentions and motivations for doing so can be suspect. Alcira was furious that "it was not one of us."

Ana was devastated when she first heard and wept hard. "Dear God, help me!" she cried. She worried that William, her favorite son, would abandon her and the rest of the family. She thought about the difficult life William had had, laboring long hours on the farm and never going to school because the family couldn't afford to send him. Ana felt especially distraught at the knowledge that William would never meet his biological parents. And she worried about whether Carlos had been well cared for.

The news was also hard on Carmelo, who did hear it for the first time from William—suddenly his son by mistake—but Carmelo is much less expressive than Ana. The poor man was puzzled at first, thinking that Ana had delivered all four boys and two had been taken away! When we met Ana and Carmelo at their home six months later, Ana was still crying, unable to fully assimilate what had happened, but slowly gaining acceptance. Her somber mood was occasionally interrupted when her tough, hot-tempered Santanderean nature broke through, as when she insisted that the four brothers file a lawsuit against the Hospital Materno Infantil. A lawsuit made perfect sense to Ana, an idea she underlined by asking, "Do chickens crow?" This sarcastic touch matched the feisty nature of this small woman. But Ana also had a warm, sweet side that William and Wilber's childhood friends told us about, and she was ready to show it whenever Carlos came around. Carmelo stood by silently, but his eyes were wet. By now he knew that William would always be his son, but months had passed and he still didn't know whether Carlos ever could be. Still, he felt connected to the son he hardly knew.

Paternity Uncertainty: Who's the Father?

In contrast to mothers and maternal grandparents, fathers and paternal grandparents have some reason to doubt their genetic relatedness to their children and grandchildren, giving rise to the term *paternity uncertainty.* That is because ovulation is hidden, fertilization is internal, and women can have sex at any time. Thus, males can never know for sure whether the child delivered by their partner is truly theirs. Paternity uncertainty is of considerable interest to evolutionary psychologists—it is well known that mothers generally invest more time and care in their children than fathers do and that fathers may invest more in some children than in others. The different levels of investment fathers extend to each of their children results from many factors, but one may be their certainty of relatedness to a given child.[15] Perhaps Carmelo's preference for Wilber was partly tied to the familiar features he recognized in this son.

Jorge and Carlos: "Our Family Has Grown"

Jorge and Carlos had to tell their aunts—their mother's five sisters—what had happened. All the aunts had been with the boys for birthdays, baptisms, graduations, and other significant events in their young lives. Two, Blanca Cecilia and Maria Teresa, were like their second mothers, having lived with them for nineteen years in their two-story home. Even the sisters who had married and raised families of their own—Leonor, Maria Esther, and Ana Rosa—were closely involved.

Although he was reluctant at first to act on the evidence Jorge had shown him, Carlos took the lead. He called Leonor and Maria Esther and invited them to lunch. The occasion, he said, was that "the family had grown." Leonor, cool, elegant, and interested, assumed that "Carlito's" girlfriend was pregnant, but he promised her that was not the case. He told her to just come to lunch.

When Leonor and Maria Esther arrived at the restaurant, Carlos showed them the photographs and described the probable mix-up at the hospital. His aunts were stunned—they had known their nephews all their lives, and nothing like this had ever come up, in their family or in anyone else's. The two aunts adored

Carlos and Jorge, both so well behaved, studious, and professional. The aunts knew that their sister Luz had brought the
boys up well and that neither one had been in serious trouble at
school or in the neighborhood, unlike some of their peers. Like
everyone who knew Jorge and Carlos, Leonor and Maria Esther
recognized the huge personality and physical differences between the twins, but they never suspected that anything was
amiss because fraternal twins can differ by quite a lot—their sisters
Blanca Cecilia and Maria Esther were fraternal twins, and they
were quite different. Leonor and Maria Esther eventually laughed
to brighten things up, and announced that they had just gained
two nephews.

Carlos's mood that day was a mixture of unease and appre-
hension. Leonor assured Carlos that God does things his way. She
believed that her sister Luz Marina would have been sad but accepting of what had happened. In the end Leonor stopped laughing and left her favorite fish dish untouched.

Because she had helped raise Jorge and Carlos since birth, Blanca
Cecilia identified as a kind of mother, but her feelings of affection
may have also reflected her own status as a fraternal twin, a relationship that her nephews believed they shared until recently.
Most twins develop a quick rapport with other twins because they
recognize that they have something fundamental in common,
although the attraction is greatest when the twin types are the same.
Twins run fairly rampant on the maternal side of the brothers'
family. Luz was born a twin, but her twin sister died shortly after
birth, so whether she was an identical or fraternal twin is unknown. Luz walked with a limp, supposedly because of her own
mother's difficult multiple birth delivery. Twin boys also appeared
in the next generation, delivered not just by Luz but also by
Blanca Cecilia's twin, the brothers' aunt Maria Esther, although

one of these twins also died soon after birth. Birth information was unavailable for the paternal side of the family.

Twins run differently in the La Paz family, but they are plentiful there too. The grandmother who brought the baby to Bogotá did not deliver twins, but one of her five children delivered fraternal twin sons when she was nineteen—Edelmira, the aunt who brought the wrong baby back to La Paz. Mothers of twins are exquisitely sensitive to twin development and twin relationships, so while the exchange was not her fault, Edelmira's role in the mistake was difficult for her to bear. Another of Ana's sisters delivered male twins when she was about seventeen, but both died shortly after birth. Ana delivered identical twins, and one of her sons fathered identical twin boys.

All the mothers in both families had conceived their twins without medical help. However, assisted reproductive technology (ART), the medical procedure that produced the first "test tube" baby in England in 1978, is largely responsible for the dramatic rise in mostly fraternal twins in Western nations.[16] Twins now occur in about one in thirty births in the United States, compared to one in sixty in 1980, and about one-third result from fertility treatments.[17] Several procedures are now available. In vitro fertilization (IVF) combines an egg with a sperm in a laboratory dish, then implants the embryo in a woman's uterus after a few days. Or sometimes a sperm is injected directly into an egg, a procedure known as intracytoplasmic sperm injection (ICSI). One or more fertilized eggs can then be implanted into the uterus.

Fertility treatments are not the only reason for the rise in twinning rates. The peak period for conceiving fraternal twins is when women are in their midthirties, and women are now having children at older ages. By delaying conception women run the risk of simultaneously releasing two eggs, which would produce fraternal twins if fertilized by two separate sperm. But other factors also affect the chances of conceiving fraternal twins, such as being a taller and heavier mother, engaging in frequent sexual intercourse—especially after periods of abstinence—being of African descent, and having a family history of twinning. The causes of identical twinning are less well known, but they do seem to run in some families, suggesting a genetic link.[18]

Who has twins and why leads to fascinating debates in the medical world and entertaining stories everywhere. I know a woman who naturally conceived quadruplets—two sets of identical twin boys—and thinks her two fertilized eggs divided because she had been baling hay for hours in extremely hot weather. Some residents of the "Street of Twins" in Havana, Cuba, claim that the fruit of the siguaraya tree is responsible for the twelve twin sets (both identical and fraternal) that live on their two-block strip.[19] These stories engage our imagination, but they do not inform our understanding. Luz's mother, Leonor Chavez, was thirty-eight when she delivered her fraternal twins, Blanca Cecilia and Maria Esther, and forty when she delivered Luz and her sister, whose twin type is unknown. Luz herself was thirty-six when she had her twin sons, Jorge and William—the perfect age for a fraternal pair—but her twins were identical. The La Paz family also shows a mix of identical twins, fraternal twins, and deceased twins. Chelmo's partner, Martha Castañeda, and Ana's sisters, Edelmira and Maria Eva, were young when they delivered their twins, somewhat increasing the chance of identical twinning— although Edelmira's twin sons appear to be fraternal according to family members.[20] Based on their identical appearance Martha did in fact deliver identical boys, but she was not a blood relative; the type of twins Maria Eva delivered is unknown. However, Ana was forty-five when she delivered her identical twin sons, Wilber and Carlos—she was not at high risk for bearing identical twins and had passed the peak period for conceiving fraternal twins. Her birth history adds to the mystery and wonder of human twinning, keeping us captivated and hungry for more information. Meanwhile, another expert was Blanca Cecilia, who believed she had predicted the switch.

When Blanca Cecilia has bursts of nervous energy, her long graying ponytail whips rapidly around her head. Blanca Cecilia had been with her twin nephews ever since they were discharged from the hospital—she was certain that they came home at different times, Jorge before Carlos. The babies were breast-fed, but she gave them bottled milk in between. Blanca Cecilia lived with them and cared for them until they left home when they were nineteen. Therefore, it seems strange that, even though Blanca Cecilia was living with the boys' sister, Diana, when the switch first became known, she didn't find out about it until her sister Leonor told her. By then DNA test results had identified the true twins, finally convincing Diana that it was true. It turned out that Blanca Cecilia didn't know until later because Carlos and Jorge each assumed that the other one had told her. Blanca Cecilia now lives with Carlos and Jorge—and Carlos blames his expanding waistline on his aunt's great cooking.

Blanca Cecilia was shocked and excited by the news. Reflecting on her feelings six months later, with greater knowledge of how each person was affected, she could not help feeling sad for William, who would never meet his parents and who had lost the education he craved—she had watched Jorge and Carlos advance to the university level and could see how much that experience meant to them. Blanca Cecilia was also unhappy for her sister Luz Marina, who would never know her other twin son, William. But with great fanfare Blanca Cecilia described a dream she had had several months before the discovery. In the dream Luz came to her and asked her to care for all four twins. There had been an exchange and now each twin had a double, brought together by Luz's spirit. Luz worried that Blanca Cecilia would not love each one, but she assured Luz that she would.

Blanca Cecilia's dream exemplifies magical realism, a type of fiction that injects elements of fantasy in otherwise realistic settings. It goes beyond entertainment to present observations of social and political conflicts in Latin American countries and in the developing world. The truth of some stories may be questioned, but they are real to the people who believe them, functioning to unite them and help them to overcome fears and restrain violence.[21] This style of writing was made famous by Colombia's Nobel Prize–winning author, Gabriel García Márquez, in his 1967 novel *One Hundred Years of Solitude* and in his other works. Márquez claimed that "surrealism comes from the reality of Latin America." Today, some promoters of Colombian tourism have recast the term as a brand, "Colombia, Magical Realism," to attract visitors from abroad.[22]

Blanca never mentioned the dream to anyone because she was sure no one would believe her.

The Bogotá household was always packed with relatives, among them the brothers' aunt Maria Teresa, their mother's younger sister. She and her daughter, Gloria Andrea, were two of the eight residents in the brothers' childhood household and lived with them until the boys left home. Maria Teresa recalled that Luz's doctor felt her sister's rapidly thickening abdomen during an early prenatal exam and detected two heartbeats. He pronounced the twins identical, although how he reached that conclusion without an ultrasound is unknown. As a twin herself, Luz was pleased but concerned about the financial burdens posed by multiple birth babies. Of course, she delivered identical twins, but brought home a "fraternal" pair. That explains why Maria Teresa "went crazy" when she saw the photographs of the mismatched twins.

She cried along with her neighbors, who had known her two nephews since they were infants.

Looking back, some seemingly innocuous observations assumed new meaning. Maria Teresa had entertained the children when they were young, tickling them and making them laugh, but Carlos was more reserved than the other two, neither playful nor participatory. He was just different, playing more with his cousin Gloria Andrea than with his siblings. Then there was the stuffed toy cow named Angélica María that Luz had brought home for her children. Diana, then twelve, and Jorge, eight, loved it, with Jorge becoming Angélica's voice so the toy could speak to them. But his brother didn't like such games; he preferred to play school, with his sister as the teacher and he as her student.

According to Maria Teresa, when the twins got older, Carlos was a serious student and stylish dresser, whereas Jorge was a somewhat more relaxed pupil and casual dresser. Their athletic preferences and musical choices also diverged—Carlos liked basketball and rap, Jorge liked football and rock. "They were not typical twins," she said. The differences between them, while pronounced, are not unusual for fraternal twins, because genetic factors influence personality, sense of humor, sports participation, and musical interests.[23] The stuffed cow toy did not hold the same appeal for both brothers, nor did the game of basketball. Everyone responds differently to the things around them, filtered through their own genetic lens. Still, the brothers had some common traits—both were interested in school and in eventually getting advanced degrees, although to different extents. Their mother's firm hand and strong support helped both of them along, but she probably had to lean harder on Jorge.

Like her sister Blanca Cecilia, Maria Teresa had also had a dream.

How would Luz have reacted to news of the exchange? Apparently, she had a temper, so she would have tried hard to find the nurse responsible for the switch. And she would have done everything in her power to be with William, but she would never have abandoned Carlos.

Aware that Jorge and Carlos's friends had teased them terribly about their differences, I wondered how their friends reacted to the news that they weren't twins after all. One evening, on the spur of the moment, I rounded up two of Jorge's best friends, Andres and Ricardo, and invited them to my hotel for beer and snacks. This was in July 2016, during my second visit to Bogotá, so the friends had had nearly two years to reflect on how they had reacted to news of the switch, what it meant to Jorge, and how it had affected him.

Long before the switch was known, Jorge, Andres, and Ricardo had formed an exclusive triumvirate that they call the Trio Miseria (the Miserable Three), a chat group that they use for exchanging personal news, stories, ideas, and jokes. The three also take trips together throughout Colombia and Brazil and have supported each other through girlfriend breakups, family deaths, and financial crises. Both Andres and Ricardo hold Jorge in high esteem for his generosity, support, and ability to find solutions to his problems and theirs. His chronic tardiness makes their eyes roll and their hands clench, but they put up with it because they value his friendship so tremendously.

Andres Sanchez Torres was the first to arrive. He is a warm, friendly guy who eats and drinks with great gusto, which made me wonder whether I had enough salami, cheese, and brew to last the night. He and Jorge have known each other for eight years, ever since they took a drafting class together, and they display the kind of easiness and familiarity with one another that comes from their long history of shared experiences.

At first, Andres thought that Jorge's crazy tale of the twin switch was just that, nothing more than a silly joke. Andres, a project analyst, was busy at work when Jorge's message, marked IMPORTANT, showed up on his computer screen, announcing that "our family has grown." Andres instantly thought that Jorge had had another child, exactly what Aunt Leonor had assumed when she heard those same words from Carlos. Next, Andres examined the Facebook photos and profiles of Jorge and William to which Jorge had directed him. Then he called Jorge. "Come on, don't fuck around!" Andres shouted, knowing his friend was a perennial prankster. Andres was certain that Jorge had used Photoshop to create an identical image of himself or had set up a fake Facebook page, but when he saw the pictures of Carlos and Wilber, "it went from being just a story to being *something*." At first Andres wondered if there might merely be lots of look-alike people in Colombia or maybe in the rest of the world. But he knows Jorge well enough to know when he is being serious, and Andres came to understand that there was a real possibility that Jorge had an identical twin brother, William, who had been switched at birth with another infant. It was crazy.

Jorge had invited Andres to come with him to Lourdes Plaza that night for the twins' first meeting, but Andres couldn't go because he had a test in one of his university classes. "I think I failed my quiz because I couldn't stop thinking about it," Andres said.

Ricardo Andres Rincón Castro is tall and lean, with big eyeglasses, a mustache, and a trimmed beard, and exudes a more thoughtful and serious demeanor than Andres. A part-time project manager and part-time engineering student, he had logged on to the Trio Miseria chat site when he saw the message flagged as important and assumed it was something personal, having to do with Jorge's family, maybe his son, Santi. "Why can't Jorge be more specific?" Ricardo wondered. Jorge had also directed him to Facebook, and when Ricardo came across the photos of the two accidental brothers, he correctly figured out that Jorge and William, not Jorge and Carlos, were the real twins—but it took Ricardo a few extra minutes to realize that Carlos also had an identical twin who had grown up somewhere else. Feeling shocked and overwhelmed, Ricardo was eager to meet William and to support his friend, but Ricardo had to miss the reunion because of his uncle's fiftieth birthday celebration.

After more beers, meat, and cheese, Andres and Ricardo started a lively discussion of the behavioral similarities and differences between their old friend, Jorge, and his new twin brother, William, whom they had gotten to know. Politeness and kindness led the similarities list, followed by fondness for injecting humor into most situations, even serious ones. But when they go clubbing, the twins' differences become apparent. William is outgoing, but less so than his twin, displaying a quieter version of Jorge's social spark. Jorge is quicker to approach pretty women, but they say that William is a better dancer and can be found more frequently on the dance floor. (I have danced with both twins myself and found them to be equally adept in this area. In fact, twin studies show that physical skills and athletic performance are substantially affected by genetic factors.)[24] William is fond of traditional Colombian country music, whereas Jorge is fanático about hard rock, especially that of Iron Maiden. And, of course, their different accents reveal their different backgrounds, although William speaks more clearly and less rapidly than his other family members. Above all, both twins are expressive about anything they love, such as William's seeing the ocean for the first time on a trip to Cartagena, when his unabashed joy turned him into a little kid, bursting with glee.

When the two are together, Jorge does most of the talking, leaving William to read his text messages or walk away. This might strike some people as selfish or unfair, but the twins say they are content with this arrangement, which reflects trust and comfort on both sides. Not surprisingly, William speaks up a lot more when he is not with his identical twin, which often makes it hard to remember which twin you are talking to. It is often the case that when identical twins are apart, they seem more alike than when they are together. In fact, a 1962 study reported the same paradoxical finding, that identical twins reared apart are more alike in extroversion (assertiveness, gregariousness) and neuroticism (anxiousness, moodiness) than identical twins reared together. It may be that because reared-apart twins have not had a lifelong relationship with one another, they can express themselves more freely and similarly away from the influence of the other, when they have less need to distinguish themselves. William and Jorge have many traits in common, such as kindness, thoughtfulness, and leadership, and they may have expressed these so clearly because they were raised apart. Recent twin research has not replicated the finding of greater personality similarity in reared-apart than reared-together twins, perhaps because these studies have used different inventories and questionnaires.[25] However, anyone who knows identical twins can sense the subtle behavioral changes that surface when they are apart or together.

There is little question that the twins' drastically different rearing environments created some differences between them, such as William's greater trust in people and Jorge's constant vigilance. People in remote rural towns know everyone for miles around, not just because their families have deep roots, but because they need companionship, resources, and assistance. In contrast, city dwellers move around, live in closed-off apartments, lock their doors, and watch out for assailants—recall that Jorge chose to meet William near a police station.

* * *

Several weeks after the twins first met, they rented a hall for friends and relatives from both families to meet the switched twins for the first time. One person present who was not part of either family commented that there were no moments of sadness, only joy. Jorge and William dressed alike, whereas Carlos and Wilber did not. Hilarity followed initial confusion when people mistook William for Jorge and thought that Carlos was Wilber. People were dancing and hugging amid the bright balloons that were everywhere.

But unreasonable expectations, tough challenges, and unsettled questions resurfaced once the party ended. For one, Carlos could not instantly become Ana's son, despite the love she promised him. When he was first introduced to his biological parents, Carlos said how nice it was to meet them, but his words were not completely heartfelt. The parent-child bond grows out of years of caring and companionship, and Carlos had lost his beloved mother to cancer five years earlier, when she was fifty-seven and he was just twenty. He needed to wait and see, taking baby steps toward establishing a meaningful parent-child relationship so long past due. William had to confront his lost educational and professional opportunities, aware that his difficult farming and military life had really belonged to someone else. Everyone wanted to know how the switch had happened. It would not have made a difference, but it might have provided some closure. And all four twins had to get used to calling someone else's twin brother his own.

Jorge's friends, Andres and Ricardo, increased their social capital through their association with him after the twins' story became known—their prospective dating partners were impressed that they knew a person as famous as Jorge. However, fame brought a dark side when Ana and Carmelo's home was robbed in the summer of 2016. Masked thieves carrying weapons stole cell phones and attacked their grandson, and one robber warned the couple not to come after them because they all knew each other. Wilber believes his family was targeted because people in their town had seen the twins ferried around in expensive cars by the foreign TV producers who eventually found their way to the twins and their story. Consequently, neighbors assumed that the family was rich, and even Ana's doctor told her she no longer needed national health insurance because she could pay for medical care herself. This robbery was the first anyone can remember, either in La Paz or in the towns nearby. Ana and Carmelo are no longer comfortable talking about the twins' opportunities outside their four walls.

All four twins are amazed that their lives have attracted so much attention—so it is worth thinking about why their story has captivated the world. I believe that identical twins are intriguing because the sight of two people who look and act so much alike challenges our beliefs in individual differences. And people often envy the ease with which most identical twins develop mutual love and trust. Therefore, when parents cannot keep identical twins, their adoption by different families strikes us as wrong and unfair. But the Colombian twins were accidentally switched, and the exchange involved two identical twin pairs, the odds of which are impossible to calculate. Furthermore, two twins had to meet for the truth to become known, raising the odds even higher. And the right sequence of events had to unfold—if Wilber rather than William had been working at the butcher shop the day Laura walked in to buy barbeque meat, the twins might never have met—because Laura knew Jorge, but she did not know Carlos, Wilber's identical twin. The seemingly minor occurrences that happen in our lives can have profound consequences.

Meeting the Families: A Celebration—of Sorts

Wilber and Carlos climbed the stairs to Wilber and William's apartment, where their parents were waiting. Wilber entered first, then turned to Carlos and said, "These are my parents—and these are *your* parents." Carmelo, wearing his best suit, stood up, put his hand on his new son's neck, and hugged him, the first time Carlos ever experienced genuine fatherly affection. Ana covered her face because she was crying, then reached for her son's hand. She asked God to bless her precious son and to be with him every day. He gently asked her not to cry, saying that such things come from God. Ana, Carmelo, and Carlos held their heads close together.

William entered next, followed by Jorge. William then introduced his parents to his brother. The rewriting of relationships was staggering.

Several days after Ana learned the truth, she arranged and paid for a special church mass commemorating Luz Marina, William's biological mother and the mother she now knew had cared so well for her son Carlos. All four twins were with her at the service in Bogotá. In her heart Ana felt Luz's presence and prayed that God would keep her in peace. Ana was grateful for all Luz had done so selflessly to make sure that Carlos would grow up to be a fine young man. Ana received some wise words from the priest who led the service: to keep conversations going with all four young men, and she has.

On everyone's mind were a lot of what-ifs. What if Ana or Carmelo had had relatives in Bucaramanga? Then their sick baby would have been treated closer to home and never would have traveled to the hospital in Bogotá. What if Bogotá's preemie nursery hadn't been so crowded? There would have been less chance of a switch. And what if Ana had delivered her babies at home?

Home deliveries have their own risks, but baby switches are not one of them.

Having Babies: Hospitals and Homes

In 1900 most deliveries of newborns took place at home, but their frequency fell to 44 percent by 1940 and to 1 percent by 1969.[26] Home deliveries in the United States now represent less than 1 percent of all births, but their frequency increased by 60 percent between 2008 and 2012. Their frequency grew even though infants born at home experience more complications, such as neonatal seizures, and more mothers receive blood transfusions.[27] Perhaps the general public is less familiar with the hazards of home births than the benefits. However, in a curious twist, 2012 national health statistics show that home births may pose a *lower* risk than hospital births, but that could be because birth attendants purposefully select low-risk women to deliver at home.[28]

The human female psyche's absence of baby-switching fears is clear if we listen to women who planned for a home delivery. Women delivering at home do so mostly to avoid unnecessary medical procedures, exercise control over the birth, and enjoy an intimate experience; they rarely mention worry about receiving the right child.[29] A 2001 study found that 9.1 percent of a small group of new mothers acknowledged that baby switching was a predelivery concern, but much higher percentages of women felt anxious about the pregnancy, the delivery, and the hospitalization. In fact, the small percentage of concerned women may not have even thought about baby switching until they heard about their hospital's practices for matching mothers and babies— perhaps they suddenly worried that an ID bracelet might fall off their baby's thin wrist.[30] I know a new mother who caught a glimpse of her newborn daughter just after delivery, before the infant was taken for a checkup, noting that the baby had an unusually high hairline. When the infant was later taken to her room for breast-feeding, the hairline seemed lower, but the mother assumed that her faulty memory reflected her exhausted state and began nursing the infant, falling madly in love with her. Suddenly, a nurse burst into her room with another baby, one with a high hairline. The mother began breast-feeding the child, learning to love a new baby all over again.

Now that most women in the United States deliver their babies in hospitals, there *is* some reason to be concerned that the right babies are matched with the right mothers. As I indicated earlier, it has been estimated that twenty thousand to twenty-three thousand infant misplacements occur in US hospitals annually, for example, when babies are returned to mothers after examinations or after mothers are allowed to rest. These figures are staggering and should be taken seriously because they were arrived at independently by a consultant hired by Talon Medical Ltd. in San Antonio, Texas, and the DNA Diagnostics Center in Fairfield, Ohio. Nicholas Webb, head of Talon Medical, claimed that the vast majority of these errors are corrected quickly—but because the misplacements are so numerous, it is likely that each year several families unknowingly receive someone else's child.[31] Most of these switches will never come to light because the children involved do not look alike. Identical twin switches have a far greater chance of detection, because of the twins' matched appearance, relative to switches involving fraternal twins or unrelated infants.

Multiple pregnancies and deliveries require optimal care because of the risks involved. The recommendation that twins and triplets be born in hospitals brings a bit of irony to the conversation because hospitals are where baby switches occur.

Chapter 6

Finding the Colombian Four

Twins and Other Curious Pairs

You're traveling through another dimension—a dimension not only of sight and sound but of mind. A journey into a wondrous land whose boundaries are that of imagination . . . a land of both shadow and substance, of things and ideas.

—Rod Serling

As a child, I loved this magical introduction to the weekly television show *The Twilight Zone*, whose episodes portrayed ordinary people in extraordinary circumstances. Each thirty-minute episode blended science fiction, high suspense, and great drama, giving viewers a fanciful white-knuckle ride through exotic places with infinite unforeseen possibilities. The current stream of online and on-air reruns attests to the show's universal and enduring popularity.

The story of the switched Colombian brothers could be an episode from that series. From the twins' perspective the discovery was a sudden and unexpected rewrite of their life histories, a complete revision of their childhood memories and the heartbreaking business of squaring opportunities lost with opportunities gained. Studying their experience and its aftermath also promised an adrenaline-charged ride for me, a journey to a new land to hopefully meet a type of foursome that no researcher had ever encountered. Without doubt, these brothers would leave an indelible mark on our understanding of how interactions between genes and environments affect our abilities, job choices, eating habits, and physical strength. Events in the twins' lives would also expand knowledge of how new mothers know who their babies are, the status of legal procedures and rulings regarding switched-at-birth infants, and the emotional impact of finding out that you are living someone else's life.

Questions Without Answers

The only information about the Colombian twins came from Caracol TV's two-part series produced by *Séptimo Día*, a *60 Minutes*-style newsmagazine that told the story to the people of Colombia and the adjacent nations of Ecuador and Venezuela.[1] The report, "Crossed Lives," was not broadcast widely, although Yesika, who is from Bogotá, saw it when it first aired in October 2014. She knew of my previous work on switched-at-birth twins and emailed to see if I was interested in this case—I was!—and we soon agreed to work together on one of the most fascinating projects either of us could have imagined.[2] My research experience with reared-apart and switched-at-birth twins in Minnesota and elsewhere had taught me what information we would need from the twins and the types of interviews we would use and questionnaires we would administer. Yesika's social work training and professional associates in Bogotá would facilitate contacts and interactions with the twins and their families, as well as meetings with the psychological examiners, geneticists, hospital staff, and attorneys we hoped to visit. We also hoped to write a series of scientific articles and a book that would describe the findings and events that so radically changed the life histories of four young men.

It turned out that William, assisted by his then girlfriend, who had some television contacts, was responsible for bringing the twins' story to the media; he called every department at Caracol TV until he found the right one. Jorge was enthusiastic about his twin's idea, but Carlos and Wilber were not. Carlos had strong reservations about involving the media, concerned that he would lose control of what was aired, and he was largely correct. "Some TV people wanted me to act really sad, do this, do that, act like I was depressed and really exaggerate my feelings. I dislike sensationalism," Carlos said. Jorge also has his limits; he did not want to be "turned into a clown," but he was eager to share his story with the world. Each brother's reared-apart twin held attitudes about public attention that aligned perfectly with his own. Nevertheless, Carlos and Wilber, while reluctant, agreed to go along, most likely because of *Séptimo Día*'s offer of free DNA testing, a costly but vital step toward confirming beyond a doubt that a baby exchange had occurred. Everyone had to know because their life histories, personal identities, and family relations hung in the balance.

How the exchange of babies actually happened was the great unanswered question, just as it was in the seven other cases of switched-at-birth twins I have known. These mysteries are rarely solved, so imagination and speculation run wild. We learned that babies like the four twins, born prematurely at seven to eight months, were routinely placed together on a large table in the newborn nursery of the Bogotá hospital, so perhaps William was lying closer to Wilber than to Jorge, and a staff member forgot which twins belonged together. Or perhaps an overworked assistant misread the babies' identification tags, or maybe the tags fell from their wrists and were incorrectly reattached.

Séptimo Día producers dramatized these possibilities when they filmed part of the report in the baby nursery of the Bogotá hospital where one set of twins was born. Two incubators were positioned several feet from each other, each with a pair of infant twin dolls dressed in striped pajamas and matching caps with small white ears protruding from the top, giving the impression of tiny bears. The incubator on the left held the La Paz pair dressed in blue, the one on the right held the Bogotá pair dressed in purple, and each twin doll had a different name emblazoned across his belly. The narrator walks toward the incubator on the left, removes Carlos, and brings him to the incubator on the right, placing him between Jorge and William. Moments later he picks up William and delivers him to the incubator on the left, setting him next to Wilber. Then we see the four adult twins sitting alone, slumped between incubators and looking forlorn. Of course, this was all done for effect because no one really knows what happened in the nursery a quarter of a century ago. This imaginary scene embodied all that Carlos disliked about media attention and Jorge's cautious, but less intense, reservations.

Despite this dramatic depiction, or perhaps because of it, many new questions arose. Did the exchange of babies happen on the day the baby from La Paz arrived in Bogotá or later in the week? And why didn't his grandmother notice the difference between the baby she brought to Bogotá and the one that came back to La Paz? Or perhaps the nurses were tipsy, as one of the twins' aunts truly believed.

None of these hypotheticals and unknowns was as haunting as the statements made by Gilma Ospina, a nurse who appeared on the program and had worked in the premature care unit in

1988, the year the twins were born. She acknowledged that she could have inadvertently switched two of the twins, but she did not feel the need to apologize for such a mistake because no one can know whether she was truly responsible. She speculated that the two babies' identification tags, just simple pieces of tape, had fallen off and were incorrectly reattached. Even if she had misplaced the babies, she was happy to see that the switched twins were doing so well as adults.

The program also equated Jorge and Carlos's city life with wealth and opportunity, and William and Wilber's country life with poverty and deprivation. It made for a great television story, but a crucial aspect of the difference in their childhood environments is easy to miss. In terms of material possessions and necessities of life, both sets of accidental brothers did differ—except that each pair believed they were living in homes comparable to others in their area. Both families worked hard to maintain the standard of living they had set for themselves, and both families were successful in that respect.

Turning to science, *Séptimo Día* interviewed the geneticist Dr. Emilio J. Yunis of Bogotá, whose Institute of Genetics performed the DNA analyses. Yunis was stunned by the striking physical resemblance of each reunited set of twins, half-seriously suggesting that a DNA test was probably not necessary. But the seriousness of the twins' expressions as they listened to the results reminded viewers of the far-reaching implications of this news for the twins and their families.

Tracking Down the Twins

Séptimo Día included a short interview with the Colombian attorney Francisco Bernate, who was not officially involved in the case but was prepared to offer an opinion.[3] We never met him, but on-screen he looked professorial in a gray jacket and purple tie with his long dark hair swept back from his face. He commented first on the slim possibility of the twins' receiving compensation from the hospital where the switch had taken place; he believed this was unlikely because more than twenty-five years had passed since the mistake was made. He opined that the damage began when the truth was first known, asserting that everyone has a right to their identity and to know where they have come from.

We had been unsuccessful in trying to reach the twins because we were unable to find the twins' phone numbers, contact the TV show producers, or find additional information online. But we realized Bernate could connect us and after weeks of waiting he did. It helped that Bernate was a professor of criminal law at the Universidad del Rosario's law school, where Yesika's sister, Alexandra Montoya, who is famous for her impressions of Colombian celebrities, was working toward her second career. This personal connection probably was responsible for the lawyer's email message to Yesika that included Jorge's email address and cell phone number.

Yesika and I were now on an exciting journey together, with the dual goals of finding the four brothers and convincing them to participate in the first-ever research on doubly exchanged adult twins. By the end of December Yesika had flown to Bogotá for the holidays and met with three of the four twins; Wilber was unable to attend because he was covering the butcher shop. The three young men and Yesika discussed research plans, when they might be available to us, and a little more about their getting to know one another. Later I received a photo that showed Yesika and the three twins seated around a table, as well as a little boy who was cuddling up to Jorge. That was Santi, Jorge's then four-and-a-half-year-old son, whose mother was Jorge's former girlfriend.

The recently reunited twins Jorge and William were seated together, while Jorge's accidental brother, Carlos, sat apart.

For two tense months, October to December, we waited to find out whether the twins would meet with us. But as 2015 approached, Jorge told us we would be welcome in Bogotá. We arranged for a ten-day stay in Bogotá in late March and early April, including a one-day trip to La Paz. Information gleaned from doubly exchanged twins, especially those raised in such contrasting environments, would be a unique addition to the rich history (since 1922) of reports, articles, and books about reared-apart twins, as well as to my own ongoing research about reared-apart Chinese twins and other separated pairs.[4] The first mention of twins reared apart was not in the scientific literature, but in a play by the Roman comic dramatist Plautus (254–184 BC), *The Menaechemi* (The Twin Brothers), a hilarious tale of separated twins, mistaken identity, and widespread confusion.[5]

Twin-Family Relations

Seeing the photo of the twins and Santi suggested to me that William, Jorge's identical twin, might be rejoicing at the sudden acquisition of a nephew. In fact, he is Santi's genetic father as well as his uncle, because William's biological relationship to Santi is exactly the same as Jorge's. Parents transmit half their genes to each child; because identical twins share 100 percent of their genes, either twin could have fathered little Santi. Until recently genetic testing was unable to distinguish an identical twin father from an identical twin uncle, but in 2014 German investigators figured out how to do this. If one twin develops a mutation after birth it could be passed down to his child, and since the other twin would not have that mutation he could not be the father.[6] This technique would be handy in cases of disputed paternity in which both twins had sexual relations with the same woman and she became pregnant or if a twin was suspected of having an affair with his brother's wife. Before 2014 judges were powerless to assign responsibility for child support in such cases, but now they can because ten to forty mutations can be expected in each paternal generation.[7]

An array of other curious relationships emerges when identical twins raise families. When William has kids, they will be cousins to Jorge's kids, but all the children will have a genetically identical parent. This quirk of birth transforms close cousins into genetic half-siblings, who share an average of 25 percent of their genes, whereas ordinary first cousins share just 12.5 percent. Family relationships grow even stronger when identical twins marry identical twins because all four spouses turn into the genetic parents of their nieces and nephews. In one such family that I know the wives became pregnant at the same time and delivered their children on the same day, changing these legal first cousins into the equivalent of genetic fraternal twins.[8]

Not surprisingly, one of my ongoing studies shows that identical twin uncles and aunts feel socially closer to their nieces and nephews than do fraternal twin aunts and uncles. I suspect that behind those feelings are identical twins' perceptions of the behavioral and physical similarities between themselves and their nieces and nephews. The growing field of evolutionary psychology adds an intriguing explanation: it makes sense to "be nice" to your close relatives as a way of getting your common genes into future generations, namely the concept called inclusive fitness. Of course, people do not make genetic calculations in their head as they go about their daily interactions, but they act as though they do.[9] In contrast fraternal twin aunts and uncles share an average of 25 percent of their genes with their nieces and nephews, the same as in nontwin families. Thus, investigators would expect to find more variability in the nature of their perceptions of similarity and social closeness.

I wondered whether Jorge's accidental brother, Carlos, was suddenly grieving the loss of a nephew he had loved for nearly five years, now that he was no longer the uncle he had thought he was. These were among the hard questions for which I hoped to find answers in Bogotá.

Transformers and Matryoshka Dolls

I occasionally teach a graduate-level seminar about twin research, and one of the exercises I assign students is to dream up an ideal experiment for figuring out the extent to which genes and environment affect our different traits. "Be creative," I tell them. "Really stretch your mind and go beyond the classic twin study." At this point in the course the students understand the logic of the classic twin study design, which involves comparing similarities of pairs of identical twins (who share 100 percent of their genes) and pairs of fraternal twins (who share an average of 50 percent of their genes). Greater resemblance between identical than fraternal twins in any trait, such as solving math problems, participating in sports events, or attending religious services, shows genetic influence on those behaviors.[10] We find that genetic influence affects virtually every trait we have measured, but the environment also plays a role, affecting some behaviors more than others. For example, genetic factors more strongly influence general intelligence, accounting for 50 to 75 percent, whereas their influence is less on personality (50 percent), self-esteem (38 percent), and longevity (33 percent).[11]

Genetic and environmental influences work together to shape our behavioral and physical traits, and in the case of intelligence we can say that about 50 to 75 percent of the variation is associated with genetics and 25 to 50 percent is associated with the environment. It is impossible to divide the intellectual makeup of a single person into genetic and environmental components because they are completely intertwined within an individual.[12]

I have been pleased with my students' proposals, but my favorite is a study of sets of same-sex triplets comprising an identical twin pair and a fraternal cotriplet. That trio poses a great natural experiment because all three triplets share the same environment, but only two share all their genes. If the identical twins are more temperamentally alike and socially closer to each other than to the fraternal member of the pack, this tells us that genetic factors influence our personality traits and friendship choices. Research using twins, who are far more plentiful in the population than triplets, shows exactly that.[13]

This triplet experiment can be extended even further. Let's say that one identical twin was raised by the biological family, while the other identical twin and the fraternal cotriplet were raised together in an adoptive home. If researchers found that the separated identical twins were more alike than the reared-together nonidentical pair, this would show even more convincingly the genetic influence on the traits being measured. Researchers would need to study many of these rare sets to find definitive answers to nature-nurture questions, but even one case or a few can provide important insights that can be further explored in large-scale studies. When it comes to triplets' social activities and relationships, identical partners generally align more closely with each other than they do with their fraternal ones. For example, my colleague's triplet children, Mike and Mark love to indulge in overeating, whereas Matt is proud to not be a member of that culinary club.

None of my students' ideas, or my earlier ones for that matter, came close to the exceptional research possibilities offered by the switched Colombian brothers. I began thinking of the four twins as Transformers, the popular toy that assumes different forms and features by manipulating its parts. The potential experimental contrasts the Colombian twins generated also reminded me of matryoshka dolls, the painted Russian figurines that fit inside one another in increasingly smaller sizes. I grabbed some paper from my printer and started mapping out the myriad relationships and comparisons that were possible.

Reared-Apart Twins, Virtual Twins—and the New Replicas

In mathematics a combination is a selection of a specific number of items (e.g., two people) from a larger number of items (e.g., four people) without attention to who comes first or second with respect to order. Higher-order multiple births—triplets, quadruplets, and more—are fun to work with in this regard. When thirty-three-year-old Nadya "Octomom" Suleman of southern California gave birth to octuplets in January 2009, I wrote a paper showing that her eight babies yielded twenty-eight unique twin pairs when they were organized into groups of two.[14] The situation is even more amazing when we consider that Suleman had had six fertilized eggs implanted in her uterus and two of those eggs divided, producing two identical twin sets in the bunch.

I performed similar calculations for the four Colombian brothers and came up with three results, two that were not surprising and one that was completely unexpected and exciting. By pairing the brothers every way I could, I ended up with six distinct sets:

- Two identical reared-apart twin pairs, Jorge and William, and Carlos and Wilber. These pairs share their genes but did not share their environment.

- Two unrelated, or virtual twin, pairs: Jorge and Carlos, and William and Wilber. These pairs shared their environment but do not share their genes.

And for the first time in any study:

- Two replicas: Jorge and Wilber, and Carlos and William. These pairs share neither their genes nor their environment, but they replicate the unrelated, or virtual twin, pairs, who share only their environment.

Reared-apart twins are easy to define—they are twins separated at or soon after birth and raised by two different families. They are genetically identical, actually clones by definition, but because they do not share an environment, their behavioral and physical similarities are the result of their common genes. All of us can use this information to understand why we are the way we are and how we got that way. In addition, reared-apart identical twins give us direct estimates of how much genes matter, making these twins a cleaner, neater twin research design than twins reared together, whose shared experiences could enhance their similarities. No wonder reared-apart identical twin pairs have high status in the hierarchy of twin research methods.

However, despite some critics' claims that most identical twins are alike because they are raised together and are treated alike, it would be incorrect to assume that they are alike because they were raised together. It would also be incorrect to suppose that increased contact between reunited reared-apart twins makes them alike. This has been shown repeatedly, but was revealed most dramatically by the first-ever personality study of four groups of twins that my Minnesota colleagues and I conducted in 1988.

This project included identical twins reared apart, fraternal twins reared apart, identical twins reared together, and fraternal twins reared together. As expected, we found that the identical pairs were more alike than the fraternal pairs. The surprise was finding that identical reared-apart twins are as alike in personality as identical reared-together twins.[15]

This counterintuitive finding means that personality similarity between family members in traits like traditionalism and aggression come from their shared genes, not their shared environment. There is no other way to explain why separated twins like Lily and Gillian, who were scared of Santa Claus and clowns, dressed up as ballerinas at Halloween, why Samantha and Anaïs chew on their hair when they get nervous, why Bridget and Dorothy wear more rings and bracelets than anyone they know, or why Todd and Josh both identified as female and independently underwent surgical transformation to have their biological sex and gender identity align.[16]

Todd and Josh are the only known pair of separated identical twins who have experienced gender dysphoria (the persistent discontent with one's birth or assigned gender and identification with the opposite gender) and have undergone surgery to change their sex. After their birth their forty-year-old mother was diagnosed with facial cancer so, following advice from various hospital staffers who believed that caring for more than one newborn would be too taxing, she placed one twin up for adoption. By the time the twins reunited at age fifteen, both felt uncomfortable living as males, had engaged in cross-dressing, and were apprehensive about developing secondary sex characteristics in adolescence. These twins make a powerful statement about genetic influences on transgenderism (the transient or continued identification with the gender that is different from one's birth gender) and transsexuality (the social or surgical transition from male to female or female to male). Genetic effects on gender dysphoria are also shown by the finding that one-third of transsexual identical male twins have a transsexual twin brother, whereas no transsexual fraternal male twins have a twin who is also transsexual.[17] Of course, environmental influences before and after birth also play a role because identical twins' similarity is less than 100 percent.

It seems reasonable to attribute parent-child or brother-sister similarities to shared experience, but researchers cannot disentangle genes and environment when biological relatives live together. The only way to do this is to compare resemblance in kinships that are genetically and environmentally revealing, and the best pairs are twins raised together and apart. Upon doing this we find that environment matters nearly as much as genes when it comes to personality, but it is mostly the individual experiences that we do not share with our relatives, such as being mentored by an inspiring professor, taking an exotic vacation, losing assets in a Ponzi scheme, or being attacked by an unknown assailant, that influence our personality traits. However, nonshared experiences work in unpredictable ways—after being attacked, one person might be energized to improve public safety, whereas another might be too fearful to leave home.

By now scores of twin studies have shown that genes affect just about every human trait that anyone has ever measured. A curious exception is love styles—it seems that how quickly or slowly we fall in love with someone is mostly experiential in origin.[18] However, the only twin study to look specifically at love styles was conducted nearly twenty-five years ago, and recent findings about the brains and personalities of people in love could make for great twin research. The anthropologist Helen Fisher, who is an identical twin, and her colleagues found that certain neural mechanisms are associated with mate attraction and mate choice, and that, based upon a personality questionnaire, people might be classified as one of four love types—negotiator, director, builder, or explorer—although the types overlap.[19] Comparing the similarities and differences between identical and fraternal twins could reveal genetic influences on brain processes and personality traits that affect our love lives.

The wealth of genetic findings does not surprise me, perhaps because I shared my home environment with a fraternal twin sister who was, and still is, quite different from me in most respects. As children our preferred cereals were Rice Krispies and Kix, our favorite ice cream flavors were chocolate and coffee, and we rarely, if ever, sampled our sister's choices. Our differences in eye color, height, and running speed were apparent from an early age, and I had fun seeing the surprised looks on people's faces when I told them we were twins. I witnessed genetic effects before I knew what genes were.

Researchers have found other, more surprising results. Since the mid-1980s studies of adult twins, raised apart and together, have shown that genetic factors influence political perspectives, social attitudes, divorce tendencies, financial decision-making, and religious involvement, behaviors previously thought to reflect how our parents raised us.[20] Earlier twin studies did not detect genetic effects on these behaviors because they studied children still living at home, under the thumbs of their families. But as children approach adolescence and adulthood, their actions, tendencies, and choices speak more clearly of their natural preferences. For this reason it is paradoxical, but true, that the older we get the more important our genes become. Most people are surprised to hear this because their logical mind says that as people age they accumulate a wealth of different experiences that should affect their behavior. But logic and reason do not replace what the data tell us: we become more selective about where we go and what we do as we get older, reflecting genetically based choices, some of which may be kicking in for the first time. Consistent with these findings is that adopted siblings who grew up together become less alike in general intelligence over time as genetic effects grow stronger in the environments they individually seek. That is because as people move from childhood to adolescence and beyond they gain freedom and choice over what they do and who they do it with, allowing their genetic predispositions greater expression.[21]

Two sets of unrelated, or virtual, twins are among the different pairs generated by the Bogotá brothers. I like the term *virtual twins* because it's clever, timely, and fits the novel, twin-like pairing I first came across in 1990.[22] I wish I had thought of this term myself, but it came from a smart mother who offered two such children for study. Virtual twins (the same-age, biologically unrelated individuals raised together soon after birth) should not be confused with so-called Irish twins, children born nine or ten months apart to the same parents. Virtual twins are much closer in age, and some are even born on the same day. Furthermore, they have no common genes, but Irish twins do.

Most virtual twin pairs are made up of two adoptees, but about 25 percent of the more than 160 such sets in my files include one adoptee and one biological child—many seemingly infertile women say that once the adoption process was under way, they relaxed and became pregnant. I have even known couples who adopted a child just before or just after delivering triplets conceived by assisted reproductive methods, generating three pairs of virtual twins in one family. Some virtual twin pairs came into being through even more exotic means, such as adoption plus surrogacy, adoption plus embryo donation, and marriage of same-sex partners whose children had different dads.

Virtual twins are closely matched in age and time of arrival in their family, but they have no genetic connection. These defining features make them an ideal contrast to identical twins raised together and apart. In fact, they are reared-apart identical twins in reverse because virtual twins share their environments but not their genes, whereas reared-apart identical twins share their genes but not their environment. Most adoption researchers study ordinary adoptive siblings who differ in age and time of entry in their new home. They do so largely because they believe that these pairs are more plentiful and easier to find than virtual twins, and perhaps they are, but I am still finding virtual twins. They are excellent subjects for determining the degree to which living together could make people display similar, as well as dissimilar, habits and behaviors, and they outperform ordinary adoptive siblings on these measures because their ages and arrival times match so closely.

Virtual twins are much less alike in general intelligence and in their strengths and weaknesses in specific verbal and spatial skills than are identical and fraternal twins, even those raised apart. The modest intellectual resemblance that virtual twins show in early childhood probably reflects their common rearing, but it fades as they approach adolescence when new genetic effects and unique experiences kick in. One dad told me he expected to see some behavioral differences between his two daughters, Judith, who was adopted, and Sally, who was biological, but the extreme contrasts in the girls' abilities and personalities astonished him.

Virtual twins come into being one other way, and that is why the Colombian brothers are so important: the switching of Carlos and William that separated the identical twins simultaneously crafted two virtual twin pairs: Jorge and Carlos in Bogotá, and Wilber and William in La Paz. But there is more to this story: when twins are inadvertently switched, an exclusive and exceptional class of virtual twins emerges because its members believe they are fraternal twins, as do their parents and other relatives. After all, their mothers gave birth and took two babies home from the hospital. The math adds up and no one asks questions. The brothers of Bogotá and the brothers of La Paz became unwitting members of this unusual group.

True, these virtual twins and their families were puzzled by the striking physical differences between these siblings. Friends of the Bogotá twins would sometimes ask, "How could you be twins?" or joke that "you're too handsome to be in your family!" Even more prescient, relatives in La Paz told Ana, "Maybe one of your kids was switched at birth? Ha ha!" She would sometimes say, "My poor little son [William], it seems he has been exchanged." And when her boys threw fists at each other, as siblings sometimes do, Wilber would yell, "You're not my brother!" or "You were picked up on the street, and my mom and dad fed you for free!" But everyone knows that fraternal twins can be quite different, so the jokes and threats were neither made in earnest nor taken seriously.

I think of these exclusive virtual twins as the most exceptional of unrelated siblings, whose research status parallels that of reared-apart identical twins, who are the most exceptional among multiples. If these particular virtual twins, who always believed they were fraternal twins, are more alike in taking tests or running races than ordinary virtual twins (who always knew they were unrelated), perhaps belief or investment in being a twin enhances similarity. I would not expect the two types of virtual twin pairs—those who believed they were fraternal twins and those who knew they were not—to differ in how much they resemble one another for traits significantly affected by genes. Parents who think that their identical twins are fraternal still find similarities in their children's behaviors, so their misbelief about twin type does not affect their perceptions of their children or the children's outcomes.[23] Still, the degree of resemblance across characteristics of the ordinary and extraordinary virtual twins is an empirical question that researchers could and should address. However, the very small number of such extraordinary virtual twin pairs precludes a proper test of this notion—the newly found Colombian twins increased that number from seven to just nine.

The multiplicity of relationships generated by the Colombian twins continued to expand and included two sets, William and Carlos, and Jorge and Wilber, who have never been studied before because they were unknown to researchers until now. We have no word to describe them, so I chose *replicas*, because they truly are replicas, not originals. If you think of two people standing together in front of a mirror, the reflection in the glass is a re-creation of the original; it preserves the important elements, but it is still a copy. Replicas are an entirely new kinship, created accidentally and for the first time in Colombia because of the switching of two twins from two identical pairs.

The members of each replicated pair share neither their genes nor their environment. However, each of the four individuals can be paired with an identical copy of his accidental brother:

- Jorge was raised with Carlos, but they share no genes. Because Carlos is genetically identical to Wilber, Jorge and Wilber are replicas.
- William was raised with Wilber, but they share no genes. Because Wilber is genetically identical to Carlos, William and Carlos are replicas.

Replicas make possible a new research design, and a little reasoning reveals the great value of these rare pairs. If, for example,

Jorge and Carlos are more alike as accidental brothers than the replicated pairs in choice of clothes, taste in food, or pick of women, this would tell us that a shared environment enhances the similarity of those behaviors. If they are not more alike, this would suggest that a shared environment does not make siblings the same. Both Bogotá brothers had professional goals in mind, but were Jorge's inspiration and drive more like Carlos's or Wilber's? Neither La Paz brother advanced beyond the fifth grade, but would William's verbal skills more closely match those of Wilber or Carlos?

Keeping Them Straight

Experimental psychological research shows that it's easier to remember faces than the names that go with the faces. Researchers still debate why this is so, but this truism about memory comforted me when I found it difficult to remember which brothers were the real twins and which ones were raised in Bogotá and La Paz.[24] I had trouble keeping the four individuals, accidental brothers, reared-apart twins, and replicas straight until I saw them for myself. A chart with pictures and captions would have helped me greatly at the beginning.

As convoluted as the twins' different relationships appeared to be to us, they paled in complexity relative to their relationships with their parents and siblings. The Bogotá brothers grew up with a sister, Diana, who is four years their senior. Once the switch was uncovered, she was still Jorge's biological sister but instantly became Carlos's unrelated sister, William's biological reared-apart sister, and Wilber's replicated sister. The accidental pair in La Paz had four older siblings, whose characteristics yielded even more genetically and environmentally varied and complex comparisons. And we could compare the La Paz parents with the son they raised and the son they did not.

Putting It All Together

Having worked with reared-apart twins before, I had access to the life history booklets, personality questionnaires, and twin relationship surveys we would need. One of my students, Lissette Bohorquez, who is of Colombian descent, and Yesika helped translate into Spanish several forms for the brothers to fill out, and my Barcelona colleague, David Gallardo-Pujol, provided me with some surveys and inventories that were already available in Spanish.

Interpreters, Translators, and Testers

There is a critical distinction between interpreters and translators. Interpreters transform spoken words from one language into another, usually on the spot. Their accuracy depends not only on their expertise in both languages, but also on their familiarity with a particular subject. In contrast, translators typically work at their leisure from written materials and can consult grammatical texts, seek advice from native speakers, or type expressions into Google Translate.[25] We were hoping to find a professional interpreter with a background in psychology, and we did.

Alberto Orjuela is a Colombian-born interpreter and translator who was seven in 1960 when he relocated to New York City, where he lived for nineteen years. He earned a bachelor of arts degree in social psychology at New York's Stony Brook University in 1974 before returning to Bogotá in 1979 "to practice what I love—both translation and interpretation." He is also punctual to a fault, a trait I value in anyone I hire because I suffer from it myself.

After a series of introductory emails, we "met" Alberto for the first time during a three-way Skype interview in March 2015.

Alberto, in his early sixties, has dark hair, a ruddy complexion, and a pleasant smile. He agreed to work six or seven full days with unpredictable hours and accompany us on the arduous journey to La Paz.

Finding an interpreter was just one of several tasks to complete before leaving for Bogotá. Another was to have the twins complete a standard general intelligence (IQ) test, namely, the Wechsler Adult Intelligence Scale-IV, or WAIS-IV. Comparing the college-educated city boys with their identical country-raised counterparts who had not advanced beyond the fifth grade would be a unique addition to reared-apart twin research because I could not recall any other reared-apart twins with this degree of educational difference. One of Yesika's former instructors, Ligia Gómez, and her associate, Diana Ramos, would do the testing.

Controversies about the relative contributions of nature and nurture to IQ scores are often bitter and contentious and have surrounded IQ findings from reared-apart twin studies for decades. One of the biggest disagreements is whether the similar IQs of reared-apart identical twins reflects their shared genes or similar features of their different home environments and educational backgrounds.[26] We knew the Colombian twins would shed some light on this issue.

DNA: Identical, Fraternal, or None of the Above?

We learned that both pairs of twins were identical (monozygotic), based on the DNA findings Yunis discussed on *Séptimo Día*. We would later gain access to the full report, which shows that Jorge and William, and Carlos and Wilber, match perfectly on twenty-one different DNA factors, a nearly impossible feat for any other two people.

Pictured are the vast uneven terrain and poorly marked paths we had to traverse during the one-hour walk from La Paz to the barbeque at William and Wilber's childhood home in Vereda El Recreo. The La Paz brothers had also arranged police protection for our visit. Wilber is third in line behind the mother and child.

PHOTO BY N. L. SEGAL

At left is one of many photographs of Carlos (left) and Jorge (right) at age five, when they graduated from preschool. At right is the only childhood photograph of Wilber (left) and William (right), at about the age of six near their La Paz home.

PHOTOS COURTESY: JORGE AND CARLOS; WILLIAM AND WILBER

William and Wilber lived in this house in Vereda El Recreo, near La Paz, between the ages of five and eighteen, when they joined the military. Five other family members, including the brothers' parents and older sibling Edgar, also lived there during those years. The house had neither running water nor electricity. Photo by Y. S. Montoya

Jorge and Carlos lived in this modest two-story house in Bogotá with their mother, sister, cousin, and three aunts. From left to right are Jorge; his aunt Maria Teresa; the author, Nancy L. Segal; and Jorge's identical reared-apart twin, William. This was William's first visit to his biological family's home. Photo by Alexandra Yang

William and Wilber attended a school that looked much like the one in the photograph at the top. Between the ages of five and eleven, every weekday they walked an hour to school and an hour to return home. Photo by N. L. Segal

The bottom photograph shows the Colegio Restrepo Millan, the prestigious high school Jorge and Carlos attended in Bogotá. Photo by N. L. Segal

The switched twins, Carlos (left), born in Vélez but raised in Bogotá, and William (right), born in Bogotá but raised in La Paz, at the Unidad Neonatal (Neonatal Unit) of the Hospital Regional de Vélez. This was Carlos's first visit to his actual birthplace and William's first visit to his assumed birthplace. Photo by N. L. Segal

Carmelo and Ana, shown at their former home in Vereda El Recreo. The couple now resides in another town, a move that required them to walk three hours in order to host the barbeque on the day of our visit. Photo by Alberto Orjuela

Crossing this suspension bridge with its missing rungs and uncertain support was one of only two options for getting to William and Wilber's childhood home. The other was to wade through the mud and water of the creek just below. On the way there I chose the bridge, walking closely behind Carlos (shown in a black tank top and blue shorts). On the way back I took the creek. PHOTO BY N. L. SEGAL

(Left to right) Wilber, Carlos, William, and Jorge at the March 29, 2015, barbeque held at William and Wilber's childhood home. Except for Carlos, they are wearing the high boots and long pants necessary in the rugged countryside. This picture was taken just six months after the twins' first reunion, so Carlos's dress may have reflected his inner turmoil and reluctance to embrace the truth about his life. For lunch, William and Wilber's father Carmelo had slaughtered a cow that was roasting on spits behind the four brothers. Photo by N. L. Segal

William (left) and Jorge (right), after the long hot walk back to La Paz from William's childhood home. Jorge's chest bears tattoos of his brother Carlos and his mother, Luz, with the inscription MI SAGRADA FAMILIA (My Sacred Family). To assure Carlos they would always be brothers, Jorge acquired the tattoo of Carlos soon after the switch was revealed. Photo by N. L. Segal

In 2017 Jorge (left) formed a construction company with longtime friends. He now develops plans for their new business, which includes constructing a house for William's parents, Carmelo and Ana Delina. PHOTO COURTESY: JORGE

William (right) managed the small butcher shop, Carnes Finas de Colombia (Fine Meats of Colombia), at the back of La Gran Manzana (The Big Apple) supermarket until he entered law school in 2016. William remains involved in the business, but Wilber is the new manager. PHOTO BY N. L. SEGAL

As a professional in the world of finance, Carlos (left) manages accounts and other financial records in his well-appointed office. PHOTO COURTESY: CARLOS

Wilber (right) now works as manager of the Carnes Finas de Colombia butcher shop. PHOTO COURTESY: WILBER

The identical reared-apart twins Jorge (left) and William (right) arm-wrestle. In the end William's greater strength and stamina brought Jorge's arm crashing to the table.

PHOTO BY N. L. SEGAL

Jorge (left) and William (right) at the February 2016 wedding of Jorge's friend and coworker Laura, whose mistaking of William for Jorge led to the discovery of the switch. The twins' physical resemblance is so striking in this picture that I had to ask them who was who.

PHOTO COURTESY: JORGE AND WILLIAM

Jorge with his young son, Santi. Several months before Laura mistook William for Jorge, he had been wearing his hair long and had a goatee. Laura probably would not have confused them if Jorge had not cut and shaved his hair when he did.

PHOTO COURTESY: JORGE

The twins gathered in William and Wilber's apartment on the evening of July 17, 2016, to celebrate the thirty-second birthday of Jorge and Carlos's sister, Diana. From left to right: William, Jorge, Diana, Wilber, and Carlos, with Jorge's young son, Santi, in front. PHOTO BY N. L. SEGAL

I wanted to extend the genetic analyses to the burgeoning area of epigenetics, a hot spot in the genetics field concerned with how and why some genes are expressed, or "turned on," and how and why other genes stay silent, or "turned off." The finding that identical twin similarity is less than 100 percent for major psychiatric disorders, such as schizophrenia (50 percent) and Alzheimer's disease (60 percent), has led researchers to explore epigenetic events that may explain why one twin is affected and the other is not.[27]

Epigenetics was originally tied to the unknown processes that enable a fertilized egg to develop into a mature organism, but since the late 1960s it has focused on changes in gene function and expression that vary among our different types of cells and that do not involve changes in DNA. The prefix *epi* means "above," so it is reasonable to think about epigenetic processes as acting above, or outside, the full array of a person's genetic sequence.[28] Epigenetic changes do not alter the DNA sequence, so they have been called soft inheritance.

The possibility that the urban versus rural environments and exposures of the reared-apart identical brothers could be linked to differences in their epigenetic profiles was of great interest. Chemical pollutants, more common in cities, may have affected the Bogotá brothers more than the La Paz ones, whereas animal and plant products from the family farm may have uniquely affected the La Paz pair.[29] Which genes are expressed, as well as when and why, are topics of great interest to geneticists, with significant implications for members of the general public.[30] Researchers conducting epigenetic studies focus on the regions of the genome that are thought to affect the expression of a particular gene.[31]

Identical twins who differ in a behavior or a disease are ideal for uncovering the epigenetic factors responsible for that difference.

Identical twins share their entire genetic sequence, so if one twin is overweight or one twin is diabetic, the difference must be tied to a nongenetic event. Knowing what silences gene expression in one twin or activates it in the other may help researchers find ways to manage or mitigate behavioral and medical problems experienced by members of the general public.

It is likely that identical twins have similar genetic susceptibilities to some conditions and that a nongenetic event triggers the condition in just one twin. In 1987 the health science PBS series *Bodywatch* featured identical twins Jane and Joan, only one of whom developed diabetes. Diabetes had affected some members of their family, but only Joan developed the condition after contracting an infection that seemed to linger. Studying twins has, in fact, provided support for epigenetic contributions to schizophrenia, bipolar disorder, dental characteristics, and liver disease.[32] And researchers have found specific epigenetic changes in female identical twins with breast cancer whose sisters were not affected. This knowledge can help identify warning signs in individuals at risk and offer insight into the origins of this and other medical conditions. Of course, epigenetic differences in identical twins show that, strictly speaking, they are not exact genetic duplicates of one another. That is, despite their identical genes, environmental influences inside and outside the womb can intervene, making identical twins differ in body weight, heart functioning, and perhaps sexual orientation.[33]

Researchers have also found evidence suggesting that epigenetic changes can be passed down through generations. People exposed prenatally to famine in the Netherlands during the terrible winter of 1944–45 showed less methylation of genes—the addition of a methyl group to DNA that affects how genes are expressed—involved in growth and development than did their unexposed siblings when measured sixty years later. And epigenetic differences between identical male twins, one gay and one straight, may help explain these twins' sexual orientations.[34] The challenge is to separate the effects of epigenetic mechanisms from other possible explanations.

An epigenetic study of reared-apart identical twins, comparing their genes that have been turned on or turned off, had never been reported, so ours would be a first. Adding to the novelty of this analysis would be information from two virtual twin pairs, two replicated pairs, and an older sister paired with the biological and unrelated brothers with whom she had been raised, as well as from a biological brother she had never known. These unique pairings within the same family would allow us to compare the similarities and differences of pairs who shared genes but not environment, environment but not genes, and neither genes nor environment. We would face limits to what we could conclude from just a few pairs, but epigenetic differences between the separated identical twins could suggest that any health differences between them might be tied to their environment, both inside and outside the womb. It was also possible that the separated identical twins would be more alike than the accidental brothers raised together, evidence of genetic influence on genetic expression. We planned to map out the different twin and sibling pairs with regard to epigenetic resemblance.

My friend and colleague Dr. Jeffrey Craig of the School of Medicine at Deakin University, Geelong, Australia, is an epigenetics expert. Originally from the United Kingdom, he has been a trailblazer in using twin studies to address epigenetic questions. One study looked at newborns with reference to how maternal nutrition, assisted reproduction, and alcohol intake can affect how genes are expressed (methylation pattern).[35] Identical twins showed more similar gene expression profiles at birth than fraternal twins, although each twin had a unique pattern. For example, the greater resemblance among identical than fraternal twins for the expression of a particular gene suggested genetic influence on which genes are turned on or turned off. However, the profiles of some identical twins were less alike than the profiles of some fraternal twins and even of unrelated pairs, showing that genetic expression is a complex process. In a related study twins with a shared placenta had more discrepant methylation profiles than those with separate placentae.[36] The reason for this is unknown, but greater twin-twin competition for resources in the womb may be one explanation.

Jeff provided me with special tubes for collecting cell samples (buccal cells, from inside the cheek) from the four Colombian twins and older sister Diana to be analyzed in his laboratory.

The Rest of the Schedule

We hoped to compare nearly everything about the twins, including their mental abilities, personality traits, and physical skills, not to mention their past endeavors, current concerns, and future dreams.

Woven throughout the twins' communications was a sense of their growing excitement about a visit from an American psychology professor (me) and social worker (Yesika). We were just as eager to meet them, anticipating that their unique situation might reveal new information about human behavior and family relationships. Research participation would be a new experience for the brothers, and they weren't quite sure what to expect, but all four had checked out my credentials and seemed impressed. Jorge, ever the leader, emailed messages with warm words of welcome. We had warned them in advance that their days would be filled with interviews, inventories, body measurements, and videotaping, but the stack of materials we set before them would still seem daunting, as it is to most reunited twin participants. But like other reared-apart twins, they were eager to learn more about the factors affecting their abilities, predispositions, likes, and dislikes, and how they measured up against each other. They also knew that by engaging in the various tasks, sharing their life stories, and just being themselves, they were bringing us closer to answers to complex developmental questions. All four young men distinguished themselves as among the most enthusiastic and charming of the study participants with whom I have worked.

The Bogotá brothers had never been to the La Paz brothers' childhood home, a journey that Jorge was especially eager to make to gain a better appreciation for his twin's past and present life. In fact, setting aside a full day for travel to La Paz, a trip that took us nearly twelve hours from Bogotá (longer than the usual seven hours because we stopped along the way), was both an essential part of our visit and William's precondition for participating in the project. He wanted us to experience the home environment in which he and Wilber had been raised.

As the date for our departure for Bogotá drew closer, I sensed the enormity of this story more than I had before, perhaps because the groundwork was done, leaving me time to reflect. Clearly, this mission would electrify my twin studies colleagues, who thrive on gathering and interpreting new data. But the twins' story also captured the universal themes of family, loyalty, love, disappointment, heartache, and reconciliation that move the hearts and minds of general audiences. Who among us has never questioned our relationship to our family members? And who has never experienced the loss of a loved one?

I wondered constantly how the Colombian twins were handling their discovery and its aftermath. Based on the television interviews and email correspondence, I sensed adaptability and liveliness in the four twins who were trying desperately to right an unimaginable wrong. It was not easy for them, especially for the exchanged brothers, who were questioning their past and future relationships with their parents, siblings, aunts, uncles, and accidental twin. The four brothers were also learning that reality can be a kind of twilight zone—a land of both shadow and substance. And they wanted to learn more about how their minds and bodies compared with one another's and with the minds and bodies of other reared-apart pairs. Researchers are not the only people who find twins intriguing—the fascination that twins have with themselves and with each other is endless.

Chapter 7

Discoveries

Twins' Physical and Behavioral Traits

Getting Physical

Mia and Alexandra, fourteen-year-old identical twins born in China, but raised separately in the lively capital city of Sacramento, California, and the quiet fjord village of Fresvik, Norway, are one-and-a-half inches apart in height and fifteen pounds apart in weight. They exceed the average differences of 0.58 inches and 11.60 pounds for identical female twins reared apart, as well as the average differences of .62 inches and 11.53 pounds, for identical female twins reared together.[1] Perhaps Alexandra's greater exposure to fresh air, natural food, and daily exercise in Norway combined to produce her taller, more robust build, whereas Mia's need to keep her weight down as coxswain for her rowing team in Sacramento may explain her slimmer figure. However, possible differences in the twins' intrauterine environment cannot be dismissed. Kelli and Missi, identical twins raised together outside Chicago, differed by four inches at age eight and seven inches by age eighteen. Kelli's shorter stature resulted from a marginally attached placenta that delivered less prenatal nutrition to her than to her twin sister; Kelli also suffered from cardiac problems. These twins have the same blonde hair, blue eyes, and facial features, but one twin is a smaller version of the other.

Identical twins are more alike than any other pair of people, but they do not show perfect similarity. Identical twins result when a single fertilized egg divides, but a host of prenatal events can interfere with the identical expression of their identical genes. Unequal blood supply in the womb can occur when fetuses' blood vessels become connected, affecting the two-thirds of identical twins who share a placenta. Known as twin-to-twin transfusion syndrome (TTTS), this condition can create differences in twins' size and health. It is likely that the twins born in La Paz were seriously affected with TTTS because one La Paz newborn was sent immediately to the Bogotá hospital for treatment. When it comes to birth order, naturally delivered second-born twins are at higher risk for respiratory distress and infection than firstborns. Second-born twins are also at higher risk for newborn death. Not all second-born twins experience difficult births, but their average risk is higher, partly linked to the decreased size of the uterus after delivery of the first twin.[2]

All four Colombian twins were delivered by caesarean section so they avoided the hazards posed by vaginal deliveries. But the twins give us a glimpse of how life in a modern city and in a remote community can yield close copies but not exact duplicates.

DNA Revealed: Not Another Clone!

In August 2005 Susan and her husband, Steve Kay, had traveled to China with thirteen other couples, including Karen and Tom Lewis, to adopt one of the many thousands of abandoned little girls. China's one-child policy, instituted in 1979 to curb population growth, restricted urban couples to one child and rural couples to two. That policy, and China's preference for sons, explains the forced sterilizations of some women and abortions of female fetuses, as well as the widespread abandonment of baby girls. Among the abandoned babies were twins, some of whom were lucky enough to stay together, but others were separated. I am tracking the behavioral and physical development of such twins—they now include Mia and Alexandra and twenty-one other pairs—in the only ongoing study of young separated twins conducted in real time as the children grow up.

When Karen and Tom received their new baby, whom they named Kathy, they and their traveling companions noticed the striking resemblance of Kathy and Sarah, Susan and Steve's daughter. Both babies had brown hair, a round face, round eyes, and tiny chins, and they were extremely petite, actually "waif-like," with estimated ages that were only seven days apart. Both families suspected that they had received half of an identical twin pair. Susan contacted me, and we obtained saliva samples to compare the girls' DNA. As I noted earlier, the most accurate way to determine twin type is by comparing twins' resemblance across about fifteen DNA markers, the small segments of DNA that vary enormously from person to person. The only two people to match completely across all fifteen are identical twins.[3]

Everyone was shocked when the two little girls did not match on any of the DNA markers, so I persuaded the lab to repeat the test. When they did, the samples matched. It seemed that one of the samples had been contaminated, but which test could we trust? The lab agreed to perform the test again with a fresh set of samples, but this time the results showed that the girls were not related. So, just to be sure, a different laboratory repeated the test a fourth time and confirmed that the girls were not related.

Sarah's mother, Susan, was especially disappointed, asking sadly and hopefully whether they might be cousins.

Because of the profound implications of the DNA test results for all four men and their families, we had to address the real, but unlikely, possibility that the Colombian twins were chance look-alikes. Analysis of their DNA confirmed what everyone could see, that Jorge and William, and Carlos and Wilber, were the real twins, and both pairs were identical.[4] When I explained the actual procedure to Carlos over drinks, he joked, "Just don't give me another clone!" In fact, identical twins are clones by definition—genetically identical organisms—but human clones would not be identical twins because they do not meet the unique criteria that define twinship, such as simultaneous conception, common intrauterine environment, and shared date of birth.[5]

Dr. Juan J. Yunis, a medical geneticist, has worked with several Colombian families after single babies born to different mothers were inadvertently switched. "We see many things in our laboratory, so I am not surprised by much," he acknowledged, but nevertheless he called the Colombian twins' situation "a spectacular case." The father of Juan J. Yunis, Dr. Emilio J. Yunis, was the geneticist who performed the analyses of the Colombian twins' DNA.

Chorions, Amnions, and Placentas

One of the great myths surrounding twins is that fraternal twins always have two placentae, whereas identical twins share one. The placenta enables the transmission of oxygen and nutrition from mother to fetus, as well as the release of waste materials and carbon dioxide from the fetus. The truth is that some fraternal twin pairs have fused placentae, giving the appearance of one, and about one-third of identical twin pairs have two, such that each twin has his or her own. A related myth is that all fraternal twins arrive individually encased in their own chorion and amnion, the outer and inner protective membranes surrounding the fertilized egg, whereas identical twins always share these structures. In fact, some unusual fraternal twins—and we don't know how many—and about two-thirds of identical twins have a single chorion, although their amnions are separate. Only a tiny percentage of identical twins, perhaps 1 to 2 percent, share their chorion *and* their amnion, and would be at high risk for transfusion syndrome, or TTTS.[6]

Birth Records and Birth Weights: Telltale Signs?

The birth records for Carlos and Wilber, born in the small country hospital in Vélez, could not be found. However, Carlos was probably delivered first because the twins' mother, Ana, claimed that William was born first but, of course, William and Carlos had been switched.[7]

The complete chart for the identical twins William and Jorge, born at the Hospital Materno Infantil in Bogotá, was available and shows that William was delivered first, followed by his brother seven minutes later. The twins were classified as "monochorionic-diamniotic" (one chorion, two amnions), making them members of the identical twin majority at some risk for TTTS, but they exhibited no symptoms of this condition. The only possible sign was that William was anemic, but he was the larger twin, and the smaller twin typically shows anemia if TTTS has occurred. This made me wonder whether their birth orders written on their charts had somehow been switched, a possibility that could be a telltale sign that one baby had been replaced by another, which fits with something I learned a little later. However, their birth weight difference was less than the 18 percent threshold that currently identifies twins at risk for TTTS or other health concerns, so physicians don't usually worry about twins' condition unless their birth weight difference reaches this threshold. This difference is lower than that indicated in the past.[8]

The Bogotá twins' birth weights were slightly below average for male twins delivered at thirty-five weeks. William weighed 5 pounds, 1 ounce, while Jorge weighed 4 pounds, 8 ounces. However, both twins' Apgar scores (values reflecting a newborn's physical condition on a 1 to 10 scale) of 7 and 10, presumably taken at one and five minutes after their birth, show that their physical health was good, so the twins probably went to the premature nursery for precautionary reasons.[9] But William and Jorge's medical charts contain something strange that was apparently overlooked.

A reasonable assumption is that the larger twin at birth was the larger twin at discharge. If that was so, William gained nearly a pound, whereas Jorge lost just about one-tenth of an ounce. Babies often lose 5 percent of their weight in the first few days, start to gain weight by days 3 and 4, and end up back at their birth weight by day 5. So far, nothing was amiss.[10] But the records do not make clear which discharge weight goes with which twin. Reversing the discharge weights means that William would have lost about nine ounces, while Jorge would have gained a little more than 1 pound, 5 ounces. Newborns can be safely released from the hospital even if they have not fully recovered their weight loss, but a more prudent plan is to wait until babies put on some pounds.

What could have happened? Because we know that William and Carlos were switched, a possible—and, I believe, likely—scenario is that the medical chart contains William's *birth weight* of 5 pounds, 1 ounce, and Carlos's *discharge weight* of 4 pounds,

5 ounces. Ana, Carlos's biological mother, said that Carlos weighed about two pounds at birth. The discharge weight of 4 pounds, 5 ounces, is more consistent with Carlos's low birth weight than it is with William's. However, it is unlikely that Carlos would have nearly doubled his weight in four or five days, so he may have weighed more than two pounds at birth; Ana was in surgery and may not have recalled this information correctly. Regardless, if someone had carefully checked these numbers, then William's possibly erroneous weight loss of 9 ounces—and the exchange of babies—might have been detected almost immediately.

It seems extraordinary that a baby delivered at thirty-five weeks and weighing more than five pounds was switched with a baby delivered at twenty-eight weeks and weighing about two pounds, especially a newborn who needed immediate medical care. *Seven* different nurses made notes in the medical chart on December 22 and 23, suggesting that no one in the hospital really got to know Luz Marina and her babies. And, interestingly, in places the medical chart reads as though it concerned only one baby.

Growing Up

All four premature twins thrived physically with the love and care they received. Seeing them today as grown men belies the fact that they had once been small and fragile. Their body builds follow their genetic lines—Jorge and William are shorter and slighter than Carlos and Wilber. However, William is physically the strongest, a legacy of his years of hard work on his father's farm; he surpasses the other three in endurance, stamina, and arm wrestling. He showed impressive speed in beating his twin in a good-natured arm wrestling joust. Neither competition nor ill will was evident in this interaction—it was just twins at ease being together and having fun.

Two people may weigh the same, but a tall person might appear to be too thin and a short person might look too fat. Body mass index (BMI), calculated as weight in kilograms divided by height in centimeters squared, is a convenient way to know whether your weight is too low, too high, or just about right for your height. Genetic influence on BMI is about 85 percent, evident in the greater similarity of identical than fraternal twins.[11]

Identical twins are the privileged few who can really know how they look sporting a new outfit, a different hair style, or an extra twenty pounds since they have only to look at their twin. One of the reared-apart female twins in the Minnesota study always thought she was too fat, but when she met her twin sister, who was ten pounds heavier and quite attractive, she changed her view of herself. And a reared-apart male twin showed up at the study weighing eighty pounds less than his identical twin brother. Seeing his twin made him grateful that he had stuck to his diet.

The BMIs of the four twins were similar in 2015, seven months after they met, because the shorter twins weighed less than the taller twins. But during the next year William gained nearly twenty-one pounds by pumping iron and guzzling high-protein cocktails, which reset his BMI to just short of overweight. Here we have compelling evidence of how a lifestyle change can reduce identical twins' physical resemblance. With his broader face and larger torso, William did not resemble his twin as much as he did the year before. What if he had started working out a year earlier? Jorge's coworker Laura might not have confused them, they might never have met, and we would not have written this book.

Despite his weight gain, William's new BMI was still closer to his twin's than to those of the unrelated brothers with whom he was raised in La Paz. Carlos's BMI was closest to Wilber's, reflecting the effects of their genes, although Wilber's BMI was slightly closer to that of his biological brother Chelmo.

William likes his new body because women take greater notice than they did of his skinnier self. His twin brother, Jorge, is also pleased with his own appearance, but hopes to reduce his "big belly," hardly noticeable to others (and maybe not even to Jorge until William buffed up). Jorge walks and rides a bike, but he won't exercise like his twin, whom he criticizes as being obsessed with fitness.

Identical twins often monitor one another, tracking the physical changes that make them more or less alike. Carlos likes his appearance, but growing up he lacked self-confidence because he thought he was too skinny. Adding weight took care of those feelings, but now he is at an impasse—he wants to lose fat but not weight, although he knows that losing weight will help him lose fat. He also would like to have larger legs, but that would be possible only by gaining weight or working out, neither of which he finds an attractive option. When it comes to legs, when Carlos and Wilber walk side by side, their calves show a similar outward curvature, an expression of their identical genes.

"Carlos is fatter now," Wilber observed in 2016, aware that his twin could also see that Wilber's stomach had grown. Wilber eventually flattened his middle by forfeiting afternoon naps and evening meals. Then he lost too much weight, resumed eating his favorite foods (catfish and pork ribs), and regained several pounds. Overall, Wilber likes his looks, and both twins call special attention to their deep reddish lips, teasing their girlfriends about how *deliciosos* they are. The field known as cheiloscopy studies lip prints, which are made by pressing the lips against a special surface. They are actually like fingerprints because the patterns of lines and creases are unique to each individual. And the lip prints of identical twins are alike, but not exactly alike.[12]

The high-end clothing choices of Wilber and Carlos—which between them include a Diesel watch, Zara shirt, Gucci bag, and Kenzo jeans—reflect their focus on style and appearance. These two always look like they have just been to a hair stylist. Carlos sometimes tells his twin to stop imitating him, but Wilber is just doing what comes naturally. Their preferences encourage us to think about why we dress as we do. Choice of clothing arises from a combination of genetic and environmental factors, including body type, fabric texture, item availability, fashion trend, and purchasing power. Manner of dress also partly reflects behavioral attributes, such as self-monitoring (observing and managing one's own behavior—high self-monitors tend to use attire to manage the impressions they make on others) and self-perception (one's sense of value and self-worth—those who believe they are competent and dependable at work generally dress to impress). Genetic factors partly influence both self-monitoring and self-perception.[13]

Identical twins raised in different environments probably end up alike in these surprising ways because of active gene-environment correlation, the purposeful seeking out of opportunities and events compatible with genetically influenced interests, personalities, and temperaments. We all do this, creating our own environments from what is available to us. In La Paz, Wilber wasn't privy to the fashion trends and clothing choices his twin brother, Carlos, enjoyed in Bogotá, but Wilber made the most of what he could see and learn. Once he moved to Bogotá, the many choices and trends around him amplified his fashion interests, resulting in a good gene-environment fit.

Hands and Fingers

Twins are a curious group when it comes to which hand they favor. About 20 percent of twins are left-handed, about twice the percentage of nontwin lefties in the general population. A once-plausible but now contested theory is that late splitting of the fertilized egg, at or after day 8 postconception, is unlikely to yield precise copies of the original, perhaps causing left-handedness in one twin. Twins are, however, more likely than nontwins to experience birth hazards, such as difficult delivery and low birth weight, which have been linked to left-handedness in some pairs. Parents of twins are more often left-handed than their own siblings who are parents of nontwin children, although none of the parents of the Colombian twins wrote with their left hand.[14]

About 25 percent of identical twins are opposite-handed, meaning that one twin is right-handed and one twin is left-handed. This same minority of identical twins variously shows mirror-image eye dominance, fingerprint patterns, dental characteristics, and/or hair whorl, the direction in which the hair spins at the top of the head. Unusual biological events affecting laterality (sidedness) as the fertilized egg develops might cause identical twins to mirror one another in these ways. Environmental influences after birth, such as differences in smoking habits, tooth extractions, and denture wearing, have also been tied to facial reversals between twins. For example, when one twin smokes and the other does not, there can be differences in the deviation of the nasal septum, the wall separating the two nostrils.[15]

All four twins are right-handed, but not to the same degree. William is the strongest right-hander, followed by Wilber, Jorge, and Carlos in that order, with Carlos on the brink of ambidexterity, followed closely by Jorge. Both Carlos and Wilber are among the minority of "inverted right-handers," pointing their pencil downward and holding their hand above the line of writing. Santi, Jorge's young son, does this too. The little boy is not biologically related to the identical pair Carlos and Wilber, but links between twinning and left-handed tendencies have shown up in some families, and Santi's father, who is not a strong right-hander, is a twin. Perhaps when Carlos and Wilber, as well as Santi, were younger, their parents, caretakers, or school system discouraged their attempts at using their left hand for writing or drawing. Forcing them to use their right hand instead of their left may have affected their hand posture for reasons still not understood. Interestingly, the percentage of left-handers in Latin American countries is smaller than the 10 to 12 percent found in the Western world.[16]

Fingerprints

One of the great myths surrounding identical twins is that they have identical fingerprints, leading to the assumption that if one twin commits a crime, the other twin could be falsely accused. But that just isn't so. Identical twins do not have identical fingerprints because of variations in the womb such as temperature and positioning. However, their fingerprints are more alike than those of fraternal twins, indicating some genetic influence, especially for patterns known as arches.[17]

The science of fingerprints is called dermatoglyphics. Fingerprint ridges are the raised lines found on the tips of our fingers and are formed continuously between the tenth and twenty-fifth week of gestation.[18] Analyses may consider the total ridge count (sum of the ridges crossing the ten fingers) and pattern types (arch, loop, whorl, and variations of these three main types present on each finger).

As expected, the smallest differences in total ridge count are between the real identical twins, Jorge and William, who differ by twelve, and Carlos and Wilber, who differ by seventeen. And the greatest differences are between the unrelated brothers who grew up together, Jorge and Carlos in Bogotá (thirty-one), and William and Wilber in La Paz (sixty). Genetic effects are clearly at work, although neither identical pair matches perfectly (identical twins rarely do). This raises the question: What is the likelihood that they would be classified as identical based on their ridge count alone?

Kevin Haroian, my former colleague at the University of Minnesota, computed a number called Slater's Z score that could give us a hint. These scores say that the probability that each Colombian twin pair was identical was more than 50 percent (that is, greater than chance) and that the unrelated pairs were unlikely to be classified as identical. Still, reputable researchers would never rely solely on fingerprint ridge count for determining twin type, because identical twins could have markedly different fingerprints if one were especially stressed while in the womb.[19]

When the same unusual print is found on the same finger of both twins, it points toward their being identical. The identical twins born in Bogotá had the same unusual pattern on their left index fingers, a tented arch, an image that appears to have a tent pole rising in the middle. This print is found on fewer than 5 percent of human fingers and thumbs, and the twins were delighted to be part of this select group.[20]

Twin Type Revisited

My late colleague Dr. David T. Lykken developed a tidy formula for predicting twin type that combined twins' resemblance across eighteen blood groups, fingerprint ridge count, and two measures of body size, the cephalic index (head width × 100 divided by head length) and the ponderal index (height divided by the cubed root of weight). Using these numbers, the probability of misdiagnosing a pair of twins is less than 0.1 percent.[21] Just for fun, we tried this with the Colombian brothers, pairing them every which way, first using their ridge counts alone, then adding their first set of body size measures. The two pairs' chances of being identical went up as we added information, with the highest probabilities going to the real twins—Jorge and William scored more than 87 percent, and Carlos and Wilber scored more than 89 percent.

Also, just for fun, we reran the calculations using the twins' second set of body weights. This time the chance that Jorge and William could be identical twins fell to 47.7 percent. William had gained more than twenty pounds, nearly tripling the weight difference between him and his twin from the year before. Of course, the DNA findings are more accurate than the physical measures, showing that they are identical twins with virtually 100 percent certainty.

Epigenetics: City and Country

Numerous studies have compared the epigenetic profiles, or patterns of gene expression, in identical twins, looking for clues to why some pairs differ in complex traits and diseases like smoking or depression, but our study was the first to do this using identical twins and siblings raised apart.[22] It turned out that the twins in one identical pair were similar to each other even though they had been raised apart, and Diana was similar to her biological brother William, whom she had never known. However, one of the city-raised twins differed greatly from his country-raised twin, perhaps because he was affected by an unusual event in the womb, but there was no way to test this. A finding of special interest was that the expression of genes that may have been affected by radiation and pesticides was different for the brothers from the city and the brothers from the country. It is too early to know whether the city-raised pair was more adversely affected than the country-raised pair, or even whether these effects are harmful and, if so, to what degree, but such questions can be explored in the future. For now, simply finding this difference in reared-apart identical twins is important.

General Health

Each reared-apart identical twin was much more like his twin brother healthwise than the accidental brother with whom he was raised. William and Jorge's three-page medical inventories were nearly blank, showing no allergies, no surgeries, no medications, and no broken bones. Neither twin had ever been a smoker. *"Gracias Dios no me duele nada!"* (Thank God nothing is wrong!), William said. Aside from the leishmaniasis he had contracted in the army, his only complaint was a small benign mass under his right ear that he would have removed. Jorge had nothing to discuss in regard to his health history.

The other identical pair, Carlos and Wilber, had many affirmative answers on their medical forms, perhaps linked to the risks posed by their early birth at twenty-eight weeks to a relatively older mother, such as their low birth weight and her hemorrhaging.[23] Both reared-apart twins were self-described crybabies from the start, and their discomforts continued. As young boys each twin had had difficulties pronouncing *r* and *g*, but speech therapy corrected Carlos's problem. Wilber, raised in far more modest circumstances, did not receive therapy so his mispronunciations are still evident. Carlos had worn braces on his teeth to correct poor alignment, whereas his brother wears them now as an adult.

Carlos also experiences pain in his wrists, ankles, arms, and fingers from playing basketball and has had hives.

Carlos uses eyeglasses to correct for astigmatism and myopia, while his twin claims not to need them. In fact, when Wilber tried on Carlos's glasses, they made his vision worse. People who were born prematurely often experience vision problems, the result of early stimulation of the immature visual system, insufficient nutrition from losing contact with the placenta, or other birth complications. And infants born at twenty-eight weeks, like Carlos and Wilber, are at greater risk than infants born later for retinopathy of prematurity, a blinding disease and major cause of visual loss. Carlos's first few days of life were more challenging than Wilber's, but it is curious that only one of these early born twins was visually impaired. An early study of twin and nontwin children found that twins are more likely to wear eyeglasses and that twins' visual problems seemed linked to their prematurity. These identical and fraternal pairs did not differ in their need to wear eyeglasses as a result of a nongenetic cause: their early birth. However, twin studies have found genetic influence on other eye problems, such as refractive error or the eye's improper bending of light resulting in blurriness.[24]

Wilber produced an extended list of health issues, the first dating to when he fell off a horse as a young child and required two days of hospitalization. He was riding the horse with William when the horse suddenly jumped. William threw himself to the ground and was unhurt, but Wilber clung to William's waist and hit his head on a rock. This incident changed the shape of a bone in his head. In addition, Wilber has sought treatment over the years for ear problems, respiratory difficulties, and for a pulled muscle in his back.

Both Wilber and Carlos have histories of smoking, consistent with a genetic influence on this habit. Carlos had his first cigarette when he was ten, smoked spontaneously from time to time after that, and now enjoys only an occasional cigarette. Wilber began smoking when he was eighteen and smoked two or three cigarettes a day for two years before quitting completely. As for alcohol, Carlos drinks less now than he did several years ago because he dislikes having a hangover, but he still enjoys his favorite cocktail, a *cabeza de jabalí*, a combination of vodka, white rum, gin, tequila, triple sec, and orange juice, garnished with a red cherry. All four twins relish a few beers.

Food Fights and Other Culinary Curiosities

Twin "culture" refers to the habits, rituals, likes, and dislikes that uniquely define each identical twin pair. The reared-apart Chinese twins Mia and Alexandra eat several times during the day, growing hungry each time but filling up fast. The reared-apart Scottish twins Caroline and Margaret routinely left one uneaten square of toast on the plate when they were finished with breakfast. And Tony and Roger from upstate New York seemed to eat just one continuous meal a day. These reared-apart identical men took advantage of an all-you-can-eat pizza restaurant by substituting for one another while one hid in the restroom. They kept this prank up until the harried server who delivered each order refused to comply, but laughed heartily when she realized she'd been had by twins. These quirks are seen much less often in fraternal twins, suggesting that genes play a role, although we do not know how they guide people toward these particular behaviors.

Carlos and Wilber like to "out-eat" each other, which is not surprising because they are the bigger twins and rank eating second in importance to women. Food consumption contests are a large part of Wilber and Carlos's unique culture, evidenced by an eating contest several months after they met that Carlos won by polishing off his portion and some of Wilber's. Neither twin could or would engage his respective accidental brother in such activities because each would find these contests unappealing.

Carlos, in particular, defends his individuality, and food is one way he does this. At Bogotá's trendy Local Gastronomia Nacional, a server handed out lunch menus, but chalkboards posted on the walls listed the specials. Carlos and Wilber studied these offerings and decided on the same meal, shrimp with rice. "We will have . . . ," Carlos said, then suddenly grew indecisive before telling the server they would both be having rice, but with different main courses.

Jorge and William are foreigners in their brother's kitchens and never stage food-eating contests or compete in any apparent way. They do not always order the same dish, although William can be persuaded to have a glass of wine when Jorge does. But they eat off of each other's plate and sample each other's meal with the same fork, all done naturally and effortlessly. This level of intimacy is usually displayed by significant others, close relatives, lifelong friends, and twins who have grown up together, so it is striking to witness this interaction between twins who have not been together for long.

Life events can significantly affect how we eat, with some people turning to food for comfort and others refusing to eat at all. All four brothers had gone through a major upheaval in their lives that may have affected their eating habits. Restrained eaters might refuse to eat for fear of becoming fat, uncontrolled eaters might find it hard to turn down a tempting dish even when they are feeling full, and emotional eaters would consume extra portions and snack when they were feeling anxious. Researchers have found both genetic and environmental influences for these three measures, but a study of the eating habits of Spanish university students may be especially revealing.[25]

William expressed the highest level of uncontrolled eating, not just among his three brothers, but also higher than these university students. Furthermore, all four brothers outdid the students when it came to emotional eating, possibly reflecting the upheaval in their lives. Of course, we don't know the brothers' eating habits before the switch was discovered, so it is impossible to say whether that ordeal explains William's lack of control or everyone's emotional eating. We do know that William, one of the switched twins, did not eat well during the first few days after the revelation despite his godmother's tempting him with his favorite dishes, so his emotional and uncontrolled eating could have reflected his emotional state, even though six months had passed since his history was known.

Scribbles and Scrawls

When Wilber puts pen to paper, he rotates the page counterclockwise until he achieves a perfectly horizontal, or landscape, view, but none of the other three twins does this. I wondered whether this habit might affect his handwriting but, more generally, whether handwriting features were more similar between the related than the unrelated brothers. Of course, both pairs of accidental brothers had learned to write in the same school system, which may have increased their resemblance.

Little recent research has looked at twins' handwriting similarities, although early twin studies found that identical twins were more alike than fraternal twins in the general quality and speed of their penmanship. But identical twins were not more alike than fraternal twins in individuality or general style of their penmanship, suggesting that genetic factors influence the "coarser outlines of behavior," whereas the "finer details" are more susceptible to environmental influences and chance.[26]

Eileen Page is a certified graphologist with years of experience in handwriting analysis. At her suggestion the twins and four of their siblings wrote several sentences about the significance of family, a topic that has the same meaning for all of them.

In fourteen handwriting categories, such as the space between words and the direction of the slant, the three most-similar pairs were biological siblings, even some who had grown up apart, and the four least-similar pairs were biologically unrelated, even those who had grown up together. Most remarkable, the two separated identical pairs were in the top third when it came to similarity. Thus, this modest exercise suggests that genetics may influence some handwriting features to some degree, although graphologists would need to examine handwriting samples from many more twins and their siblings. Curiously, Wilber was the only one who applied heavy pressure to the page.

Becoming Men

In some areas of Colombia, even large cities, fathers or older brothers arrange for their sons or siblings to lose their virginity when they are as young as fourteen. I asked our interpreter, Alberto, about this and he said it was true, then shared a story about a "devirginizing" that he had witnessed in his younger years. A friend's father had invited the schoolmates of his son Fernando to be at a brothel when he lost his virginity. The boy was about seventeen at the time and certainly no virgin. But Fernando played stupid to make his dad proud, and everyone had a good time on the father's dime, enjoying a bottle of scotch whiskey to commemorate the occasion. A French schoolgirl "who was neither French nor quite a schoolgirl" came around, but she was a great actress and feigned a heavy Parisian accent. Fernando had a good time drinking, groping the woman, and playing innocent. Alberto wasn't sure, but he thought Fernando got a "jumbo-deluxe-combo" that night.

A variety of factors, including one's genes and the environment in which one is raised, influence age at first intercourse. Just how much genes play a role is not clear, with estimates ranging from 0 to 72 percent. Genetic influence seems to be greater among younger people, because many societies have relaxed their sexual restrictions.[27]

All four Colombian twins were relatively young when they had their first sexual experience. Three twins were fourteen and one twin was seventeen. Their ages are consistent with the 10 percent of Colombian adolescents from Bucaramanga, the capital city of Santander, who have had sexual experiences. The same percentage holds true for teens from Santa Marta, located 450 miles north of Bogotá.[28] The Colombian twins' sexual histories do not allow general conclusions about how much genetic and environmental factors affect age at first intercourse, but twin studies support contributions from both.

Chapter 8

Another World

La Paz and Beyond

C arlos, the switched city-raised twin, called La Paz "nothing and nothing and nothing," but not in a negative sense. He meant that the small town was simply far from the center of things, "another reality." This may explain why William, the switched country-raised twin, insisted that we see the home and town where he grew up.

They lived somewhere between the tiny towns of Vereda El Recreo and Vereda Colon, another world in our eyes. No one had computers, and the town had no paved roads or grocery stores. The twins' house had no running water, or any plumbing at all, and stood surrounded by trees, plants, and other wildlife. The house now belonged to Chelmo, one of the older La Paz brothers, because their parents had moved a three-hour walk away to La Guayabita, an area closer to stores and neighbors. The journey to Chelmo's farm is one that people in the area make without hesitation because they know no other options. Even small children scoot up the uneven hills and wade through muddy puddles without fear of falling. Crowded buses and fast cars disturb people from La Paz when they venture into Bogotá or the nearest big city, Bucaramanga, while city kids in Bogotá clamor to sit in the front seat to watch their world pass by. And city kids, used to buses, cars, and taxis, complain about having to walk more than half a mile.

Despite its isolation the areas around La Paz have a rich and complex culture. Residents celebrate the annual Festival for the Virgen del Carmen, the patron saint of all vehicles, curious because most people in the surrounding areas do not have cars since there are no roads, although some drive motorbikes. They also hold various religious services and political demonstrations for peace, but the festivals and other events are hours away and happen only occasionally.

Getting There

Traveling from Bogotá to the twins' childhood home in La Paz is challenging. Under normal conditions it means a five-hour ride by highway to Vélez, followed by a one-hour drive to La Paz through rough woods and over large rocks and muddy streams in a four-wheel-drive vehicle, then a one-hour hike through the same treacherous terrain to the house. Horseback is an option for the final leg of the trip, but most people who live there just walk. Residents say the walk takes fifteen to thirty minutes, but while we walked, they kept greatly underestimating the time remaining, perhaps to reassure first-time visitors to the area like us. This is understandable because the people in La Paz are used to getting around on foot. In contrast, city folk tend to overestimate distances and arrival times, probably because they include walking speed and traffic in their calculations.[1]

Being There

We were headed to a barbeque at William and Wilber's childhood home hosted by their parents, Ana Delina and Carmelo. The four twins had different feelings about this Sunday afternoon affair. The biological brothers Jorge and William, ever the extroverts and social butterflies, anticipated it eagerly, seeing it as an opportunity to bask in the attention of the one hundred or so friends and family members whom William had insisted on inviting. Among them would be the La Paz brothers' former teacher, who had made the one-hour walk to school with them each day; their friend Edgar Pardo, who owned the Bogotá butcher shop where they worked; and the town's former mayor, Ermes Amado, who had political connections that appealed to William. The more private, pragmatic, and self-described mature identical twin pair, Carlos and Wilber, disliked the attention-seeking tendencies of the other two, believing that the switch and its aftermath were serious life-changing events, not the stuff of show business or political ambitions. They grudgingly allowed themselves to be dragged along, but worried that the crowd of guests would turn the four twins into local entertainment. That each twin would have the same reaction as his recently reunited double is not surprising, because genes have a significant influence on how we process information.[2]

Many people around La Paz would have been unaware of the twins' story on *Séptimo Día* because they didn't have TVs, but news of the switch had spread quickly among area residents by cell phone or during visits. Everyone was excited to see the mirror images of the two boys they had known since childhood and felt honored to be visited by university faculty from the United States. In this respect the people of La Paz and Bogotá were no different, obsessed as they were with the twins' story and eager for more details. After the first televised segment aired, *Séptimo*

Día had received a flood of calls from doctors, psychologists, sociologists, and general viewers, literally forcing the station to produce a follow-up.

Given the attention the story had attracted in Bogotá the reluctant twins, Carlos and Wilber, anticipated that the guests, intrigued by the switch, would have them repeat the sequence of strange events several times. People might not listen closely to how the confusion and its resolution unfolded, but everyone would stare unabashedly at the twins' faces, bodies, and gestures in search of similarities and differences. Wilber and Carlos were just not into stardom, celebrating their newfound behavioral and physical likenesses privately and quietly, scoffing at their brothers' occasional attempts to sport matching clothes, shoes, and goatees. Most important, Carlos would have little precious time to get to know his biological parents and siblings in a calm, intimate setting, which both he and Wilber felt was essential if those relationships were to move forward.

What some people later interpreted as frostiness toward his La Paz parents and siblings, even rejection, was a disoriented young man who was trying to wrap his head around a life that truly had been his destiny if not for a careless mistake made years earlier. The alternative world that Carlos saw for the first time was far removed from the one in which he was living. Bogotá allowed him to fulfill his dreams of getting an education; he became a financial analyst and earned a good income. He enjoyed clubbing with friends, attending rock concerts, and watching football games. None of this would have been possible if he had returned to La Paz where he was born. He somehow sensed that he would have been a different person, but at the time he would not acknowledge this and even denied it. His life in Bogotá was also a poignant reminder of the mother he had loved so completely, buried all too soon, and mourned so deeply. With time, Carlos became reconciled to his situation and established new family ties on his own terms, but crowds were not part of that, and until he was able to assimilate his past and present circumstances, people misunderstood what he said and did.

Jorge did most of the talking during the trip to our first stop in Vélez, a pattern that persisted even after we arrived at his brother's home turf in La Paz. Several times the driver pressed William for directions, but he seemed uncertain, even though he had made this trip many times. Some might suspect that the country boy felt overshadowed by the city boy, who generally took command when they were together, but there was genuine trust between these two and they were fine with it. Of course, maybe the early hour prevented William from responding to the driver's constant call for directions—William nodded off several times, as did his twin, who fell asleep with his head in William's lap.

This degree of physical comfort between identical twins, even those who have been raised apart, may seem surprising, but I have seen this kind of physical closeness before. In 2010, I met a twenty-year-old Asian American identical twin who had reunited with her South Korean sister for the first time, in Seoul, before boarding a train to Busan to visit their birth family. The American twin realized only later that the two had fallen asleep while leaning against each other and holding hands. She said she usually is standoffish about physical contact with others, but dozing off with her identical twin sister felt peaceful and familiar. And this was how it was for the Colombian twins—when Jorge's head dropped into his brother's lap, it was natural and effortless, comfortable and familiar. Their physical ease with each other may explain why the members of both identical reared-apart twin pairs share a bed when sleeping at each other's homes, as do many identical twins raised together, even as adults, because it just feels right.

During their moments of wakefulness as we drove toward Vélez, I heard about William's political ambitions to be elected to the city council and eventually become mayor of La Paz. He felt closely tied to the people of his town and wanted to improve their lives in any way he could. Amado, the former mayor, was his close friend and stoked the young man's desire to be in public service. William was already bringing computers to the schoolchildren of his town through a program set up in the city, and he would eventually help with road construction that permitted easier access to the area. At the time he also thought a lot about getting a law degree, a credential that would boost his standing as a professional and give him greater understanding of the legal processes behind the projects he hoped to put in place.

Jorge is a strong advocate of his identical twin's political goals and dreams but has none of his own, preferring to focus on his engineering career. But he has the makings of a politician: an outgoing personality, good public-speaking ability, considerable self-confidence, and readiness to provide assistance when it is needed. The twins' similarities in this respect are not unusual because genes influence political participation, leadership skills, and helping behaviors.[3] Both twins expressed the same tendencies, tailoring their behaviors to the circumstances of their particular environment.

I learned more about Jorge and William as we approached Vélez to visit the hospital where Carlos and Wilber were born. They have the same bump in the same spot on the bridge of their nose, and until they met, they were certain it had come from an early injury. These surprise revelations are the rare perks of being a reunited identical twin. The "Jim twins," Jim Lewis and Jim Springer, the premier pair of the Minnesota study, were raised in different Ohio cities and met each other for the first time when they were thirty-nine. Both their adoptive families had been told that their child's twin had died, but when one mother, Lucille Lewis, went to court to sign some adoption papers, the clerk blurted out that the other twin had also been named Jim. When her son turned five, she told him what she had learned, but he wasn't psychologically ready to find his brother until he was nearly forty. Aside from their same names, nail-biting habits, light-blue Chevrolets, and interest in woodworking, both twins suffered from severe headaches, which they attributed to stressful events. But that was only partly true because their symptoms began when the twins were teenagers, and they described the pain in the same way, as a great blow to the neck. We now know that headaches have a partial genetic basis, making them likely in people susceptible to stress.[4]

On the way to Vélez I also learned that Jorge and William share some dietary preferences, such as a fondness for chicken, but they will eat only the drumstick. Maybe it is the flavor, the ease of holding it, or the shape that is similarly appealing to the twins, but they were too tired to explain this preference. While they slept, I took a closer look at their ears, confirming my first impression that both twins had ears that stand out from their heads at the same sharp angle. But no identical twins are exactly alike: Jorge wears eyeglasses and William does not. As I explained, some eye problems such as near-sightedness are partly genetic in origin but may also be linked to premature delivery and/or extensive schoolwork.[5] Both twins were born somewhat early, but one stayed in school and the other left school at age eleven to work on his family's farm, lifestyle differences that could explain their vision differences. Even so, the behavioral and physical matches outnumbered the misses, no doubt why these twins were quick to call each other brother while sticking to a first-name basis with their accidental ones.

* * *

At 6:00 a.m. we approached our first scheduled stop, the Hospital Regional de Vélez, the public facility where Carlos and Wilber had been born. The conversation turned to the circumstances of their birth and delivery, with William certain that the switch had happened soon after Carlos had arrived in Bogotá, given the chaotic conditions in the preemie nursery. Jorge recalled his mother's saying how much he and Carlos looked alike as babies, as some premature babies do, and he showed me a photograph to prove it. The photo showed the twins when they were extremely young infants, and they did look somewhat the same, although not all premature babies do; it depends partly at what point in the pregnancy they are delivered. Babies born at thirty-five weeks, like Jorge and William, look like small full-term infants, whereas babies born at twenty-eight weeks, like Carlos and Wilber, are small and skinny with translucent skin.[6] Photos taken during their first weeks and months show that Jorge and Carlos, the accidental Bogotá brothers, quickly diverged in size, coloring, and facial appearance. And before she delivered, Luz had been told to expect identical twins, so perhaps she was unconsciously trying to match her perceptions to her doctor's diagnosis.

Hospital Regional de Vélez

The tiny hospital, dedicated to providing quality health care to local residents, looked like a collection of different-sized shoeboxes placed alongside one another. The building and its surroundings were a bit eerie, not just because it was still somewhat dark, but because this was where the twins' strange saga began. We entered through a door marked URGENCIAS (Emergencies), and hospital staff escorted us through white, dimly lit corridors to the Unidad Neonatal (Neonatal Unit).

As we peered through the glass partition, we saw an empty space with only an incubator and two baby cradles placed side by side, perhaps where Carlos and Wilber had spent their first few hours together. This was also Carlos's first visit to the place of his birth and William's first visit to the hospital where, until six months before, he believed he'd been born. *Séptimo Día* had shown this unit in one of the televised segments, but seeing it in person was an emotional experience that many of us, most of all the two switched twins, were not prepared for. It was one of those "should have been, could have been" moments—if only the baby had not been so sick, or if only the family and hospital staff had paid closer attention to the appearance of the newborn who left and the one who returned. Imagining the events that took place in that nursery twenty-six years earlier was painful, but hard to resist.

In one rare moment the two switched twins stood together just beyond the entrance to the nursery, and I observed them closely. Seeing William and Carlos so close to one another was unusual because an obvious uneasiness lingered between them at that time, born of their uncommon connection. Their ambivalence was grounded in the knowledge that, while neither could be blamed for the switch, each embodied a life and a lifestyle that belonged to the other one, and their presence was a forceful reminder of that. William hungered for the opportunities that Carlos had had instead, and Carlos could not contain his impatience with William for not climbing the professional ladder. They eventually would resolve this tension, but it colored their relationship in the early months.

More what-if questions probably raced through everyone's mind: What if the small hospital had been better equipped to handle tiny babies? What if the twins' grandmother had stayed with the baby in Bogotá? What if the twins' aunt Edelmira, who had brought William back to La Paz, had had more discerning eyes? Their aunt answered a lot of questions over breakfast at a family-run restaurant in the center of La Paz, called El Campesino (The Country Man). It is a popular place, with long wooden tables and benches, perhaps because the surrounding area has few restaurants. The server brought us a typical Colombian morning meal of *caldo de costilla* (beef broth) and bread, and we ate dinner there later before heading back to Bogotá.

Aunt Edelmira

"The baby had a digestive problem, which is why his grandmother brought him to Bogotá," Edelmira told us. "He couldn't defecate or urinate. His mother never saw him until he came home, because she was recovering from a caesarean-section delivery. . . . When I brought him back to La Paz, he was well wrapped and I was told not to unwrap him until we arrived and his mother could feed him."

These recollections of visiting her newborn nephew in the hospital in Bogotá only add to the mystery of how one twin was switched for another. Edelmira claims to have seen the *same* baby, in the *same* crib, every day for the seven days he stayed there. When she first saw him, she had the presence of mind to ask the nurse if this was "Ana Delina's baby," and the nurse said it was and that the infant had a problem urinating. Upon hearing those words, she was satisfied that this newborn was truly her nephew. "I fixed my eyes on him, only it was the wrong baby."

In those days newborns at the Hospital Materno Infantil were identified with a handwritten tape placed around their wrist. One day Edelmira noticed that the baby's wristband was missing. After she called attention to this important detail, a nurse told her that the infant had probably "moved around," causing it to fall off. When Edelmira returned the next day, she saw that the baby's wristband had been reattached; when she checked it, she saw that it matched the one she had seen two days before. There was no cause for concern, but when she was ready to take the baby home, a problem arose. Because the last name on her identification card didn't match the last name of the baby, the hospital refused to release him. It took the persuasive powers of a nearby relative to convince the staff that Edelmira was the baby's aunt and that his parents had asked her to bring him home. "I received medication and instructions from the doctor for how to care for him, but maybe they were the wrong instructions because now he was anemic and it seemed strange," Edelmira said. "By the time I got the baby, the doctor didn't notice that there had been a switch." No one did, and to this day no one knows what really happened, and it is likely that no one ever will. Even if the nurse in charge were found, her memory of the premature babies she cared for twenty-six years before would be dim, like the recollections of the nurse who was interviewed for the TV program.

William's belief that the twin exchange happened early is probably correct because Edelmira had supposedly memorized the baby's face and wristband data early on. But because premature newborns sometimes look alike, perhaps Edelmira didn't notice the switch, or maybe the right wristband was always on the wrong baby. Aside from a lawsuit pending against the hospital, none of this matters now because the clock cannot be rewound. Everyone accepts that, but knowing what happened could replace futile speculation with some peace of mind.

Vélez to La Paz

When we left the restaurant, we found a lot of activity outside. It was late Sunday morning and most people were off from work, so some had come to sit outside and enjoy the warm weather and a

first chromosome that fails to separate from the others as the egg or sperm matures, or it can result from the inheritance of a translocation from a parent whose twenty-first chromosome has another chromosome attached.[8] Researchers have identified some clinical differences between the two types.[9] Different gene combinations giving rise to the same facial contour, ear shape, and skin tone could explain why the young man from La Paz looked so much like William and Jorge. Their similarity was especially remarkable given the circumstances: physical resemblance was responsible for realigning the right twin pairs.

This encounter also made me grateful that we had run DNA tests on all four brothers before we got there, because I know that not all look-alikes are reared-apart identical twins. I will never forget the disappointment Susan experienced after learning that a girl seemingly identical to Susan's adopted Chinese daughter was not her twin.[10] Since then I have worked with other look-alike pairs impatient to celebrate their newfound identical twinship, but I have encouraged them to keep the champagne on ice until the DNA laboratory says they have reason to pop the cork.

La Paz to Vereda: Hiking or Horseback

We had two options for getting to the brothers' childhood home: hike or ride a horse. Their mother, pregnant with twins, had made that difficult journey twenty-six years earlier on foot until she reached a place where cars could pass. Everyone said that the walk was easy, but it turned out to be dangerous and daunting to an outsider even though some sections had been cleared the day before by the twins' relatives using machetes. William had also arranged for increased security to ease any concerns we might have had.

We saw no obvious markings along much of the route, so we followed William and Wilber and their friends, who had made this journey many times. The group had to contend with sharp hills and a rusted iron fence but came across no real signs of habitation. The locals kept assuring us we were "almost there," although a considerable distance remained. At one juncture we faced the choice of negotiating a rock-strewn, fast-moving stream or traversing an aging suspension bridge with lots of missing rungs, and ropes that hung about twenty feet above the stream. I took the bridge. Although Carlos had never done this, I followed him closely, carefully placing my feet exactly where his had been. The young children who lived there moved swiftly across the bridge and the terrain, coming from behind and beating us across. Jorge said that if his young son, Santi, were there, in "two minutes he would tell me to pick him up." His view—that the children of La Paz grow up suffering and must fight harder for more things than city kids—is a bit of wisdom that took Carlos longer to understand. But Jorge was not the switched twin, so he could appraise the situation dispassionately.

I had brought along a shiny purple suitcase with gifts and supplies for the day. I soon found that while this tote is easy to wheel through airport terminals and along city streets, it was a burden along the uncharted route we were taking. William, the strongest of the bunch, slung it over his head for a while, then handed it to Carlos and insisted that he carry it. This act may have been William's way of drawing his switched counterpart into this other world, exposing Carlos to the challenges of country life that are not so easily overcome. Carlos complied, but he resisted the events of the day in other ways by wearing shorts, not slacks, and sneakers, not boots, and later exchanged his muddied sneakers for flip-flops. He sometimes stood apart when people were taking pictures or making family introductions.

* * *

After we had walked a full hour in the hot sun, we suddenly came upon a house and a lot of people. We found no gate and no entrance—we were just *there*. Outside, a wooden picnic table stood laden with what looked like vegetables, and we could see a barbeque pit constructed of large sticks where the pieces of one of Carmelo's freshly slaughtered cows, sprinkled with salt and other seasonings, were grilling about a hundred yards away. Meat in rural Colombia, like the carne a la llanera we were served, is often tough because of overcooking to destroy the bacteria on animals that are killed for food. The only bathroom was the privacy of the surrounding bushes and trees.

People looked around, eager to catch sight of the twins, two of whom they would be meeting for the first time. Some neighbors gazed at the rest of us curiously but also respectfully, knowing we had come from the United States to meet the twins and their families. The former mayor arrived and as a politician was eager to engage my help in promoting tourism in the area at some future time. A pair of five-year-old identical twin boys stood next to each other in the crowd, and I felt happy for them, knowing that they had each other to play with in this outlying area. With no other houses in sight and no reasonable roads, playdates and soccer moms simply don't exist. That kids had to walk the same distances as adults if they wanted to see their friends was just a normal part of life.

The vegetables I had spotted were actually two kinds of potatoes that Ana had prepared and placed on plantain leaves spread across the wooden table for guests to help themselves. (Plantain leaves save on tableware and covering.) Beer and a delicious homemade alcoholic drink called *guarapo de caña*, made from sugarcane juice, were available, but we had only two hours to eat, drink, and chat because returning to La Paz before dark was important. Still, we had time to talk to the La Paz parents in one of the three open spaces at the front of the house. Carmelo said little, crying silently as he followed his wife's words.

Ana wore a purple V-neck sweater, light-colored slacks, and black tennis shoes, the only sensible attire in this remote area, although dark-colored pants would be more practical for hiding any stains from soil. She had on the long earrings and beaded bracelet typical of Colombian women, and like many of them she kept her hair long and pulled back, accentuating her thin face. Aging women in the United States tend to cut their long hair short in the belief that it makes them look younger, but ages and dates are not an obsession in rural Colombia the way they are in the United States. Ana rarely smiled when she spoke, probably because the baby switch was still a tender topic. Carlos's reserve and the deaths of her two sons, no doubt brought to mind that day, might have contributed to her generally serious demeanor.

Ana wept as she retold and relived the events leading to her knowledge of the switch and its aftermath. She spoke of William's beauty, kindness, and sweetness, a son so different from his presumed twin brother in appearance and behavior, and acknowledged that he had lived a harsh life. Because she and Carmelo never had enough money to send him to school, he had joined the military to experience the world beyond La Paz. Devastated that William would never meet his biological parents, and that Carlos had never known his real father, Ana found pleasure in knowing that Carlos had grown up well and felt grateful to Luz for raising him. But it hurt her that her newfound biological son did not say hello to her "as his mother."

That afternoon we experienced a wonderful moment when the reunited twins Jorge and William stood before the guests to thank them for coming and to introduce us more formally. As expected Jorge did more of the talking, even though La Paz was where his twin had grown up, but William added freely to the conversation when he sensed it was called for. The crowd was quiet and attentive, but their eyes darted from one twin to the other, constantly comparing and contrasting, finding it incredible to see a double of the boy and young man they had known and watched for twenty-six years. I delivered a short speech with the assistance of one of the interpreters; I thanked everyone for their hospitality and for the opportunity to visit the La Paz brothers' home. People cast plenty of stares in my direction, probably because the people in this small town were not used to having visitors from abroad. Some newspaper photographers were also running around, setting up cameras and placing the twins in various poses. It was a pretty big deal.

A Day in the Life

Views of the green hills and tall trees were quite beautiful from certain locations around the house. But this was also territory over which guerillas, the left-wing rebels whose terrorist organization had waged battle with the Colombian government since 1957, had roamed during the brothers' childhood. The guerillas stole chickens, cattle, and crops from the people who lived there, rather than demand cash, because the guerillas knew that farm families were poor. But the guerillas sometimes abducted children and turned them into combatants. Approximately two hundred guerillas had combed the area where the family lived, but, as Wilber explained, "When you're a little kid you don't understand what's happening so you're not afraid." But he had plenty to fear as a sixteen-year-old when the guerillas took him and a friend and forced the pair to walk with them for about ten minutes. Upon reaching a huge hole the guerillas asked the boys their names, but Wilber was too terrified to answer, so his friend answered for them as Wilber thought about another of his friends who had been taken and held for eight days. Then the guerrillas told the boys to wait and they disappeared. "They came back twenty minutes later and told us to leave," Wilber recalled. "I thought we were going to be killed." His parents said little about what had happened because this was part of daily life in La Paz. The guerillas and the Colombian government reached a peace agreement in 2016.

Some harsh elements in the La Paz brothers' home life were related to the strict manner in which the children were raised. The family usually gathered for dinner, but Carmelo never spoke and the children had to stay silent. "When we eat, we eat" is what he said, according to Wilber. And Carmelo occasionally struck his children, three smacks with a belt or a branch when they didn't do their chores or misbehaved in some way. William and Wilber angered their father with their constant fighting, but as Carmelo got older, his sons got faster, so when he reached for his belt, they ran away and stayed hidden for several hours. Still, Carmelo had the final say when it came to what they could and could not do, and they were often afraid to ask for his permission. Ana sometimes intervened, counseling them to be good in order to get their father's approval.

Their childhood days were highly regimented, beginning with awakening at 5:45 a.m. and bathing in a tank filled with water drawn from a well. Homes didn't have plumbing, but the family had the great outdoors. "There was no privacy," William recalled. "But we were mostly men, so my mother took a bath after we left for school." The schoolhouse was a long walk each way, over the same rough terrain we had covered. When the children got home, they had chores to do, followed by dinner from about 5:00 to 6:00. "Working in the fields means that you eat early," William said. They had a little free time for play after dinner, but few distractions before going to bed at 7:30 p.m.

Their childhood was difficult; while the family had enough

to eat, the kids often walked barefoot because there was no money for shoes. Working on the farm was required, and everyone did it because they knew no other way of life—William recalled that the hardships became apparent only when he looked back.

As 3:00 p.m. approached, it was time to begin the long walk back to La Paz, which seemed slightly less intimidating now that we had done it once. But it was hotter now, and the hard-packed dirt had melted into mud in lots of places. Although a family friend guided us skillfully, I lost my balance halfway down and sat squarely in a soupy puddle that darkened my clothes and stained my handbag forever. Next came the same dizzying one-hour ride to La Paz in the four-wheel-drive vehicles and a quick stop at the restaurant. There we were all offered dinner and a sampling of the luscious Colombian treat of *bocadillo con queso*, cheese topped with sweet guava paste. These treats were arranged for by Yesika's sister Alexandra, who surprised us by making the long trip to La Paz to drive a few of us back to Bogotá.

Despite everything we had done that day, or perhaps because of everything we had experienced, we felt a lingering excitement and elation brought on by an extraordinary day that had revealed a way of life far removed from the familiar. We became aware in a deeply personal way of the ramifications of restricted opportunities for personal growth and development and understood them more clearly than is possible from reading most professional or popular articles on the topic. Poverty took on a whole new meaning— most people think that being poor means lacking money and the goods and services it buys, but poverty can also mean merely a lack of conveniences. The people of La Paz did not have paved roads, running water, or modern bathrooms, but they were not poor in the conventional sense because they raised their meat and vegetables, and they had no need to pay water or electric bills.

The visit also underlined the universal importance of family ties—that a mother can love a son she never knew; that a son could not immediately feel affection for family members despite the biological ties between them; and that another son could mourn a mother he would never know. These were important takeaways that would add layers of understanding to everything we learned about the twins.

In one of my waking moments on the ride back to Bogotá, I remembered that on the way back to La Paz we had retraced the route Ana had taken twenty-six years earlier when her twins were about to be born. That led me to thinking more deeply about an issue that had been in the background of all our interactions with the twins and their families: how mothers know who their babies are. Most mothers insist that you "just know," but the basis of mother-infant recognition is far more complex.

Who's My Baby?

Amazingly, most new mothers can pick out their own newborn from a group of three to five other infants.[11] This is an adaptive behavior because it doesn't make good evolutionary sense to care for someone else's baby at the expense of your own.

A mothers' accurate identification of her baby is based on various cues, including the infant's smell, the texture of the baby's skin, the quality of the child's cries, and the general appearance of the infant's facial features. Most mothers who spend just half an hour with their infant can tell their child from other infants, based solely on the odor of the babies' breath. However, the amount of time that mothers spend with their newborn doesn't seem to make a difference, because mothers who stay with their newborns for longer periods of time are not more accurate than those who stay with them for shorter periods. Of course, not all mothers are correct in their judgments, perhaps because of their own sensitivity to smell or the intensity of their baby's odor.[12]

The story changes when it comes to identifying a newborn based on odors lingering on the baby's clothing. When babies are one day old, mothers are not especially good at telling their own child from someone else's when sniffing a cotton vest worn by the baby for twenty-four hours. But by the tenth day after delivery most new moms are quite adept at this task, and mothers who cradled their babies on their breast for about a half hour after birth are better than mothers who handled them for less than five minutes. Early exposure to the baby made a difference.[13]

Another curious observation is that mothers of young children are better than nonmothers at detecting the odors of four-day-old infants. One explanation is that mothers experience more complex mental and emotional processes than do nonmothers, although this happens only when the mothers are exposed to the odors of infants, not to the odors of adults. Even more exciting is that researchers have found long-term changes in the part of the brain that processes information as women transition into motherhood.[14] It seems likely that these changes are a unique biological part of becoming a mother, making moms exquisitely sensitive to the condition and needs of their child.

Some adoptive mothers have described their child's body odor as strange or alien, but recognizable because of their shared time.[15] Perhaps the pleasantness or unpleasantness of an infant's odor affects the mother's recognition of, and/or bonding with, their baby, but this has yet to be investigated. Switched twins and their mothers are ideal candidates for a test of this idea because they are biologically connected to one baby but not to the other and don't know it. However, at present researchers have documented only nine switched-twin pairs, too few to obtain a definitive answer. Moreover, the critical window for conducting such a study, which would be at or soon after birth, would have passed by the time the switch was discovered.

The significance for the mother-infant bond of mothers' early exposure to an infant's odors is of great interest, but remains unclear. The nature and extent of Luz's and Ana's early physical contact with their twins is unknown, because of their newborns' premature status and the eventual baby switch. Luz may have cradled William just after delivery but only briefly until he was taken to the nursery, and Ana never enjoyed immediate physical contact with Carlos because both mother and baby were in poor health. We know that William was his mother's favorite child, although he was not her biological son. But he was, and is, the only one of his siblings who makes an extra effort on her behalf. And there was always less affinity between Carlos and Luz than she had with her biological children, although she loved Carlos dearly. Maybe his smell, his temperament, or his appearance were at odds with those of his siblings and, therefore, he seemed unfamiliar to his mother early on in subtle, nonconscious ways. Of course, in some cases a new mother's predisposition for infant care conceivably could override the unpleasantness or lack of familiarity of her baby's odor or other features, or could affect the evolving mother-infant relationship in ways too elusive to detect. Women who love newborns may gain great pleasure from giving infant care and seeing their baby smile, and some adoptive families request special needs children for exactly these reasons, knowing that some developmental milestones may be delayed.

Although smell is important, humans rely most heavily on visual cues when it comes to identifying family, friends, and foe. Thus it is not surprising that new mothers can distinguish their own babies from others in a photograph array. However, first-time mothers, especially those who have spent little time with their infants, are much less accurate than second- and third-time mothers, who are quite successful. Anxiety, fatigue, less affectionate feelings toward their infants, and/or reduced opportunities to learn which facial traits best distinguish their child from others may separate the new mothers from the experienced ones. But once new mothers spend seven hours with their babies, sometimes less, they are just as good as the veterans.[16]

New mothers can also recognize their infants by sound, evidenced by the finding that after forty-eight hours of shared time all new and experienced mothers know their baby's distinctive cries. And when it comes to touch, most mothers who spend at least one hour with their newborn can pick out their own baby from others just by stroking the child's skin, which tells us that the texture, temperature, and familiarity of the infant's skin are the main cues.[17]

These observations are especially significant in the cases of the Colombian brothers. Neither mother had spent much time with her twins following delivery, so both were unfamiliar with their babies' smell, appearance, sound, and feel. Ana, recovering from a hernia, never set eyes on Carlos, had little contact with Wilber, and didn't see William until he came to La Paz when he was one week old. Luz had limited hospital time with Jorge and Carlos and even less with William. Thus, it is likely that both new mothers would not have done as well as other new moms in identifying their babies.

Experiments are informative, but they do not mirror the real-life presentation by hospital staff of babies to their new mothers, who accept that baby as belonging to them. No one offers multiple babies for mothers to compare, so how does a mother know that a baby is truly hers?

A test comparing the DNA markers of a mother and her putative child can determine whether a woman is, or is not, the child's mother. That is because half of a child's DNA comes from its mother, so if the test finds no matches among the markers, the child must belong to someone else. Something similar happened in Switzerland in the 1940s, in the switched-at-birth twin case involving the French-speaking Joye family from Fribourg and the German-speaking Vatter family from Freiburg. DNA technology had not been developed then, so the testing consisted of comparisons of a series of blood types of parents and children, but the principle is the same. An Rh subgroup, originally called C, but now known as O, was especially informative in the case of the exchanged Joye twin from Switzerland. The nontwin child switched with one of the Joyes' identical twin sons had blood type labeled cc, but since Madeleine Joye had type CC, she could not have been his mother. However, her CC type was compatible with the switched twin, who had group Cc, because Madeleine Joye could have passed on her C gene, and her husband, who was cc, could have transmitted his c gene. But matching does not prove that a man or woman is the actual parent because other people can have that same blood type. Of course, establishing maternity or paternity involves comparing more than one blood group or one DNA marker.[18] The correct Joye twins were eventually identified by reciprocal skin grafts, as I explained earlier.

Fingerprinting of mother and baby upon delivery and discharge is a reliable and cost-effective practice for linking mothers and newborns, and some countries have actively promoted this practice. In contrast good impressions of footprints are harder to obtain, and, more important, infant growth precludes comparison of earlier and later images. Some hospitals have used more sophisticated methods for pairing mothers and newborns, such as radiofrequency identification devices. These consist of matching electronic tags that are inserted in bracelets worn by mother and baby and are used to monitor and record feedings, baths, and other activities. At the time of discharge hospital personnel compare the two tags to be certain that they match, but critics have argued that the bracelets are problematic because they can be removed.[19] In the United States medical facilities have used a variety of procedures for ensuring that the right mother goes home with the right baby.

All this raises questions of vital importance: How accurately would mothers recognize their babies if they had no previous exposure to their own baby or to other babies? And how confident would they be in their judgments? If they answered without hesitation that a child was theirs, what would be the basis of that judgment? I suspect that most mothers would not question their relatedness to a child that a nurse delivered to her room because they have no precedent for maternity uncertainty. I also suspect that we will never know the answer to these questions because posing them to new mothers would create unnecessary worries and harmful doubts in their minds just as the mother-infant bond was about to begin.

Both Colombian mothers were recovering from caesarean surgery and had older children to care for at home. They had more to think about than the rare chance that one twin discharged to their care might belong to someone else. Like most mothers, it never crossed their mind.

Fathers have more to worry about than mothers when it comes to knowing who their child is. Because of the key features of human reproduction (concealed ovulation, internal fertilization, and continuous female sexual receptivity), men can never be completely confident that a son or daughter carried by their spouse or partner is truly theirs. This makes paternity uncertainty of great interest, not just to evolutionary psychologists (who study the cues men use to assess true parenthood), but also to attorneys (who manage lawsuits about child custody and support when parenthood is disputed) and fathers (who worry about their lack of resemblance to a particular child and a partner's infidelity).

Paternity uncertainty is also of interest to clever entrepreneurs, such as the former health care marketer Jared Rosenthal. Rosenthal operates a thriving New York City mobile DNA testing lab. With the question WHO'S YOUR DADDY? painted in large letters across two trucks that he drives around the city, fathers questioning their relatedness to their children, as well as individuals searching for or doubting their relatedness to parents and siblings, come to him for testing. Rosenthal maintains contracts with ten thousand companies for drug tests, DNA tests, and background checks. He does the DNA testing from the privacy of his two trucks, as well as his two clinics, one in Brooklyn and the other in the Bronx.[20] If Carmelo ever doubted his relatedness to William, he never said so. The man who was Carlos's childhood father had abandoned his family and, as far as we know, never questioned his paternity of the three children he left behind. However, the greater tensions he experienced with Carlos than with the other two children, who were his biologically, could have had some roots in his sense of differences between him and his son, creating doubt about their connection.

Upshot

If Luz had been around when the switch was discovered, she might have mourned the reduced financial status that caused her to deliver her twins in one of Bogotá's public hospitals, rather than the more desirable public clinic where she had delivered her daughter. Ana most certainly regretted the health issues that had forced her to deliver her twins in the community hospital in Vélez, especially because all but one of her other children had been delivered at home. But had she delivered her twins at home, one or both of her premature infants might not have survived.

———

Chapter 9

Different Versions of the Same Song

W hen the separated British twins Dorothy and Bridget met for the first time, they were avid readers of the same books, especially the historical novels of Catherine Cookson. More interesting was that one twin came from an intellectually stimulating home, while her sister did not. But the less advantaged sister loved to read and used a library card to obtain reading materials on her own, essentially creating her own environment from the choices around her. We all do this—which is why researchers talk about genetic influences on the environment.[1]

As Jorge observed, kids in La Paz had to fight harder than kids in the city to get what they wanted. Coming from a home considered lower middle class, he and his accidental brother were not wealthy, but their mother insisted that they get a good education. Both benefited from the rich educational and occupational opportunities in Bogotá, while the other brothers' exceedingly limited choices meant that they indeed had to fight harder to get ahead. The chance separation of the two identical twin pairs into such extremely different environments created an ideal setting for comparing self-esteem, job satisfaction, and general ability among the various pairs.

Self-Esteem

Self-esteem is the degree to which one sees one's abilities, talents, and worth positively or negatively.[2] High self-esteem has been linked to happiness, likability, and assertiveness, whereas low self-esteem has been associated with depression, delinquency, and aggression.[3] Genetic factors account for about 21 to 49 percent of the differences among adults from all male and mixed-sex samples.[4]

The self-esteem scores for all the twins were extremely high, higher than those of individuals in other South American countries and the United States.[5] Anticipating that some or all the twins might experience emotional difficulties because of their traumatic discovery, the television producers of *Séptimo Día* offered to pay for psychological counseling. But it seems that this assistance was not needed: Carlos attended just one of his three sessions and used it to sort out his girlfriend problems, and William had the constant support of his cousin, godmother, and girlfriend. It is also possible that the attention they received from the media and everyone around them offset the difficulties resulting from learning about the switch to some degree and enhanced their self-esteem. Cab drivers recognized them and took their pictures, and Facebook fans celebrated them and were eager to visit them. It is also possible that each twin's newly discovered relationship and rapport with his identical brother raised his feelings of self-worth to some extent.

The twins in both identical pairs were quite alike in self-esteem, although the scores of Jorge and William were a little closer than those of Carlos and Wilber, but the biggest difference was between the accidental brothers from La Paz. Wilber's slightly lower self-regard may have partly reflected his role as his accidental brother's employee at the butcher shop, especially because these two rarely agreed on work-related issues or just about anything else. But the other accidental brothers were quite alike, probably because each could act on his own interests and they charted paths that did not cross.

The Twins at Work

Everyone enjoys long lunches, but that's not what is at the heart of work. Instead, jobs provide two types of satisfaction: intrinsic satisfaction, such as from fulfilling personal values and interests by having the chance to be creative, and extrinsic satisfaction, such as the gratification derived from working conditions that include long coffee breaks. Genetic influence on intrinsic satisfaction is relatively modest at 32 percent, but genes have little influence on extrinsic satisfaction.[6] Differences among people in how much they value creativity on the job is expected, so it is not surprising that intrinsic satisfaction shows a mix of genetic and environmental influences. However, everyone enjoys a friendly work environment, long vacations, and a pleasant boss, so the absence of genetic effects on extrinsic satisfaction also makes sense. It is also possible to look at overall satisfaction with one's job as reflecting a combination of genetic and environmental influences.

The job satisfaction levels of the Colombian twins were as ordinary as they were extraordinary. Like most people, all four twins expressed higher intrinsic than extrinsic satisfaction, but their general satisfaction either equaled or exceeded that of other twins and nontwins, which is unusual. This was surprising because none of the four had achieved his final career goals.

Jorge was dividing his time between working at the Strycon Company, designing lines for the transport of water and gas, and going to school. He was studying mechanical engineering with the goal of working in the field. William was the full-time manager of a butcher shop and a candidate for the La Paz city council. He dreamed of going to law school someday. Carlos was an accounting analyst by day and a student of public accounting by night. He planned to study international financial standards later in the year and perhaps advance to financial coordinator. Wilber worked mostly at the butcher shop managed by William, but also at other butcher shops in town. Previously, he had installed Internet and television services for Telex-Claro, a position he regarded as his "main job." He hoped to acquire various businesses in the future, but had no firm plans for doing so.

All four twins seemed quite satisfied with their working conditions; this may reflect their youth and adaptability, as well as the knowledge that their work situations were still temporary. The personal satisfaction they derived from their work is more interesting because the spread among them on this measure was greater. The accidental brothers from Bogotá had the highest scores here, which were much alike, whereas the accidental brothers from La Paz scored lower on personal satisfaction, but also close to one another. This makes sense because Jorge and Carlos *chose* to do what they were doing and could see their goals in sight, while the others did their jobs more out of necessity, and their futures were less clear. The politician in William seemed stifled behind the meat counter, although he did his best to charm his clients while serving them. Wilber did not love his job at the butcher shop, except for the freedom to manage his own time; he hoped to run his own business someday because bosses "work less and are better rested." Experience has also taught him that in La Paz you can get a job without studying, but in Bogotá you can study and still not get one.

Brains Reared Apart

Identical twins do not have identical brains because many factors affect brain development, some in unknown ways. Magnetic resonance imaging (MRI) techniques show that identical twins' brains can differ in volume, structure, and cortical thickness. In fact, heavier birth-weight twins tend to show greater cortical surface area, which is the folded gray matter associated with consciousness. And researchers have identified thousands of variations or changes in just thirty-six nerve cells, so it would be very unlikely for identical twins to show exactly the same variations. It is, therefore, striking that reams of studies show that identical twins' IQs, or intelligence quotients, are more alike than those of fraternal twins, full siblings, and parent-child pairs. The average IQ difference between identical twins is six points, although some twins differ by more and others do not differ at all. The average IQ difference between fraternal twins is about ten points.[7]

By now genetic influence on general intelligence, about 50 to 75 percent, has been well established so that only the diehard champions of environmental influence would disagree. But what it means is that the genetic influence on intelligence is widely misunderstood. To say that mental ability is partly genetic in origin does not mean that people cannot get better at what they can do or acquire skills they formerly did not have, because everyone can improve with practice and training; it does mean that we cannot all be the same.

Studies have consistently supported the finding that years of schooling boosts IQ, on the order of about one to two IQ points per year. When identical twins are raised apart, the one with the better education usually does better on tests of intelligence, but genes still matter because identical twins in the same pair usually end up scoring closer to each other than they do to twins in other pairs.[8]

Before we arrived in Bogotá, the four Colombian twins took the Spanish version of the Wechsler Adult Intelligence Scale-IV, known as the WAIS-IV. All were tested on the same day so they could not discuss questions and answers. Only two examiners were available, so we insisted that each tester remain unaware of the relationship of the two individuals she would test. As a further precaution neither examiner tested the real twins because we had assigned one twin from each set to each examiner.

All four twins were curious about what the tests were for because we had kept the purpose of the test hidden—we didn't want them to start studying or begin thinking about who might be the smartest of the bunch. One tester called Jorge a dreamer because he asked more questions than the others, "like a child who wants to know everything." All our twins appeared motivated, especially Carlos, who was in a hurry but still did his best, managing to outscore the other three, while Wilber had the flu, a factor that might have affected his performance. And William, always gracious and kind, turned to his examiner and said, "God bless you," once he had completed his test.

Levels and Shapes, Highs and Lows

General intelligence information is sensitive and personal, so we can report only the levels and shapes ("ups" and "downs") of the ability profiles, but they were just as fascinating as the twins' overall scores. Ability profiles capture each twin's strengths and weaknesses across four areas tapped by the WAIS-IV, namely, verbal comprehension, perceptual reasoning, memory, and processing speed.

Each city-raised twin mostly scored higher than, but sometimes similarly to, his country-raised twin brother across the four measures. Nothing is intellectually significant about being raised inside or outside a big city, except for the kinds of opportunities available and one's ability and motivation to take advantage of them. Both La Paz brothers had left school when they were eleven, although William eventually completed a high school equivalency course, whereas the Bogotá brothers were pursuing college degrees. This is an extreme difference, with years of schooling one of many factors associated with test performance. And the causal connection between the two is unclear, because we can ask if brighter people stay in school longer or if longer schooling makes you brighter.[9] Of course, the La Paz brothers did not have a choice about staying in school because their parents could not afford to send them. If William had had a choice, he would have stayed in school, whereas Wilber probably would not have.

Jorge's and William's ability profiles show some similarities, but their verbal comprehension scores diverge. Carlos and Wilber show a somewhat closer pattern, except for Wilber's high memory score; their more similar pattern is somewhat more consistent with findings of genetic influence on the shape of ability profiles—identical twins are more alike than fraternal twins, even from a young age.[10]

The difference in overall ability between the unrelated brothers raised in Bogotá was typical of the difference between full siblings, while the difference between the brothers raised in La Paz was more typical of identical twins. Carlos's education may have amplified his natural abilities and motivation, whereas Wilber (and William's) lack of schooling seemed to have reduced their

scores by a similar degree. The ability profiles of the two accidental pairs show both similarities and differences in shape, whereas
the performance of one pair of replicas (the twins from each pair
who were not raised together) was a real surprise. Jorge and
Wilber differed considerably in level and in shape, as expected
for people who share neither genes nor environment, but Carlos
and William, while different in level, were quite alike in their
profile pattern. This result, which is probably a chance finding
based on the tiny sample of two, comes with the warning that we
should only base firm conclusions on many pairs.

Aside from their extremely different environments, what else
might explain the score differences between the identical twins?
Premature birth, especially low birth weight, has been linked
to lower intelligence test scores. These scores may mask subtle
deficits in visual-motor abilities, language functions, and at-
tentional skills, especially among males. Jorge's and William's
weights at birth were just slightly below the average weight of male
twins born at thirty-five weeks of gestation, but we know only that
the birth weights of the other brothers, as recalled by their mother,
were two pounds each. However, the relationship of twins' birth
weight to IQ is not straightforward because researchers showed
long ago that identical twins who weighed nearly two pounds less
than their twin at birth did not lag behind them when tested at
the age of six. Accelerated maturation of the lungs and brains
of fetuses with modest nutritional deficits might shield these
newborns from adverse birth events, and Carlos may have been a
winner in this regard.[11]

Another explanation for the reared-apart twins' ability differences is regression to the mean.[12] This describes the phenomenon that researchers have noted time and again: people who

score high the first time around tend to get lower scores if they take the same test again later. Factors like good health, luck, and chance may help some people on the day of testing, whereas people who score low but move up when they repeat the test may have gotten a better night's sleep, prepared better, or benefited from chance events—or a mix of all three. If the Colombian twins are tested in the future, and the city boys were to lose a few points and the country boys were to gain some it would not be unusual.

I hear more different versions of the same song about the Colombian twins' intellects than I usually do. Both separated identical pairs showed greater difference than I expected, given my experiences with reared-apart twins. However, before I visited Bogotá and La Paz, I neither appreciated nor comprehended the enormous discrepancies in the two environments, which is why I described La Paz as an alternative world. It is important to appreciate that previously separated twins have generally grown up in middle- and lower-middle-class homes, with access to education, culture, and the amenities of twentieth-century living, features that were absent from William and Wilber's experience, making them outliers among reared-apart twins. And research with seven-year-old reared-together twins from low socioeconomic classes found that genetic influence on general mental ability dropped to near zero, while the shared effects of the home and school environments went up, an example of how particular environments can overwhelm genetic factors.[13] Nevertheless, the Colombian twins do not challenge existing findings of genetic influence on intelligence, confirmed by countless twin studies, but these findings are better informed because the Colombian twins offer insight into how extreme environments can affect mental performance.

Is a Picture Worth a Thousand Scores?

The Draw-A-Person Intellectual Ability Test, or DAP:IQ, was developed to estimate the intellectual ability of children, adolescents, and adults by using a drawing of a human figure.[14] An IQ score derived from this test is based on attributes in the drawing such as the presence of eyes, number of fingers, and shape of the torso. The Colombian twins completed the Draw-A-Person test twice, fifteen months apart, with both unstructured and standard sets of instructions. The drawings were evaluated by the original creators of the test, who were kept unaware of the identity and relatedness of the individuals involved.

IQ scores can be estimated only from the drawings completed under standard conditions, that is, standard instructions, such as "draw a picture of yourself . . . draw your whole body . . . draw how you look from the front." The differences between scores based on these drawings and on the WAIS-IV were large and overestimated the twins' actual test performance. However, the ordering of the estimated IQ scores, from highest to lowest, matched the ordering of the actual IQ scores.

Differences in the size and likeness of the human form between the individuals raised in Bogotá and the individuals raised in La Paz, especially in the first set of drawings completed with the unstructured directions, are striking. Also compelling is the general resemblance of the first set of pictures produced by the accidental brothers from La Paz. We can only speculate about the reasons for the tiny size and lack of detail in these drawings. They may reflect submissiveness among people living in isolated areas of Colombia, especially when they meet people from higher socioeconomic brackets or better-educated individuals. The brothers' home did not have books and pictures portraying people realistically in terms of background and dimension (the house also lacked a dictionary and world atlas), and such pictures might have been unavailable or in short supply at their school. William made his second drawing, which was his self-portrait, after he had enrolled in law school, and it was much larger and more detailed than the first, whereas Wilber's drawing changed only slightly. (Clinical interpretations of these pictures with respect to body image, self-esteem, or depression are likely to be tentative at best.)[15]

The use of human figure drawings for estimating standard IQ has been controversial, with hosts of supporters and detractors.[16] Although the correspondence in ordering between the estimated and actual scores is of interest, I am not ready to concede that a picture is worth a thousand scores.

Chapter 10

"Twin-Bred" Cultures

Personality Profiles and Twin Relations

I have witnessed many memorable moments that reflect the unique "twin-bred" culture and personality of every identical twin pair—the use of paper clips to scratch an itchy ear; the staccato-like laughter that erupts spontaneously from two mouths; the hair chewing that eases the worries of anxious young women; and the flirtatious glances and expressions of reunited male-female twins. These quirky behaviors are harder to study than height, intelligence, or self-esteem because they vary so greatly across pairs, but each quirk affects researchers' thinking about why people do what they do.

The Personal Ad

Asking people to describe themselves presents them with a tortuous task because people worry about bragging or putting themselves down. So I had the Colombian twins compose a personal ad for a dating service, an exercise they enjoyed immensely because all four are interested in meeting women and are sensitive to the qualities that attract women to them. During these conversations I also learned about the kinds of women they seek and the qualities they like and dislike about themselves.

* * *

Women like Jorge and he knows it, especially because he was the most sought-after of the four when news of the twin switch appeared on Facebook. He describes himself as "very happy, intelligent, and good-humored." "Girls like to laugh," he said, adding that when women talk to him, they realize he is cool company. Getting married and having two more children are two of his key goals, although his perfect partner has yet to appear. Always the diplomat, Jorge will choose the best man for his wedding from outside the band of brothers to dampen within-group jealousies.

An ideal partner would love him a lot, showing neither a complex nor a bad-tempered side, and would never stay mad for long. Having a professional degree, while not required, would "add points." Jorge once thought that he and his twin gravitated toward the same sorts of women, but when he introduced William to various potential partners, Jorge changed his mind, realizing that William goes for traditional women from rural regions whom Jorge finds somewhat naive.

Jorge's last comment exemplifies one of the most curious findings about twins: identical twins generally do not choose partners who resemble one another in personality and interests, leaving mate choice to follow the random process of romantic infatuation.[1] This is surprising because the interests, values, and friendships of most identical twins are closely aligned, but it seems that subtle differences in whom we meet can become huge differences when picking dates and mates. Furthermore, few identical twins say they could have fallen for their twin's husband or wife. During a long weekend I spent with the identical Texas twins Mark and Craig, who are married to the identical twins Darlene and Diane, each spouse insisted that he or she could never have married their spouse's twin. What drew Craig to Diane over Darlene were her "sweeter, gentler features," and what drew Mark to Darlene over Diane was her greater assertiveness, which complemented his laid-back approach to life. These twins' experiences help us make sense of the Colombian twins' individual dating preferences.

Jorge is happy most of the time, focusing on doing what he likes to do; he and William share this sunny disposition. Facing problem situations squarely before stepping back to find solutions makes Jorge proud and no doubt increases his self-esteem. He believes that Carlos and Wilber are happy as individuals and as a pair, even though their bad temper is their hallmark trait. Jorge also knows that Carlos, the brother with whom he grew up, enjoys his job as a financial analyst, but Jorge wonders how much his brother's twin, Wilber, enjoys his job as a butcher and wonders if Wilber lacks Carlos's drive. Perhaps Jorge forgot about Wilber's enthusiasm for his former job installing software.

When Jorge loves or wants something, his passion spirals out of bounds. His devotion to his favorite football team, Club Atlético Nacional, has escalated to the point that the other three call it his obsession; an out-of-town game also caused him to miss one of our dinners (after he had promised to attend). His brothers worry about Jorge's altercations with crazed fans who support other teams, but Jorge tunes them out because he "loves everything" about the sport, deriving happiness from releasing his energy at the game especially when he is feeling bottled up. His favorite colors are black and dark green, the colors of Club Atlético Nacional.

His list of recent passions also includes caring for his young son as he grows up and supporting William as he fulfills his goals.

Santi, Jorge's son, is a "twenty-four-hour-a-day priority for whom I try to set a good example." When Jorge's mother was sick, she reminded him that he never knew a father during his own childhood and urged him to see what he could do with his own child. Jorge has also dedicated himself to "opening new horizons" for his twin, thrilled that William is going to law school. Jorge helps William as much as he can, not just with coursework but by introducing his twin to new foods and drinks, and correcting his use of words and phrases that are common in the country, but not in the city. Editing the text messages his twin sends to prospective dating partners is part of what Jorge does to help William. At the same time, Jorge has stayed loyal to Carlos, with whom he was raised, and is intent upon fostering connections among all four brothers.

Strycon laid Jorge off in 2016 because of the crisis in the Colombian oil industry—declining investments and a shortage of reliable reserves. Finding another job so he can pay his university fees is a lingering problem, but because Jorge financially supported Carlos and some of his own friends in the past, Jorge is certain he will find a solution to this situation too—he always does. This period of unemployment, which includes some unexpected laziness, is bothersome, but he constantly searches for something to occupy his time, such as doing laundry, cooking, seeing Santi, or visiting Santi's grandmother. Being busy and in motion is how Jorge prefers to live. For example, while we were chatting with William, we asked Jorge to wait for a half hour in a vacant room next to mine in the hotel. The room was comfortable, with a bed, television, radio, and Wi-Fi, a place where Carlos once enjoyed the amenities and downtime while waiting for us. But after a few minutes Jorge came back to say he would wait in the lobby, which was busy and had lots of people around.

*   *   *

If he had to compose a singles ad, William would advertise himself as a hardworking young man interested in having a family; he would list happy, extroverted, and charming as his best qualities. He sees his charm embodied in his universal kindness, ease at forming friendships, and desire to help people. His thoughtfulness was on display when he was the only one of the four twins to give me a gift when I returned to Bogotá; he presented me with a package of *bocadillos*, the sweet guava sandwiches that I love, and when I left he gave me a pair of soft shoes emblazed with the name of his town, La Paz.

Like his twin, William is waiting for his ideal woman to appear. She would be happy and extroverted like him, support his almost daily regimen at the gym, and, most important, come from a good family whose members are hardworking, honest, and have good principles.

The self-descriptions of these twin brothers sound like near photocopies, and William knows it. Like Jorge, William believes in being thoughtful and respectful of others, priding himself on forming friendships wherever he goes. The person is most important to him, and he makes no distinction when it comes to age, ethnicity, or religion. He also knows that immediate warmth is outside the culture of Carlos and Wilber, who are less affectionate.

William, the future politician, insisted, "I will always pose with people for pictures." Reflecting upon his run for a seat on the La Paz city council in 2016, he worried that his loss was more difficult for his disappointed supporters than it was for him. As his twin would probably have done, he confronted his loss squarely, realizing that the solution would be to better prepare for the next campaign. With this in mind he works with the mayor of the town on projects that support farmers and friends in the area.

At the same time William sees himself as a shrewd businessman, buying an apartment that is under construction and, while he is in law school, handing management of the butcher shop over to Wilber. Nothing is off-putting about what William describes as shrewdness, a trait that others might see as simply knowing how to arrange things to his personal advantage. That sounds like Jorge.

William is meticulous and careful where his identical twin is more lax. As a lawyer in the making, William reads contracts carefully now that the media, fascinated by the twins' story, wants the twins for TV appearances, biopics, and documentaries. He insisted that our interpreter read through St. Martin's informed consent statement line by line, whereas Jorge signed the form without reading it, knowing that William would read it and ensure it was reasonable. Enormous faith and trust pass between these two, and their knowledge of themselves and each other clearly makes them mirrors. When Jorge shot a gun for the first time in La Paz, he hit the target, a success that did not surprise his twin because he is a good shot himself. This moment exemplifies the ways identical twins support and encourage one another, something that athletic coaches see all the time and try to capitalize on.[2] Carlos, on the other hand, missed the shot.

William has achieved, or is confident that he will achieve, everything he has always wanted. He is happy most of the time. As an eager learner who loves studying law, he rejoices in the opportunities he had thought he would never have. William is never miffed when his twin corrects his speech, suggests new foods, or offers advice about women, regarding these as opportunities to learn new things. Meeting his identical other is the most important thing that ever happened to him.

William enjoys challenges and did so even as a twelve-year-old child, when he decided to ride a bull, "something no one ever does." He teased the bull to tame it and became the only person around who could ride it. His persistence is a hallmark of his approach to life and was especially important in expediting his first meeting with Jorge, which led to the twins' television appearance on *Séptimo Día*. And when William joined the military, he did so to experience life beyond his family's farm. He was unafraid of the guerillas, but he feared the landmines that had cost his close friend his limbs.

The current challenge for William is bodybuilding because women now regard him as "delicious," but Jorge thinks William is becoming obsessive about this pastime. Like the others, William claims that his twin spends too much time on football and should not borrow money from friends to travel to games. William also worries that football attracts some "bad people" and that his twin may get hurt. Both twins' dedication to activities they love is a quality they admire about one another, but for now they urge their twin to use moderation because of where and how he directs that dedication.

Becoming a better dancer is among William's goals. He shares his perceived lack of talent in this area with Jorge, but both have a good attitude and enjoy dancing at parties and other social gatherings. While some of their mutual friends have judged William to be the better dancer, I think they have similar potential, and I've danced with both. Other than the fault he finds with his dancing, William could not list anything he dislikes about himself, but because of his charm no one would accuse him of bragging. In contrast, Carlos is a natural dancer, moving gracefully across the floor, and Wilber could be but isn't, perhaps because he doesn't believe he could be.

William generally is not passive, but he becomes so when he is with Jorge, and during these times his cell phone can suddenly get busy. Both twins are upfront about their relationship and comfortable with who they are, both apart and together. Identical twins sometimes act in selfless ways that nontwins find hard to understand. What some people might construe as Jorge's taking over the show is William's opportunity to listen and learn.

* * *

A dating service bio from Carlos would tell readers that he is "sociable, gentlemanly, attentive, a bit bad-tempered, serious, a good dancer, and a sports fan." He joked that he is gentlemanly only when he wants to be. Carlos also fancies himself a romantic, describing the perfect evening as one in which he would light candles, prepare dinner, serve wine, and follow it all with a good movie and breakfast in bed the next morning.

An ideal partner would be twenty-four or twenty-five years old and a professional like him, with well-defined interests. But as he thought about a previous relationship with a thirty-three-year-old, he acknowledged that he finds that mature women are attractive and know what they want.

When a relationship ends, Carlos tells the woman he doesn't care, but inside he is "dying," he said. He hasn't discussed this with his twin, but he knows that Wilber, who seemed to be going through a breakup at the time, also reacts this way. In early 2015 Carlos ended his relationship with his long-time girlfriend, a breakup that brought him significant heartache. He was hoping to date someone new, but insisted that candidates not know about the switch because after the TV story aired, Carlos met lots of women who seemed interested in him because of the show, and he shut down in response to their questions.

When I saw Carlos again, he had been in a new relationship with a woman for about a month and a half. She knew nothing about the switch when they met, but Carlos eventually played the *Séptimo Día* program for her and found that they could discuss his situation openly. He admires her independence, likes hearing about her work with atypical children, and enjoys her cooking. At the same time they are polar opposites—she is from Córdoba Montería, where people tend to be loud and colorful, and Carlos is serious and down to earth. He likes to make plans and she doesn't, but a significant area of commonality and connection is that both have lost their mothers, which enables Carlos and his girlfriend to share and understand this sad experience.

Carlos plans to marry a woman he loves and have a family with her. "If assisted reproductive technology was available to men," he said, "I would have had kids by now!" But his maturity then overtook his enthusiasm, and he declared that having kids is not of primary importance, while knowing with whom to have them is.

Independence and individuality lead his list of important ingredients for happiness, at least right now. The four brothers had discussed moving in together, but Carlos nixed the plan, mostly because he didn't want to move anywhere far from the city's center. When people visit the apartment he shares with Jorge, Carlos heads to his room if he doesn't know them. In this respect, he says, Wilber is more sociable than he is, although people who know both twins say that Carlos is the friendlier one. Perhaps Wilber becomes more passive when Carlos is around, just as William grows more subdued when he is with his twin.

Self-confidence is Carlos's best quality, but it masks a fear of failure. Carlos is certain he will achieve his goals but worries that he will fall short, even though he tries his best. A consequence of trying hard is his perfectionism, what he calls his "psychorigidity." He also sees himself as egocentric, the center of it all; when he ends a relationship with a woman and she acquires a new beau, he regards his replacement as a cheap copy. I wondered what he would say if his twin brother were dating one of his former girlfriends.

If Carlos could change any aspect of his personality, it would be his lack of concern about things that seem ordinary to him, but might seem odd in other people's eyes. Pride also figures into this. His boss was rather argumentative and on one occasion Carlos asked his boss to stop yelling at him, insisting that he was not like the other employees, and it worked. Later, when Carlos was leaving for vacation, his boss asked if he was coming back. Carlos replied, "God willing." But he did not return to that job because he accepted a job offer from a friend. Carlos loves his new job because it provides him with not only more income, but also greater challenges and opportunities for advancement.

Life is generally good for this young man because he is doing well professionally and is coming to terms with having a biological family in La Paz. He has some sad moments, especially when memories of his beloved mother and former girlfriend surface, but he tries hard to stay level. His efforts to maintain equanimity may explain his cautious side—if he and Wilber, rather than Jorge and William, had been mistaken for one another, Carlos never would have arranged to meet as quickly as Jorge and William did. Carlos would have wanted to take more time to examine the events and consider their consequences.

Carlos values kindness, calling it Wilber's best trait (although William might disagree), and Carlos can be generous and kind (although Jorge might disagree). Several significant actions show Carlos's self-assessment is correct: he stayed at a job he disliked because Jorge had been laid off and needed financial support, and Carlos helped William apply to law school when he was ready to do so. Modesty is part of the twin culture that Carlos has created with Wilber: they are reluctant to sing their own praises, but are willing to name their best qualities when asked.

Identical twins sometimes see their own worst traits in their twin brothers and sisters, although they like to think otherwise.

The reared-apart twin Jack, who was raised in Trinidad, asked his wife if he was aggressive, critical, and demanding like his brother, Oskar, who had been raised in Nazi Germany. "Yes," she replied, "but you are less extreme."[3]

According to Carlos, Wilber's worst trait may be loving women too much; Carlos complains that his brother "loves them all" and often overlooks the serious side of a relationship. But a flirty nature characterizes all the La Paz males, including Carlos. This was captured in a classic moment. Carlos and Wilber were talking quietly together at a party we held at a trendy Bogotá restaurant, but what was passing between them? They were then six or seven months into their relationship and did not seem as closely bound to one another as William and Jorge. But Carlos and Wilber's less demonstrative manner may have masked a deeper bond. Regardless, they were talking about women, one in particular, the attractive daughter of one of our interpreters—and both Wilber and Carlos were watching their other brothers to see what they would do.

* * *

"A slim man, about five feet, seven-and-a-half inches in height, with darkish skin and thick lips" would be Wilber's self-description in an ad to attract prospective dating partners. It would go on to describe the young man as "simple, humble, direct, and hot-tempered," and would encourage contacts from women who would be understanding and accepting of who he is. He would enjoy dating a professional woman, but considered her having a career less important than her ability to provide love and support, especially if she is from Santander, where women are less outspoken than in Bogotá.

At the first mention of his love life, Wilber just laughed somewhat nervously because at the time he was not doing as well in his relationships as he would have liked. Partners tend to love him too much or too little, a conclusion he reached because "when they love you too much, you don't love them, and vice versa." One of his recent love interests was quite attentive to him until he began investing more time and effort in their relationship. At that point she returned to her former boyfriend. Another woman took their relationship more seriously, but to Wilber she was just someone to hang out with.

Humbleness is the trait he values most in himself, explaining that he does not hide who he is or make himself out to be someone who he is not. He does not conceal or deny his bad temper but tries to control it, although when he explodes, he really explodes. His "what you see is what you get" approach is at odds with his twin's pride, which gets in Wilber's way. In this respect Wilber feels he is different from Carlos, who he says "changes female relationships every twenty days," rather than acknowledge a misstep and face the consequences. Wilber and Carlos see some of their less favorable traits in each other but not in themselves.

Among Wilber's least favorite traits is his tendency to become easily stressed. Things like glitches at work, being yelled at, and William's disorderliness set him off, whereas having to wait for a taxi or getting a stain on his shirt are not problems. Given Wilber's attention to his appearance, it seems out of character that a spot on his shirt was not at least a minor stressor. When Wilber was a teenager in La Paz, he carefully scrubbed the dirt off his hands before heading to the local bars on weekends, and if soap failed to do the job, he used a knife to scrape off the dirt.

Wilber manages stress by pushing away unpleasant thoughts or falling asleep. He is aware that he sometimes speaks harshly and hurtfully in a style that is too loud and too fast for Bogotá, although more in line with the conversational styles of La Paz, and when this happens, it is stressful for him. But like the brother with whom he was raised, Wilber is a willing learner, accepting of his twin's corrections of what he says and how he says it. He once called brown shoes "browns," but in the interest of protecting and not embarrassing Wilber, Carlos gently explained that they are simply called brown.

The lesser-known side of Wilber is his sentimentality and emotionality. When Colombia lost the 2014 FIFA World Cup to Brazil, Wilber broke down as he watched James Rodriguez, winner of the Golden Boot award as a top goal scorer, cry on live TV. Wilber also wept while watching the televised true story of a vocally talented young boy whose envious classmates killed him. Wilber himself is puzzled by his odd combination of a bad temper and strong sentimentality.

Trust is a trait that he values highly, and it has evolved quickly between Wilber and his twin, evidenced by their confidence in each other and deep respect. Like Carlos, Wilber values his independence and uniqueness, but he is less upset than Carlos is when people confuse the two of them, perhaps because Wilber was not the twin whose identity was severely challenged. But if Wilber had been the switched twin, what would his life have been like? Would he have entered the financial world like his identical twin brother? Wilber concedes that this could have happened because like his identical twin he always enjoyed math and is good at it, but he finds it hard to imagine such a different existence. His twin and others have encouraged Wilber to return to school. That seems unlikely, but he has not completely abandoned that idea. Still, unlike his accidental brother, William, Wilber harbors no regrets about what he never knew and never had. If he had been the switched twin, Wilber, like Carlos, would have approached the situation with care and caution.

One incident in particular led me to fully grasp Wilber's regard for and loyalty to his friends. I needed a taxi to go from his apartment to my hotel, so he arranged for a friend from La Paz, who is a cabbie, to drive me. I knew that the standard fare for the trip is about 25,000 Colombian pesos, or US$7.60, so it was stunning when the fare climbed to 40,000, or US$12.60, nearly twice as much. Wilber just laughed about it because his good friend rips him off too.

HEXACO, Not TEXACO

A kiosk at Colombia's El Dorado Airport sells T-shirts and souvenirs that read COLOMBIA, NOT COLUMBIA. Similarly, whenever I type HEXACO, an acronym for a group of personality traits, into a search engine, the spell checker insists that I search for TEXACO.

Researchers have organized human personality traits into what are now known as the Big Five, which are easily recalled with the acronym OCEAN: openness (to experience), conscientiousness, extroversion, agreeableness, and neuroticism. In 2001 Canadian researchers added honesty-humility to the mix and replaced neuroticism with emotionality, yielding the acronym HEXACO; now the *E* stands for emotionality and the *X* for extroversion.[4]

Genetic influence on the six HEXACO personality factors ranges from 41 percent for openness to 68 percent for conscientiousness.[5] Sharing an environment with someone doesn't make you alike in these traits, but sharing genes does. Still, environment matters—the environmental events affecting personality are the unique experiences we have that make us different from our family members.

The reared-apart twins William and Jorge match closely in their level and patterning of the HEXACO personality factors, except Jorge's test results showed an unexpected dip in agreeableness, or cooperation and compromise with others, his hallmark tendencies except when it comes to football. The other reared-apart pair is closely matched across all six factors, with Wilber showing a slight lead on some, but Carlos leads on honesty-humility and openness to experience. This makes sense because, as a financial analyst, Carlos is bound more tightly by rules and regulations than Wilber, who works in the butcher shop. Carlos is also somewhat more interested in travel than Wilber, who prefers to save his earnings, but Wilber plans to invest money in a pyramid scheme. Carlos suggested that they do this, and Wilber trusts his brother's plans.

The accidental brothers Jorge and Carlos, who grew up together in Bogotá, show similar levels of each trait, but they differ in extroversion and openness to experience, which is consistent with Jorge's greater enthusiasm for solving social challenges and his following his favorite football team around the world. The accidental brothers raised together in La Paz show less resemblance in the various HEXACO traits—William's higher scores on extroversion, agreeableness, and openness match his social and political aspirations, his confidence and drive, and his desire for occupational and personal growth. Both pairs of replicas show the least resemblance, as expected, probably because they shared neither their genes nor their environment.

The Birthday Party

William and Wilber hosted a birthday celebration for Diana, the older sister of Jorge and Carlos, and now William. It was July 17, 2016, and she had just turned thirty-two. The party in the apartment over the butcher shop began with a beautiful cake and was followed by fried chicken, crackers spread with a potato and ham mixture, and soda. In attendance were the four twins, Diana and her boyfriend, Jorge's young son, Carlos's current girlfriend, Aunt Blanca Cecilia (the Bogotá twins' second mother), two La Paz cousins, and a new butcher shop employee. Diana opened her presents, and everyone took pictures amid a lot of laughing, teasing, and hugging. People sat or stood around the small living room, which doubles as Wilber's bedroom, or drifted in and out of William's adjoining bedroom.

Few would guess that the history of the reunited identical twin pairs was less than two years old because their familiarity and ease of relations suggested that they had been together all their lives. Jorge and William hugged and kissed as was their custom, and they often put their arms around each other. Carlos and Wilber kidded around, playfully calling each other names, and mostly reclining on a bed with their drinks. Wilber continued to kid his twin that he resembled a Jehovah's Witness selling Bibles, dressed as he often was in a suit and tie. These different postures and exchanges reflect the unique twin culture of each pair—early on Carlos and Wilber branded Jorge and William "the lovers," and Jorge and William faulted Carlos and Wilber for their reserve. Jorge and William tease each other occasionally, but it is not the jeering, mocking tone so characteristic of the other two. William and Jorge are closely attuned to each other's feelings. For example, one night as we left a restaurant, Jorge mentioned William's gullibility about a poorly produced television segment about their lives, and William seemed embarrassed. His behavior triggered an immediate apology from Jorge, who conceded that agreeing to participate was a mistake anyone could have made, and then Jorge bumped his head against William's in their special "twin way."

Twenty-two months after the switch was discovered, the four twins understood and accepted that family relations grow and flourish according to the temperament and timetable of each individual and pair. They had all grown in their own ways, both separately and as two and four.

Chapter 11

———

Twins, Pairs, and Pedigrees

G iven past tensions between the switched twins, it was surprising when Carlos pulled out his cell phone during lunch to call William just to say hi. Even more surprises were waiting.

The upheaval in their lives changed all the twins, but the two who were switched at birth, Carlos and William, were changed more significantly than their accidental brothers who stayed in place. But once they got past the shock, a new maturity and refreshing optimism were evident in all four brothers during my second visit. Time had to pass before they could know how they might fare individually and together, at least in the immediate future.

Carlos

The extraordinary journey made by this young man allowed me to ask him a question I could not ask the year before. At that time he faced a constant struggle between the life that was and the life that should have been, and he reacted by distancing himself from his Santander relatives, who had tried to welcome him.

"Were you relieved that you were raised in Bogotá and not La Paz?" I asked. Carlos didn't answer directly, saying only that when the switch was uncovered, the thought of being raised on a farm made him uncomfortable. It helped when a friend consoled him by saying that Carlos is what God wanted him to be, but Carlos acknowledged that my question put him on edge, making him think more about his feelings and how he judges himself. But he also said that sitting in the hotel room with Alexandra, our trusted interpreter, and me, a familiar figure, made him want to open up. His mood was a dramatic departure from the reserve he had displayed in the past, and we just let him talk. At first he skirted some issues as unanswerable, but returned to them later with some well-conceived thoughts.

When the discovery was new, Carlos was uneasy, thinking about what his life would have been like if he had been returned to La Paz as intended. He asked himself, "Would I have been the same person?" but it is a question he cannot ever answer. Initially he made a lot of assumptions about growing up in La Paz, but making assumptions is something he doesn't like to do, because he believes it's not good for him. He then explained that the only obstacles in life are the limits you place on yourself, words from his beloved mother. When Carlos and Jorge entered high school at the Colegio Restrepo Millan, people expected them to fail like their cousins before them, but Luz told them that whether they passed or failed was in their hands, and with her support they succeeded. Pressed again to say whether he would have been the same person had he been raised in La Paz, he uttered a cryptic, "Not impossible," but he didn't sound confident.

Carlos has come to understand that he upset William by being insensitive about and unaware of William's hardships, and that his impatience with William's inability to pursue a meaningful career was misplaced. Carlos realized that education and opportunity were unavailable to the two accidental brothers from La Paz—so perhaps William's insistence that Carlos cart my heavy purple suitcase up the muddy hills gave him some understanding of what life was like there. As this part of our conversation ended, Carlos was virtually certain that if he had lived in La Paz, he would not be the financial professional he was.

I was finally able to ask the question whose answer seemed apparent, but that he had never given voice to. Was Carlos relieved to have been raised in Bogotá? Yes, he finally acknowledged, because seeing and experiencing the alternative reality of where he was born was a cultural shock. In fact, his accidental brother, Jorge, had confirmed this to me earlier, telling me he believed that Carlos was thankful to have grown up in the city, "as if life gave him a 'stroke of luck,' but he never said it. He sees that his twin [Wilber] isn't interested in an education." Carlos was finally able to answer for himself, which showed how much he had grown and learned.

The Colombian twins' answers to what-if questions reminded me of the identical reared-apart twins Jack, who grew up Jewish in Trinidad, and Oskar, who was raised Catholic in Nazi Germany. During one of their meetings they acknowledged to each other that had their home environments been reversed, each would have embraced the historical and political viewpoints they abhorred in the other. These twins exemplify the idea that the self-understanding that grounds our identity is subject to contingencies that are dependent on context.[1] So it was for the two switched Colombian twins, even if they have not fully grasped it. Today Carlos says he is *from* Santander, but that he *is* a *rolo*, a person born in Bogotá who speaks with a particular accent, and William says the reverse.

The revised relationship between these two happened spontaneously. "We never talked about it," Carlos said. But the concessions came mostly from him, not in a planned way, but gradually as he began to change. How, why, or when this happened he cannot put into words—other than to say, "it just happened"—but he had left open the possibility of forging a relationship with his family in La Paz when he felt ready. During the months that followed, as his emotions calmed, Carlos saw the La Paz brothers' situation differently, as a matter of circumstance they couldn't control, rather than as a lack of desire or drive. This insight inspired him to help William research law schools and decide which one to attend. And the two of them—*just the two of them*—planned a trip to Cancún together several months later. Carlos also started helping out at the butcher shop by grinding meat, although he didn't wear an apron, explaining, "I don't go that far!" In the last year he has taken several trips to Santander, traveling with his new cousins, but sometimes with his twin brother, with William, or on his own, no longer waiting to be asked. He has changed "100 percent" since that first visit to La Paz—William said this three times.

Carlos knew that his biological parents immediately accepted him as part of their family, and he also knew that they understood how hard it was for him so they waited until he made the first move. What began as occasional private visits, the kind Carlos and Wilber prefer, segued into more regular get-togethers, and he has come to enjoy playing a little football and basketball with his cousins. Lodging is "wherever," with his sister Alcira in Vélez or his cousins, brothers, or parents in La Paz. Because his parents have a toilet in their new home, although no drinking water, he feels comfortable there.

He has given his mother a nickname, "Anita," and his relationship with her is good and growing. They talk, she complains, he scolds her playfully by "pulling her legs," and telephones her on her birthday. Still, he does not call her Mom, and, as much as she would love it, she understands that this is not possible. Carlos has thought about it at times but prefers to hold off until he feels completely certain about it, noting that *"Mom* is a big word." Carlos feels that he does not have a real mother-son relationship with Ana, because at his age he is independent and not in need of her care as a young child would be. But as with most things involving his new family, he is leaving the possibility open, a willingness that may be partly linked to the loss of his own mother six years earlier. Regardless, Ana is attentive to her new son, gazing at him lovingly when he is around, taking him by the arm, and making certain that he has enough to eat. According to his older accidental sister, Diana, who has shared time with her, Ana continues to cry because "her baby was taken away."

Carlos cannot know how he would have managed his relationship with Ana if Luz were still alive, and he refuses to make assumptions about how she would have responded to the switch. To commemorate his mother he has decided to get a tattoo that would run along his spine, with an inscription in Chinese to keep the wording private. The discomfort of being tattooed has discouraged him in the past, but he is willing to set that aside for Luz.

Carlos's relationship with his new father is different than his relationship with Ana because Carmelo is quiet and serious by nature. Father and son do not talk much, but Carmelo stares at Carlos a lot, as if trying to take in the extraordinary events that have affected his family. This is the first significant father-son connection Carlos has ever known, and while they may not converse a great deal, Carmelo's presence means something.

Carlos is also getting to know his older brothers and sister, bonding most closely with Chelmo because of the confidence and trust he inspires. However, Carlos feels socially and emotionally closer to his accidental brother, Jorge, than to these other siblings, which is understandable because of the Bogotá brothers' many years together. Once "fraternal twins," they are now brothers, but the label means little because of the love and loyalty between them. Jorge still makes Carlos angry by delaying his job hunting and education in favor of football and travel, but most adult siblings accept what they see as each other's flaws because of their shared life histories. At first Carlos felt slightly jealous of, and excluded from, the relationship that Jorge and his twin established so quickly, but Carlos's attitude has changed since he decided to stop worrying, start living, and "let things flow."

Like many accidental twins, Carlos believes that he and Jorge would not have become friends had they met one another socially because they are so different. But had they met by chance, Carlos feels he would have liked Jorge as a person, especially because of Jorge's constant kindness and helpfulness. Carlos's relationship with Wilber developed easily and effortlessly, but they both needed time, reflective of their cautious and less demonstrative nature. They see each other more frequently now than when the discovery was new. They get together mostly on weekends if girlfriends are in the picture, but more often if they are not. They are regular phone mates and usually call each other when both are in the bathroom. "Where are you? I hear an echo," one might say. They joke a lot, sometimes calling to ask, "How are you, my identical brother?" but in a high-pitched voice and using the feminine form. And Carlos wants to take his twin for a massage because "he'll die of pleasure." Cultural differences between them remain, but being identical twins and witness to some extraordinary similarities has the power to allow them to work through the contrasting effects of their rearing.

When Wilber took Carlos to his first cockfight in Santander, Carlos was "struck dumb," largely because he doesn't like "animal things," whereas his twin does. When Wilber killed a goat and wanted to display a picture of it on Facebook, his twin objected strongly. Carlos acknowledged that such acts are customary in La Paz, but argued that posting such a photo would offend animal rights activists. Moreover, because their story has been publicized, the twins are now recognizable and Carlos didn't want to be connected to an act perceived by some as animal cruelty. His twin listened to him.

Carlos has changed in other fundamental ways in that he is not religious in a formal sense, but has become more devoted to God and has considered attending a Christian church. After ending his relationship with his girlfriend last year, he accompanied a newly divorced friend to a religious service and was inspired by the idea that God says humans are so comfortable with who we are that we make no effort to become better. The notion that things don't just happen, and that the easiest path to what you want is not always the right one, impressed him deeply. It makes sense that Carlos would be impressed by these words. With them came the realization that he would need time and patience to develop meaningful relations with his Santanderean relatives. He was willing to change in this respect and has changed in other ways too. Carlos has burned out on clubbing, a favorite pastime for him when he was seventeen. But now he has other priorities, such as traveling abroad, dancing, and riding horses and scooters, as well as consuming less alcohol.

Because his perspective has changed so much, I was not especially shocked when he expressed a desire to live in the country someday. He thinks about the peaceful existence that city life does not offer.

William

"The switch was God's doing; it was no one's fault," William said.

Like Carlos, William has undergone profound change and personal growth and is happy with himself and the way his life is going, more so than during the first year after he learned of the switch. Fulfilling his dream of going to law school, looking forward to moving to a new apartment, collaborating with the mayor of La Paz, planning a political career, enjoying the female attention his new buff body brings, and coming to terms with the switch and its aftermath have brought him peace of mind and contentment. His drive and perseverance are why he now has achieved almost everything he has ever wanted, but he also needed the opportunities available in Bogotá and the support of his new brothers. Had the switch never been discovered, William would have been spared the shock and grief of learning about the life he should have had, but he would have been far less likely to have left the butcher shop to study law.

William's religious beliefs and commitments have helped him make sense of the extraordinary changes in his life. He was, and still is, more invested in formal religious practice than the other three; he is the only one to attend church regularly and to pray daily, although two others are heading in religious directions. It was perfect, William said, that the exchange went undetected until the brothers turned twenty-five because they were mature enough to deal with it, old enough not to be switched back to their biological families, and young enough to form meaningful relationships with one another. He is gratified that Carlos is reaching out to his parents—and to him—which had seemed uncertain for a time. "God did all this," William said. He can even joke with Carlos now, whereas he never could previously.

Despite William's overall contentment and extraordinary ability to move beyond the past, he cannot ever forget what happened. Finding out he belonged elsewhere was not the saddest thing that ever happened to him, but it certainly "hit hard." It was the missed opportunities to study and to be an identical twin alongside someone with whom he gets along so well that he felt most acutely. Meeting Jorge is the most important thing that has happened to William because, mostly through advice and example, he has been motivated in ways that would not have been possible otherwise. A huge regret is that he will never know the mother who gave birth to him ("our mother," as Jorge says), a realization that triggers feelings of inner emptiness. But William accepts this loss, believing it would have assumed greater importance if his parents and siblings in La Paz not been as loving and supportive as they were and continue to be.

As an outsider Diana has watched William's confidence grow, a change she attributes to his strong relationship with his twin brother, Jorge—in fact, all her brothers have strengthened their ties to their respective identical twins. William worries a lot about his twin and urges Diana to curb Jorge's fanaticism about football and the mad travel itinerary that he cannot really afford. Although the football excursions separate them at times, the twins' relationship has grown closer as they have started to do more things together. They have taken trips to Medellín and Cartagena, alone and with friends, deepening their trust in one another and allowing them to "joke and just hang out." William leans on his twin for help with some law school assignments, especially those in English, although Diana says neither has much facility with the language.

Another significant change is that all four twins' social ties have led to more frequent family gatherings of relatives from both sides. Through it all neither William nor Wilber has ever felt inferior to or disparaged by his twin. And while Jorge is a natural leader and the acknowledged spokesman of both his twinship and the foursome, William knows he can speak up whenever he wants to and does.

William is planning a career in politics and, like a true politician, did not fret about his slim loss in the La Paz city council election and instead is focused on a future win. Diana wondered whether his candidacy was prompted by the widespread support he received in advance, rather than by having a clear idea or concept of what he would do if elected. William was well known and well liked in his community even before he became famous as a result of widespread interest in the twin switch, but he may have presumed that the extra attention would help his candidacy. Regardless, William's law school experience and continued contacts with the mayor and his constituents will better position him for his next attempt at elected office, and Jorge is among his biggest supporters. The twins' latest collaboration is building a new house for the La Paz parents, one of the first projects undertaken by AIOM (Arquitectura-Ingenieria-Obras-Mantenimiento or Architecture-Engineering-Building-Maintenance), Jorge's new consulting and construction company jointly owned by the Trio Miseria (Jorge and his friends Andres and Ricardo—the Miserable Three).

Jorge

Friends see a positive change in Jorge as a consequence of his reunion with his identical twin and the events that followed. He has grown closer to, and more connected with, his family and friends, and he has dealt with the situation in ways that the others have not, by fielding media requests and agreeing to radio interviews. He enjoys doing these things and has a talent for them. At the end of an interview for a Canadian radio program with a Spanish interpreter, Jorge shouted out greetings in English. Having no common language poses no barrier to him in forging connections with other people—he sends out lots of smiles and thumbs-up by way of saying, "I am with you."

It took some time for Jorge to achieve this comfortable state of mind, given his initial fright and anxiety at learning that his real twin was elsewhere. But his solution was to focus on gaining two brothers, not on losing one, and to becoming an indivisible fraternity of four. No doubt, this attitude helped all the brothers weather their first disagreement, about a request from local media that the city boys viewed suspiciously but the country ones did not. The reporter had said the program would feature William's political run, but instead the segment replayed the brothers' story once again in somewhat unflattering ways. In an effort to protect their twins, because they suspected that the La Paz family would be shown as significantly impoverished when it was not, Jorge and Carlos had warned that none of them would be portrayed as promised (and were proved right). "They don't own our story—we do," Jorge had insisted. After the program aired and it proved to be different from what the brothers had been promised, they affirmed that all four would have to agree to any interview requests made in the future.

As their twin relationship progressed, one of Jorge's key goals was making certain that William gained admittance to law school. Jorge himself was on a bit of an occupational detour after being laid off by Strycon because of the oil crisis. He was offered another job but turned it down because it involved considerable travel, which would inhibit his ability to literally follow his favorite team. Jorge planned to find a new job after my second visit in July 2016, but put off doing so until he returned from the football championships in Japan in December 2016. Meanwhile, he did some freelance work from home and worked part time for Atlético Nacional's local fan club, but neither job earned him enough to cover his college tuition. Jorge then took a job in hydrocarbons, but more recently established the AIOM construction company with his friends.

William entered Jorge's life when he was feeling unique, but meeting an identical twin does not detract from one's uniqueness or individuality. Some identical reared-apart twins in the Minnesota study voiced such concerns until they spent time together, but, as researchers know and twins ultimately learn, the similarities between them, while striking, are not exact. The reunion does not damage anyone's identity as an individual, but enhances it by adding the identity of being half of a pair. Jorge now looks forward to using his twinship for pranks, as in appearing as mayor of La Paz in William's place if he wins election. But before they engage in such antics, they may want to learn more about the identical Castro twins, Julian and Joaquin, the former US secretary of housing and urban development and the current US representative from Texas, respectively. As the leading contender for mayor of San Antonio, Texas, in 2005, Julian Castro, then a member of the city council, asked Joaquin, then a state legislator, to attend the annual River Parade in his place. Community leaders knew they were sharing the barge with Joaquin, not Julian, but the crowd of 250,000 people did not. Julian's political opponents were quick to accuse the twins of deceit and immaturity, but the twins made light of this event at a press conference where they appeared in T-shirts proclaiming I AM JULIAN and I AM NOT JULIAN.[2]

As Jorge's relationship with William has grown, Jorge's relationship with Carlos has undergone some revision. Jorge is more mindful of Carlos's feelings now that Jorge and William spend so much time together. The tattoo of Carlos's image on Jorge's chest, next to the one of their mother, moved Carlos deeply, but these accidental brothers continue to kid each other constantly, usually to the point of exasperation. When Jorge called Carlos to say that he would be delayed, Carlos added more than a touch of sarcasm by announcing, "Jorge is coming late—for once!"

Jorge has thought a lot about what it means to be switched at birth. How could he not? I asked him, "What would you say to switched and nonswitched twins who came to you for advice?" To the switched twin, he would say that it is good to learn the truth, especially when you are young enough to form a relationship and learn new things about yourself. Along these lines he hopes that the four Colombian brothers will live together someday or at least travel together with no girlfriends allowed. He would tell the nonswitched twin to be happy to have grown up in the right family and to relate detailed childhood stories to the switched twin so that he or she would "know how it was."

Jorge has felt an inner spiritual growth that he links to knowing William, although Luz's death and Santi's birth have also played key roles. "Once you become a parent, you gain a whole new perspective, and you ask God for help." He doesn't go to church or practice religion in a formal way. And although he was raised Catholic, he does not consider himself to be one. However, Jorge does engage in private religious activities several times a week, something he did less than once a month before he met William. Jorge defines his personal religion as doing good deeds, having observed that some people go to church but are blind to the needs of others. Jorge enjoys visiting churches when he travels, mostly to see their architecture, but he would occasionally attend church with William if asked.

Wilber

The La Paz twin who grew up in La Paz sees himself as unchanged by the twin switch, which is understandable because he was raised in the place where he was born. Some initial shock and angry feelings gave way to curiosity about meeting his identical other and learning what the exchange would mean for everyone else. Wilber did worry that his mother, who is in her seventies, might suffer a heart attack upon learning that she did not give birth to one of her sons, so he helped others convince Ana that William would always be her child. He also told himself and William that they would always be brothers and that, because both felt the same way, nothing had really changed between them. However, Wilber gained fresh understanding of why his same-aged sibling was always so different from the rest of the family, and now he has new respect for genetic effects on behavior. "I get it now," he said.

The biggest changes in Wilber's life are his management of the butcher shop and his blossoming relationship with his identical twin. In 2016 Wilber and Carlos were clearly more focused on each other than they had been in 2015, perhaps because of Carlos's greater openness with his new family members and his recognition that having an identical twin did not detract from his uniqueness. Wilber believes his twin was changed by his first trip to La Paz because "he saw how things really were, that it was not so easy to climb the ladder in life. He became less cocky after that."

These twins can be serious together, understanding of each other, and fully supportive, but those around them see them as playful and scheming. One night, while we were having drinks with Carlos and our interpreter, Carlos received a text message from Wilber saying he needed to see him. But it was just an excuse that Wilber cooked up to get away from his girlfriend, with whom he had been arguing, and for Carlos to postpone a date with his. They decided that if the two women saw a copy of this message, they would understand that the twins had to be together and would be unavailable that night. It seemed to work.

For now Wilber's goals are to become a business owner, of either a butcher shop or a supermarket, and to settle into his own apartment. In these and other respects he is slower to make changes than the others, seemingly content to take his time and follow their lead. Although Wilber was the first brother to be interested in joining the military, William enlisted first, and Wilber arrived in Bogotá after William did and then worked in the butcher shop after his brother got the job. Wilber is also less enthusiastic about traveling than the others, and he is the only one of the four who does not have a passport, although Carlos and William got theirs only recently, for their trip to Mexico. It's likely that Wilber will follow suit once he hears about their grand adventures.

Learning about the switch, while life changing in many ways, left the La Paz brothers' relationship intact; they worked together until recently and still live together. They are brothers who have built trust and loyalty over the years. "Despite how we fight, we get along well," Wilber said, although those privy to their constant bickering might disagree. Each is free to be himself around his brother, but like many unrelated siblings, they lack the rapport that each developed so easily with his identical twin. And, like Jorge and Carlos, Wilber and William probably would not have been friends had their paths crossed outside the family.

Wilber gets along well with Jorge, but, as people who have neither a shared history nor shared blood ties, their relationship is not intimate, leaving them to converse mostly about women and sports, frequent topics of conversation for men who have little in common. But Jorge and Wilber have an inescapable connection, forged by a series of extraordinary life events. Their major breakthrough happened on July 20, 2015, Colombia's Independence Day, when William was working and Carlos was occupied. Wilber and Jorge had nothing to do, so Jorge invited Wilber to watch the annual celebratory parade. Wilber was reluctant, saying he had seen parades and he wanted to nap, but Jorge insisted, which turned out to be a good thing. Wilber was shocked by the magnitude of the parade, as he had never seen one on such a grand scale, and ended up feeling glad that he went. Although Jorge was bored after three long hours, Wilber remained enraptured. Jorge also learned something new: Wilber taught him about the two types of military designations, the high school graduates (*bachilleres*) who have high school degrees and rarely see combat during their twelve-month service, and the regulars (*regulares*) who do not have high school degrees and are often in combat during their eighteen- to twenty-four-month service.[3] Wilber explained that the La Paz brothers were regulars from the countryside whom members of the higher-ranking units regarded as disposable. This gave Jorge greater insight into the experience of his twin and his replica (his accidental brother's twin).

Wilber has also developed a close relationship with Diana and calls her to join them when the four get together. Jorge and Carlos know that she doesn't drink so they never bother to call, but Wilber does, and when she visits him at home they talk about his job, his girlfriends, and other things that matter. He introduces her as his sister if new people are around.

Was Wilber glad that the switch was discovered? He immediately answered in the affirmative and listed the many "cool things" that have happened as a consequence. He enjoys going places and being recognized, not out of vanity or pride but because he likes sharing the twins' story with people, helping them to understand what really happened. This young man has changed dramatically in this respect, compared with the early weeks when he avoided publicity because it was new and he felt uncertain about where it might lead. Wilber changed in parallel with his twin brother in this respect, and like Carlos he remains adamant about avoiding attention in Bogotá where the story was sensationalized.

Like his three brothers, Wilber believes that the twins' reunion was God's doing, and Wilber calls upon higher powers to keep his family safe, as he did when he and William were enlisted men. He wears the image of the Virgen del Carmen, the patron saint of vehicles, around his neck—he chose it for reasons of adornment but said nothing more. However, he rarely engages in religious activities, no more than several times a year.

Twin research on religiosity has been full of surprises, as we noted earlier. Since 1990, new studies have shown that religiosity is equally affected by our genes and by our individual experiences, whereas a shared family environment seems to have little influence. Earlier studies made the mistake of studying young twins living at home, under the environmental thumbs of their parents, who made their children attend Sunday services or take Hebrew lessons whether they wanted to or not. Later studies focusing on adult twins found that when people can freely choose their religious activities, their genetic predispositions come to the fore.[4] The identical twins Sarah and Susie were raised together in a moderately religious Catholic home, but their mother says these twenty-two-year-olds would be religious "even if we were atheists." And the reared-apart firefighter twins, Mark and Jerry, both went to Hebrew school and celebrated some Jewish holidays, but neither twin showed interest in religious activities as an adult.[5]

The La Paz brothers were immersed in their mother's deep religiosity, but only William followed Ana's lead when he was young and after he left home, his natural bent most likely affecting his behavior. Consistent with this view, the reared-apart twins Sharon and Debbie know they would have absorbed the beliefs and rituals of whatever faith their adoptive family had practiced. Both twins enjoy the traditions and practices attached to both holiday celebrations and regular services held throughout the year.[6]

Luz, who raised Jorge and Carlos, attended church regularly, and religion held great importance for her. As we would expect, both men engaged fairly regularly in religious activities as children, at least once a month or more. However, as young adults they participated only several times a year. More interesting is their return to spirituality and religion following the discovery of the switch and the major changes in their lives. Jorge and Carlos share no genes, but both experienced significant life events that affected them deeply.

Consistent with what twin studies tell us, the identical reared-apart twins Jorge and William have become more religious as adults, although how they express their faith differs. Carlos and Wilber also share faith in a higher power, but Carlos has become more spiritually aware than in the past, a likely outcome of his reflections on his life after learning the truth about his birth. Jorge, Carlos, and William scored somewhat higher than Wilber on honesty-humility, the elements of the HEXACO personality scale linked to religiosity.[7]

The Colombian twins help us identify factors that bend our religious paths in one direction or another. Their experiences and behaviors demonstrate that both genes and experiences, especially emotionally charged life events, are involved.[8] The beauty of these observations is how well they illuminate findings on religiosity from large-scale twin studies telling us how much of each contributes to the mix.

People have different opinions about which of the switched twins suffered greater hurt and which one overcame his difficulties to a greater degree. I believe that their situations were, and are, too different and complex to compare and that both young men gained, lost, and grew from their experience. The nonswitched twins suffered, too, in ways of their own. The twins' attorney has filed a lawsuit against the Hospital Materno Infantil on their behalf, alleging negligence in managing their care; the lawsuit is one of several major events that will engage the twins as they plot their future together.

Chapter 12

Band of Brothers

Circle Game

We can't return we can only look
Behind from where we came
And go round and round and round
In the circle game

—Joni Mitchell[1]

J orge, Carlos, William, and Wilber cannot undo the mistake that happened at the Hospital Materno Infantil many years ago, nor can they change the course of their lives in the years that followed, but they do have a say in what happens to them in the future. They can look ahead to where they are going, not "back from where they came."

The Lawsuit

Several prominent Bogotá attorneys, an uncle-nephew team, Carlos and Pablo Medellín, now joined by Carlos's daughter Adriana, have been managing the twins' lawsuit claiming negligence by the Hospital Materno Infantil and other entities. Intrigued by the case when it became public in October 2014, Carlos and Pablo have described it as "important, interesting, and rare."[2] The legal process will not be easy because precedents for switched-at-birth adult twins do not exist, although Colombian courts have heard cases involving exchanged infants.

The lawyers have two years to present the case to a judge, who will determine whether the hospital was negligent and, if so, what the award for damages should be. Making the case will be especially challenging because the mistake happened more than two decades ago; this is the first investigation of a public employee in such a case, a nurse; the passage of time makes identifying the party responsible for the switch difficult; and the chance of reaching an out-of-court settlement is low because the hospital is a state institution, under the watchful financial eye of the controller. The lawsuit was filed in January 2017, and so far the hospital has not responded.

The difficulties do not stop there, because all four twins have lived a normal life and do not appear to have suffered serious psychological damage. Specifying and determining compensation entails an element of subjectivity, and seeking too high a figure in damages could hurt the case. Public opinion holds considerable sway in such cases and could affect the final outcome in ways the lawyers cannot know. The case could also drag on for years if the first ruling is appealed, moving it up to the Administrative Tribunal of Cudinamarca. If major revisions are required it will then go to the Council of State, Colombia's maximum judicial authority in the public administrative law jurisdiction.

Under Colombian law damages are calculated from the time of the discovery, when the twins were in their midtwenties. This limitation discounts the difficulties they variously experienced during childhood, such as feeling different from the rest of their family, not knowing their biological parents, losing the benefits of a close twin relationship, and lacking access to compatible blood or organ donors if affected by a serious medical condition. I would argue that damages should be calculated from the day of the switch, when the twins were newborn babies.

The brothers could have been represented by separate lawyers to press their specific claims and concerns and, according to one of the attorneys, this arrangement may have made for a stronger case since the four were not similarly affected by the switch. The attorney also explained that the brothers rejected that option because of their good relations with one another and in the interest of presenting a unified front.

Insights and Understandings

The four Colombian twins and their families are adjusting well to their unusual situation, better than the members of any switched-at-birth twin case I have encountered. Their positive adjustment was possible, in part, because they had several critical factors in their favor. The twins learned of the switch when they were twenty-five, young enough to enjoy their surprise identical twinship, but mature enough to assess their situation rationally and realistically. All four were living in the same city so, work schedules aside, meeting and communicating were fairly easy. Ana and Carmelo, the parents from La Paz, were sensitive to their new son's feelings, willing to wait for him to open up to them and to his new siblings when he felt ready.

Everyone was helped by *convivencia*, the notion that everyone belongs to one family, a sentiment that permeates much of Colombian thought and culture. Some relationships were revised, but mostly in name only. As Carlos so beautifully expressed it, "From the beginning we focused on the positive, not the negative. This is God's doing. We were not kidnapped. No one [intentionally] stole anyone's life."

Band of Brothers

Band of Brothers is the title of Steven Ambrose's bestselling book about the E Company, 506th Parachute Infantry Regiment, 101st Airborne Division of the US Army whose members volunteered for elite service in World War II. The book reveals their true camaraderie alongside the horrific, but successful battles they fought. The Colombian four, who proudly call each other brother, replicate the spirit and dedication of E Company, albeit on a smaller scale.

In October 2016 the four twins attended a comedy show starring Yesika's sister, Alexandra, the nationally famous celebrity impersonator. It was the first time they had gotten together in a while, and it felt good to be there together, go out for drinks afterward, and catch up with each other. They had some important decisions to make, such as the type of tattoo they all will get, how they will celebrate their next birthdays, and if, when, and where they will vacation together. They have resolved to settle all such issues collectively and unanimously. Toward this end they have set up a joint email address that keeps them informed simultaneously.

The twins' experience has redefined *family* as anyone you regard as a mother, father, sister, brother, son, or daughter. How much better to feel you have gained two brothers or two sons than to think you have lost the one you lived with and loved. Time together cannot compensate for their years apart, and the joys of reunion do not erase their pain of separation, but meaningful relationships between and among the twins and their families can form and last a lifetime.

Wilber wants to know where their story ends, a concern he voiced on behalf of all his brothers. A spontaneous moment during a party on our last night in Colombia held a vital clue. Out on the dance floor Carlos executed a risky move, leaning backward at a dangerous angle. The other three surrounded him, enjoying the scene while extending their arms protectively. In that moment they were alone together, free of unresolved tensions brought on by the switch. No matter what, they have each other's backs.

Appendix A

History: Switched-at-Birth Twins

The recorded history of switched-at-birth twins includes nine cases, although there are undoubtedly more that have not come to light. Two cases involved double switches, but the Colombian brothers are the only ones that involved identical twins in both pairs and the only one in which the twins were adults when the switch became known. Exchanged female twins from Puerto Rico, involving one pair of identical twins and a pair of presumed fraternal twins, were returned to their biological families when they were eighteen months old.

History of Switched-at-Birth Twin Pairs

Location	Date of Birth	Gender	Twins' Age at First Meeting in Years
Switzerland	1941	male	5
Canada	1971	male	20
Poland	1983	female	16
Puerto Rico[a]	1985	female	1.5
Gran Canaria (Spain)	1973	female	28
Gran Canaria (Spain)	Unknown	male	unknown
Colombia[b]	1988	male	25

[a] Double exchange: Switching of an identical twin from one pair with a presumed fraternal twin from another pair.

[b] Double exchange: Switching of an identical twin from one pair with an identical twin from another pair.

Appendix B

Outtakes: Excerpts from Laura and Yaneth's WhatsApp Conversations

Two friends, Laura and Yaneth, were dazzled by the resemblance of Jorge and William and set out to uncover the truth about their birth. Excerpts from the WhatsApp conversations between the two women are fascinating.

NOTE: The entries in these text-message exchanges have been edited slightly for clarity.

TUESDAY, SEPTEMBER 9, 2014, 14:12

Yaneth Paez
Hey Laura
You know where this Jorge is from?
"the twin" of Brian's cousin

Laura Vega Garzon
mmm
where?
where was he born?
or what specialty or floor [at the office] he is from? hahaha

Yaneth Paez
where he was born, duh!
hahahaha
duh!

Laura Vega Garzon
LOL
MMM

I have no idea
Do you want me to ask?

Yaneth Paez

I showed the photos of Jorge to William, who is Brian's cousin and he was surprised. He showed them to Brian's mother and to different people who know William and everyone is very surprised.
What about if they got exchanged in the clinic?
Let's plan a reunion
hahahahah

Laura Vega Garzon

lol
yeah, it makes you want to know
Where is William from?
Get me a picture of him

Yaneth Paez

from Santander
So you can show it to Jorge?

Laura Vega Garzon

Yes, to show it to Jorge

Yaneth Paez

I am sending it to you
Done

LATER THAT DAY

Yaneth Paez

William was showing the photos to everyone in the supermarket
hahahahahahahaha

Laura Vega Garzon

yeah
So you had a picture of Jorge?

Yaneth Paez

Yes, so you see below?

Hahaha just kidding

WEDNESDAY, SEPTEMBER 10, 2014, 9:07

Laura Vega Garzon
Hello
: -o

Yaneth Paez
Hello Laura
how are you?

Laura Vega Garzon
fine and you?
I want to call you
will they scold you at work?
or better to contact you by text?

Yaneth Paez
Maybe later

what's up??

Laura Vega Garzon
I just finished talking with Jorge

Yaneth Paez
call me … they will not bother me

Laura Vega Garzon
haha

Yaneth Paez
ayyy nooo
What's up??

Laura Vega Garzon
I will call you [no call; they continue to text]

Yaneth Paez
Hurry up, you have me intrigued
jijijiji
hahahah

William just wrote to me
I'm going to ask him what type of blood he has

Laura Vega Garzon
>
> ahh
>
> God!
>
> :' (

Yaneth Paez
>
> He does not answer
>
> I have to wait ... this is the peak time at work
>
> hahahahaha

Laura Vega Garzon
>
> ahhh
>
> but do you think that William already saw the photos?

Yaneth Paez
>
> I have not sent them to him—I will not do that
>
> until you send me Jorge's blood type
>
> hahahaha

Laura Vega Garzon
>
> hahahahah

Yaneth Paez
>
> William is not receiving his messages.
>
> Only one mark is being received.
>
> hahahah

Laura Vega Garzon
>
> ahhh
>
> Hahaha
>
> What agony!

Yaneth Paez
>
> Yes

Laura Vega Garzon
>
> And now
>
> ??

Yaneth Paez
>
> nothing
>
> Foolish boy
>
> I think he is still thinking that it's a joke, but
>
> when William sees the photo he is going to faint.

THURSDAY, SEPTEMBER 11, 2014, 8:36

Yaneth Paez
Laura

Laura Vega Garzon
Hello
Tell me

Yaneth Paez
Have you spoken to Jorge?

Laura Vega Garzon
Nooo, he has not come down to my office yet

Yaneth Paez
That "son of a mother!"
You tell what he says

Laura Vega Garzon
yes
It makes me sad to call
I'll wait to see if he comes downstairs

Yaneth Paez
no no ... yes wait
I am sure he is going to come down

Laura Vega Garzon
Yes

Yaneth Paez
To look at Carlos and Jorge ... it's like seeing William and Wilber
If they do not speak, you do not know which is which

Laura Vega Garzon
hahahaha

Yaneth Paez
seriously

Laura Vega Garzon
So cute

Laura Vega Garzon
>That silly boy, Jorge! He does not come downstairs
>Do we have pictures or nothing??

Yaneth Paez
>Foolish boy
>We have nothing right now
>As soon I have the pictures I will send them your way
>all right
>hahahaha
>William has not sent them yet

Laura Vega Garzon
>And Jorge does not come down to tell me anything
>Of course they forgot about us
>

Yaneth Paez
>hahahahah
>Yes
>We did our work and now they abandoned us!
>

Laura Vega Garzon
>They are like that—men after all

Yaneth Paez
>Damn boys

Laura Vega Garzon
>hahahaha

LATER THAT DAY, ONCE THE POSSIBLE SWITCH IS KNOWN TO ALL

Yaneth Paez
>Ahh, poor them
>Carlos must feel the same as William since he was probably switched,
>too.

Laura Vega Garzon
>

Yaneth Paez
>But Jorge did not tell anything else?

Laura Vega Garzon

Well, some things like what you told me

Yaneth Paez

ahh ... too bad. Do you think that it would have been better if we had stayed silent??

Laura Vega Garzon

noooo

Jorge is now laughing hard about it.

FRIDAY, SEPTEMBER 12, 2014, 8:29

Yaneth Paez

hahahaha

William spoke with his aunt Edelmira yesterday. He wanted to talk to her to get all the information ... and it seems that she was super upset And she said that it could not be true ... that she herself took back the same baby to La Paz from Bogotá.

Of course, she feels guilty ...

Laura Vega Garzon

Of course

She will feel that it was all her fault

What a difficult situation!

Also, we all know that it was not her fault, but she will think that everyone is going to hate her

Yaneth Paez

Of courseeee

To tell you the truth, I am very concerned about how William's mom Ana Delina is going to take the news

Brian told me today she is very nervous and very sensitive

Laura Vega Garzon

Ahhhh

What a worry

They need to be very careful about how to tell her the news

LATER THAT DAY

Laura Vega Garzon
Hey, then William has been celebrating the day that is not his birthday

Yaneth Paez
Yes, and the same for Carlos

Laura Vega Garzon
hahahaha

Yaneth Paez
This is like a movie
Although, at the end of the day, it does not really make much difference

Laura Vega Garzon
Well, it depends because if I called you the day after your birthday or you call me after mine, it will make a difference.
lol hahahaha

Yaneth Paez
hahaha
you are crazy

Laura Vega Garzon
yes
Well, baby, I have to get going
We will see each other on Sunday

Yaneth Paez
If anything new happens I will call you

Appendix C

Genograms: Tracking Twins Across Generations

Both sets of accidental brothers, Jorge and Carlos in Bogotá, and William and Wilber in La Paz, had histories of identical and fraternal twinning in their families. Because fraternal twins run in families, we know that fraternal twinning has a partial genetic basis. Researchers once thought that identical twinning occurs randomly, but growing evidence shows it has a genetic basis in some families. This genogram tracks twin births in the Colombian brothers' immediate families, but even more twins were born to their extended family members.

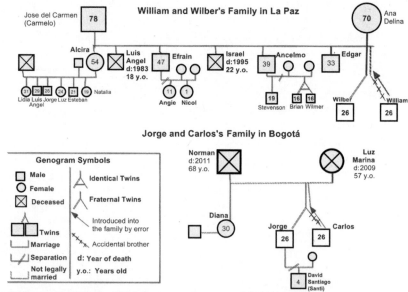

Note: The ages of the twins' family members are those at the time the twins were visited in March–April 2015. They may, therefore, differ slightly from those appearing in the text that reflect the time of Nancy's second visit to Bogotá, in July 2016.

Appendix D

Discoveries: Ability Profiles

The twins' ability profiles can be compared in three ways: the profiles of identical twins separated at birth (twin reared apart); the profiles of unrelated brothers reared together (virtual twins); and the profiles of the unrelated individuals who replicate the virtual twins, but share neither genes nor environment (replicas). Both reared-apart twin pairs in Colombia—William and Jorge, and Carlos and Wilber—show similar "ups" and "downs" in their ability profiles with one exception each, whereas the virtual twins—William and Wilber, and Jorge and Carlos—show both similarities and differences. One set of replicas, Jorge and Wilber, is quite different in their ability profile, as expected because they share neither genes nor environment, but the other set, Carlos and William, is quite alike. However, it is impossible to draw firm conclusions from only two pairs—and, in fact, scores of twin, family, and adoption studies show genetic influence on general mental ability and ability profiles.

Twins Reared Apart

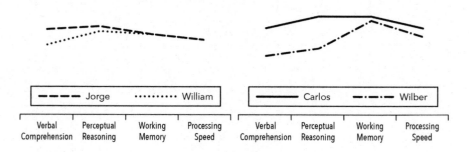

Accidental Brothers

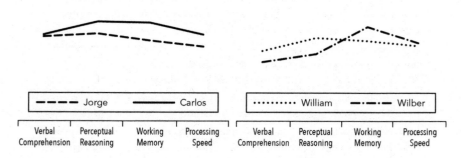

Replicas

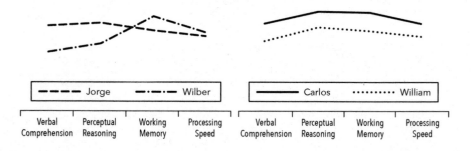

Appendix E

Interesting and Intriguing: Facts About Twins

Interesting and intriguing facts about twins are plentiful enough to fill an entire volume. Listed here are some of the most remarkable bits of information researchers have gathered over the years. I am still amazed that twins can have different fathers and that twins have been born in different countries.

- Identical twins make up one-third of natural twin births, and fraternal twins make up the other two-thirds.
- Benin has the highest natural twinning rate in the world: 27.9 twins per 1,000 births. Vietnam has the lowest natural twinning rate: 6.2 per 1,000 births.
- It is possible for twins to have the same mother, but different fathers, if each egg is fertilized by sperm from a different man—these twins are called superfecundated.
- Nine-banded armadillos give birth only to identical quadruplets.
- Twins can, and have, been born on different days (e.g., Monday, 11:59 p.m. and Tuesday, 00:10 a.m.), weeks (e.g., Sunday, 11:50 p.m. and Monday, 00:05 a.m.), months (e.g., October 31, 11:22 p.m. and November 1, 00:07 a.m.), and even years (e.g., December 31, 2011, 11:37 p.m. and January 1, 2012, 00:10 a.m.). The longest recorded interval between twin births is eighty-seven days—the twin's mother went into early labor, delivering one baby, then her contractions stopped.
- Twins can, and have, been born in different bordering countries— England and Wales, and England and Scotland—when their mothers went into early labor or experienced complications.

- The longest time apart for twins raised separately from birth is seventy-eight years.
- The chance of having fraternal twins increases with maternal age, beginning at about age thirty-five and peaking at age thirty-seven. The chance of bearing fraternal twins declines when women reach their forties.
- Approximately 25 percent of identical twins are opposite-handed. These twins may show other mirror-imaging effects, such as reversal in hair whorl, dental characteristics, birthmarks, moles, and even atypical physical features such as cleft lip and palate.
- Some women who conceive twins deliver a single baby due to the vanishing twin syndrome during the first trimester of pregnancy. This may be caused by miscarriage, but also by resorption of the twin fetus by the mother, placenta, or other twin. The frequency of this event is unknown.
- Twins often use private words and gestures to communicate with each other when they are young, but they are not creating a secret language.
- The children of identical twins are genetic half-siblings as well as first cousins. Each identical twin parent becomes the genetic mother or father, as well as the aunt or uncle, of their nieces and nephews.
- Children born to identical twins who marry identical twins are equivalent to genetic full siblings.
- Quadruplets composed of two sets of identical twins, the result of the divisions of two fertilized eggs, yield four sets of fraternal twins.
- The identical twin Charlie Duke is the only twin to have walked on the moon, and he is just one of twelve people who have done so.

The original sources for this information can be found in Nancy Segal's books, *Entwined Lives, Indivisible by Two, Someone Else's Twin, Born Together—Reared Apart*, and *Twin Mythconceptions*.

Acknowledgments

It is a pleasure to write the acknowledgments at the close of this excursion into the lives and dreams of four such amazing young men. Jorge, William, Carlos, and Wilber experienced an extraordinary, life-changing event that brought shock, uncertainty, questioning, and ultimately resolution, not to mention a few tears. Each twin handled his unique situation with grace and understanding, enabling them to come together as a true band of brothers. Their families and friends were warm and welcoming, generously sharing their observations and reflections about an event that radically revised what they had always believed to be true.

I am thankful to my coauthor, Yesika Montoya, who alerted me to this most unusual case of switched-at-birth twins. She was a marvelous collaborator during our trip to Bogotá in 2015 and continued to be in the months that followed.

Accidental Brothers went through several early drafts en route to its final form. I completed my fifth literary venture under the keen eye of my friend and colleague Lauren Gonzalez, who provided her usual insights into the material while offering great suggestions for the versions that followed. Michael Harvkey, the best-ever online instructor from the Gotham Writers Workshop, provided superb critical advice, offline at last. My boyfriend, Professor Craig K. Ihara, who came up with the title for this book, added perspective and polish to the final and "final final" versions. Dr. Cheryl Crippen, my newest friend and psychology colleague at California State University, Fullerton, was a reviewer par excellence, and I believe she has found a new calling.

Carol Mann and her staff at the Carol Mann Agency, especially Isabella Ruggiero, Kat Manos, and Maile Beal, were enthusiastic and dedicated throughout. I am especially grateful to Elizabeth Knoll, my former editor at Harvard University Press, for putting us in touch. Carol is responsible for getting the book to St. Martin's Press, especially to Karen Wolny, senior editor extraordinaire. Karen's immediate recognition of the scientific import and human interest of the twins' story allowed her to skillfully guide me through the organization, presentation, and deep editing of the material. She did not rest until I reached the stage at which "the book writes itself," a phase that I understand and appreciate because of her. Assistant editor Laura Apperson and senior production editor Donna Cherry at St. Martin's Press were helpful and insightful throughout the entire process. And the publicity team of Katie Bassel, Kimberly Lew, and Laura Clark still overflows with knowledge and support.

I am indebted to Ilena Silverman, features editor, and Jake Silverstein, editor in chief, of the *New York Times Magazine* for appreciating the significance and uniqueness of the twins' story when I brought it to their attention. They arranged for their staff writer, Susan Dominus, and photographers, Stefan Ruiz and Patrick Lyn, to cover our 2015 visit, resulting in the magazine's wonderful cover story on July 12 of that year. Associate photo editor Stacey Baker was helpful in every way possible.

Francisco Bernate, an attorney, facilitated the initial contact with the twins. Dr. Juan J. Yunis, medical geneticist at Servicios Médicos Yunis Turbay y Cia in Bogotá, offered new insights into the biological and societal significance of this case. The twins' lawyers, Carlos Eduardo Medellín Becerra, his nephew Pablo Medellín Becerra, and his daughter Adriana Medellín Cano, at the Bogotá law firm Medellín Martínez Durán Abogados, generously shared their perspectives and plans in connection with this once-in-a-lifetime case. They also allowed us the use of their beautifully appointed law offices for interviewing the twins and some family members. The interpreters Alexandra Yang and Alberto Orjuela were professional and proficient, and both developed close personal ties to the twins that continue to this day.

The staff at the Rosales Plaza Hotel was unfailingly accommodating, providing conference rooms for occasional testing, offering unlimited supplies of pens, and allowing full access to the copy machine when we desperately needed to have the twins respond to one more survey. My colleague David Gallardo-Pujol, of the University of Barcelona, forwarded several Spanish-language psychological protocols and scoring programs that facilitated the research. Yesika's father, Hernando Montoya, arranged our visit to the Hospital Materno Infantil, and staff there and at the Hospital Regional de Vélez showed us their newborn baby facilities and variously shared information about conditions in the nursery that may have led to the switch of the twins. Yesika's sister Alexandra Montoya, Colombia's celebrity impersonator who is now an attorney, helped with transportation, contacts, and other aspects of our visit too numerous to name.

My colleagues and students at CSU Fullerton were a great source of inspiration and assistance. Professor André Zampaulo, of the Department of Foreign Languages and Literatures, and Claudia Acosta, of the Department of Instructional Design and Technology, translated documents, records, and popular media. Professor Aaron Lukaszewski of the Department of Psychology reviewed selected portions of the manuscript, Professor John Patton provided calipers and other anthropometric tools for recording body measurements of the twins, and Professor Stephen Neufeld of the Department of History provided comments and sources on historical matter. Other contributors include Amanda Killian, a former member of the faculty; Linda Pabon, graduate secretary in the Department of Psychology; and the students Brittney Hernandez, Hannah Bojorquez, Lisette Bohorquez, Jaime Muñoz-Velázquez, Erika Becker, and Erika Orozco. *Accidental Brothers* also benefited from my conversations with Professor Ray Williams and his graduate student Valentín González-Bohórquez at the University of California, Riverside, and Professor James Alstrum at Illinois State University. My Australian colleagues Dr. Jeffrey Craig and Dr. Yuk Loke were instrumental in the epigenetic analyses and interpretation reported here and elsewhere, my Canadian colleague Professor P. Tony Vernon offered insights and advice, and my Spanish colleague Dr. María del Mar Gil translated the twins' birth record. Jessica Crespo, MBA, professional translator and interpreter from Gran Canaria, Spain, translated selected interview material. Yesika's former instructor in Bogotá Ligia Gómez and Ligia's colleague Diana Ramos administered general intelligence tests to the twins prior to our arrival.

Mabel Terrero, Yesika's student at Columbia University, assisted Yesika in the preparation of the genograms. The graphic artist Kelly Donovan at CSU Fullerton, who is an identical twin, added her usual magic to the photographs and charts that appear in the book.

Kevin Haroian, of the Minnesota Center for Twin and Family Research, conducted the twin type analyses based on fingerprint and body size. The late professor Irving I. Gottesman, also of the University of

Minnesota, to whom this book is dedicated, was a great source of encouragement, inspiration, and advice, and I only wish he were around to see the final product. My friend and colleague Dr. Milton Diamond, of the University of Hawaii, reviewed passages related to gender identity and development. Professor Cecil Reynolds, of Texas A&M University, and Dr. Julia Hickman, clinical psychologist, evaluated the twins' drawings, and the handwriting consultant Eileen Page compared their penmanship.

Meeting the twins and their family members was an unforgettable experience. Each added an indelible entry to our understanding of how genetic factors and life circumstances make us who we are.

Notes

Preface

1. Answers to many twin-related questions I have received over the years, and responses to many twin-related myths I have encountered are available in N. L. Segal, *Twin Mythconceptions: False Beliefs, Fables, and Facts About Twins* (San Diego: Elsevier, 2017).
2. For aerial views of Bogotá, see https://mapcarta.com/28093320/Map; and for Vereda El Recreo, see https://www.google.com/maps/place/El+Recreo,+Vélez,+Santander+Department,+Colombia/@6.1579883,-73.6805392,14z/data=!4m1 3!1m7!3m6!1s0x8e4203ccb76ef8dd:0x88581adc14f2e1d2!2sLa+Paz,+Santan der+Department,+Colombia!3b1!8m2!3d6.1898099!4d-73.57585!3m4!1s0x8e 41f7fd4e0e065d:0x2d2ebdd172403e0!8m2!3d6.1500272!4d-73.6666775.
3. B. Palmer, "Double Insanity: Twin Studies Are Pretty Much Useless," *Slate*, August 24, 2011, http://www.slate.com/articles/life/twins/2011/08/double _inanity.html; N. L. Segal, "The Value of Twin Studies: A Response to *Slate Magazine*." *Twin Research and Human Genetics* 14, no. 6 (2011): 593–97.
4. N. L. Segal, "Cooperation, Competition and Altruism Within Twin Sets: Reappraisal," doctoral dissertation, University of Chicago, 1982.
5. N. L. Segal, *Indivisible by Two: Lives of Extraordinary Twins* (Cambridge, MA: Harvard University Press, 2005).
6. N. L. Segal, *Born Together—Reared Apart: The Landmark Minnesota Twin Study* (Cambridge, MA: Harvard University Press, 2012).
7. R. Plomin et al., *Behavioral Genetics*, 7th ed. (New York: Worth, 2017).
8. P. M. Visscher et al., "Assumption-Free Estimation of Heritability from Genome-Wide Identity-By-Descent Sharing Between Full Siblings," *PLoS Genetics* 2, no. 3 (2006): e41. The range is based on a mean of 0.50 (±3 SD) and a standard deviation of 0.04.
9. C. Zimmer, "52 Genes Linked to Intelligence," *New York Times*, May 23, 2017, D1, D3.
10. Segal, *Born Together—Reared Apart*.

11. China's one-child policy, in place since 1979, was recently changed. Married couples now may raise two children. J. Marin, "China Now Sees Room for Two-Child Families," *Los Angeles Times*, October 30, 2015, A1, A4.

12. A family in South Korea could afford to raise only one child; a young Chinese twin visiting her grandmother was separated from her sister when, due to political circumstances, her family suddenly fled the mainland leaving her behind; a mother in Romania was persuaded to give one of her twins to a couple to help them avoid paying a government tax required of childess couples and to provide a better life for her daughter; and in Soviet Armenia babies were sometimes taken at birth by hospital staff and offered to infertile couples; mothers might be told that one of their newborns twins had passed away; see N. L. Segal, "Stolen Twin: Fascination and Curiosity," *Twin Research and Human Genetics* 17, no. 1 (2014): 56–61.

13. Segal, *Born Together—Reared Apart.*

14. N. L. Segal, *Someone Else's Twin: The True Story of Babies Switched at Birth* (Amherst, NY: Prometheus, 2011).

Prologue: Tales of Two Mothers

1. "Braxton Hicks or True Labor Contractions?" WebMD, 2016, http://www.webmd.com/baby/guide/true-false-labor#2-4.

2. "Preeclampsia and Eclampsia," WebMD, 2016, http://www.webmd.com/baby/guide/preeclampsia-eclampsia#1-1; ESHRE Capri Workshop Group, "Multiple Gestation Pregnancy," *Human Reproduction* 15, no. 8 (2000): 1856–64.

3. Colombia has thirty-two states.

4. "Twins and Premature Birth," University of Rochester Medical Center, 2017, https://www.urmc.rochester.edu/encyclopedia/content.aspx?ContentType ID=1&ContentID=2849.

5. R. H. Lumme and S. V. Saarikoski, "Perinatal Deaths in Twin Pregnancy: A 22-Year Review," *Acta Geneticae Medicae et Gemellologiae: Twin Research* 37, no. 1 (1988): 47–54; E. Hoffmann et al., "Twin Births: Cesarean Section or Vaginal Delivery?" *Acta Obstetricia et Gynecologica Scandinavica* 91, no. 4 (2012): 463–69.

6. "Preterm Birth," US Centers for Disease Control and Prevention, 2015, http://www.cdc.gov/reproductivehealth/MaternalInfantHealth/PretermBirth.htm.

7. N. J. S. Christenfeld and E. A. Hill, "Whose Baby Are You?" *Nature*, December 14, 1995, 669; A. Alvergne, C. Faurie, and M. Raymond, "Father-Offspring Resemblance Predicts Paternal Investment in Humans," *Animal Behaviour* 78, no. 1 (2009): 61–69. A DNA test can determine whether a man is not the father of a given child, but it cannot prove that he is. That is because other males could have genes compatible with the child's genetic background.

8. S. I. Venancio and H. de Almeida, "Kangaroo Mother Care: Scientific Evidences and Impact on Breastfeeding," *Jornal de Pediatria* 80, 5 suppl. (2004): S173–80.

9. J. Mann, "Nurturance or Negligence: Maternal Psychology and Behavioral Preference Among Preterm Twins," in *The Adapted Mind: Evolutionary Psychology and the Evolution of Culture*, ed. J. Barkow, L. Cosmides, and J. Tooby, 367–90 (New York: Oxford University Press, 1992).

10. N. L. Segal, *Twin Mythconceptions: False Beliefs, Fables and Facts About Twins* (San Diego: Elsevier, 2017).

11. B. Mampe et al., "Newborns' Cry Melody Is Shaped by Their Native Language," *Current Biology* 19, no. 23 (2008): 1994–97.

12. N. L. Segal, *Someone Else's Twin: The True Story of Babies Switched at Birth* (Amherst, NY: Prometheus, 2011).

13. K. R. Chi, "The Dark Side of the Human Genome," *Nature* 538, no. 7,624 (2016): 275-77.

14. S. Dominus, "The Mixed-Up Brothers of Bogotá," *New York Times Magazine*, July 12, 2015: 34–41, 48, 50–52, 55.

Chapter 1: A Dubious Double

1. G. S. Barsh, "What Controls Variation in Human Skin Color?" *PLoS Biology* 1, no. 1 (2003): e27.

2. R. Plomin et al., *Behavioral Genetics*, 7th ed. (New York: Worth, 2017); L. R. Cardon and D. W. Fulker, "Genetics of Specific Cognitive Abilities," in *Nature, Nurture & Psychology*, eds. R. Plomin and G. E. McClearn (Washington, DC: American Psychological Association, 1993), 99–120.

3. J. C. Loehlin and R. C. Nichols, *Heredity, Environment, and Personality: A Study of 850 Sets of Twins* (Austin: University of Texas Press, 1976); L. B. Koenig et al., "Genetic and Environmental Influences on Religiousness: Findings for Retrospective and Current Religiousness Ratings," *Journal of Personality* 73, no. 2 (2005): 471–88; N. G. Waller et al., "Genetic and Environmental Influences on Religious Interests, Attitudes, and Values: A Study of Twins Reared Apart and Together," *Psychological Science* 1, no. 2 (1990): 138–42.

4. N. L. Segal, *Born Together—Reared Apart: The Landmark Minnesota Twin Study* (Cambridge, MA: Harvard University Press, 2012).

5. J. J. Stubbe, D. I. Boomsma, and J. C. N. de Geus, "Sports Participation During Adolescence: A Shift from Environmental to Genetic Factors," *Medicine and Science in Sports and Exercise* 37, no. 4 (2005): 563–70; P. P. Fierro, "Twins in the Olympics," verywell, August 23, 2016, https://www.verywell.com/twins-in-the-olympics-2446954.

6. N. L. Segal, "A Tale of Two Sisters." *Psychology Today*, November–December 2015, 68–75, 88.

7. S. P. Whiteside and E. Rixon, "Speech Characteristics of Monozygotic Twins and a Same-Sex Sibling: An Acoustic Case Study of Coarticulation Patterns in Read Speech," *Phonetica* 60, no. 4 (2003): 273–97; M. J. Beatty, L. A. Marshall, and J. E. Rudd, "A Twins Study of Communicative Adaptability: Heritability of Individual Differences," *Quarterly Journal of Speech* 87, no. 4 (2001): 366–77.

8. "La Paz: Municipality in Santander," 2005 statistics, https://www.citypopulation .de/php/colombia-santander.php?adm2id=68397.

9. C. Moss, "Bogotá, Colombia: Introducing the Athens of South America," *Daily Telegraph*, July 4, 2014, http://www.telegraph.co.uk/travel/destinations /south-america/colombia/bogota/articles/Bogota-Colombia-introducing-the -Athens-of-South-America/.

10. "Is the Probability of Having Twins Determined by Genetics?" National Institutes of Health, September 2015, https://ghr.nlm.nih.gov/primer/traits /twins; O. Lichtenstein, P. O. Olaussen, and A. B. Källén, "Twin Births to Mothers Who Are Twins: A Registry Based Study," *British Medical Journal* 312, no. 7035 (1996): 879–81.

11. N. L. Segal, *Twin Mythconceptions: False Beliefs, Fables, and Facts About Twins* (San Diego: Elsevier, 2017); N. L. Segal, "Twin Studies in Brazil: Projects and Plans," *Twin Research and Human Genetics* 20, no. 5 (2017): 481–88; E. L. Abel and M. L. Kruger, "Maternal and Paternal Age and Twinning in the United States, 2004–2008," *Journal of Perinatal Medicine* 40, no. 3 (2012): 237–39.

12. A. Alsema, "Colombia Implements Free Primary and Secondary Education," *Colombia Reports*, February 2, 2012, http://colombiareports.com/colombia -implements-free-primary-and-secondary-education/.

13. N. L. Segal, *Someone Else's Twin: The True Story of Babies Switched at Birth* (Amherst, NY: Prometheus Books, 2011).

14. S. J. Schwartz, B. L. Zamboanga, and R. S. Weisskirch, "Broadening the Study of the Self: Integrating the Study of Personal Identity and Cultural Identity," *Social and Personality Psychology Compass* 2, no. 2 (2008): 635–51.

15. Segal, *Someone Else's Twin*.

16. E. Burnstein, C. Crandall, and S. Kitayama, "Some Neo-Darwinian Decision Rules for Altruism: Weighing Cues for Inclusive Fitness as a Function of the Biological Importance of the Decision," *Journal of Personality and Social Psychology* 67, no. 5 (1994): 773–89; D. M. Buss, *Evolutionary Psychology: The New Science of the Mind* (Boston: Allyn & Bacon, 2015).

17. E. Schein and P. Bernstein, *Identical Strangers: A Memoir of Twins Separated and Reunited* (New York: Random House, 2007).

18. Steven Pinker, interview by Sally Satel, "Inside the Psychologist's Studio: Steven Pinker," Association for Psychological Science, KMP Productions video, May 22, 2015, http://www.psychologicalscience.org/index.php/publications /observer/obsonline/inside-the-psychologists-studio-steven-pinker.html.

19. M. de la Baume, "In France, a Baby Switch and a Lesson in Maternal Love," *New York Times Magazine*, February 24, 2015, https://www.nytimes.com/2015/02/25 /world/europe/in-france-a-baby-switch-and-a-test-of-a-mothers-love.html?_r=0.

20. N. L. Segal, *Indivisible by Two: Lives of Extraordinary Twins* (Cambridge, MA: Harvard University Press, 2005).

21. N. L. Segal, "Switched-at-Birth Twins in the Canary Islands: Revisited," *Twin Research and Human Genetics* 16, no. 4 (2013): 916–21.

22. Segal, *Someone Else's Twin*.

23. R. Bailey, "Mitochondria: Power Producers," ThoughtCo.com, July 21, 2017, http://biology.about.com/od/cellanatomy/ss/mitochondria.htm.

24. Segal, "Value of Twin Studies"; R. R. Rusting, "Baby Switching: An Under-Reported Problem That Needs to Be Recognized," *Journal of Healthcare Protection Management* 17, no. 1 (2001): 89–100; "Identification Techniques for Preventing Infant Mix-Ups," DNA Diagnostics Center, n.d., http://www.dnacenter.com/science-technology/articles/infant-mix-up.html.

25. L. Belkin, "Babies Switched at Birth," Motherlode: Adventures in Parenting (blog), *New York Times*, April 2, 2009, https://parenting.blogs.nytimes.com/2009/04/02/babies-switched-at-birth/?_r=0.

Chapter 2: Familiar Strangers

1. My formal criteria for classifying biologically unrelated siblings as virtual twins are: both individuals must have entered the family by age one; the age difference between the individuals cannot exceed nine months, which is the usual age difference between classmates; if the siblings are of school age they must be enrolled in the same grade, but not necessarily the same class or school—this is to preserve the twin-like nature of their relationship; and both individuals must be free of adverse birth events that may have affected intellectual performance. N. L. Segal, "Do Parents Favor Their Adoptive or Biological Children? Predictions from Kin Selection and Compensatory Models," *Evolution and Human Behavior* 36, no. 5: 379–88.

2. N. L. Segal, *Born Together—Reared Apart: The Landmark Minnesota Twin Study* (Cambridge, MA: Harvard University Press, 2012); N. L. Segal, S. A. McGuire, and J. H. Stohs, "What Virtual Twins Reveal About General Intelligence and Other Behaviors," *Personality and Individual Differences* 53, no. 4 (2012): 405–10.

3. L. Rimmer, "Who Do You Look Like? DNA and Family Resemblance Across Generations," Abroad in the Yard, 2017, http://www.abroadintheyard.com/dna-family-resemblance-across-generations/.

4. N. L. Segal and F. A. Cortez, "Born in Korea—Adopted Apart: Behavioral Development of Monozygotic Twins Raised in the United States and France," *Personality and Individual Differences* 70 (2014): 97–104.

5. N. L. Segal, "*Twinsters*, the Movie: Reared Apart Twins in Real Time," *Twin Research and Human Genetics* 19, no. 1 (2016): 80–85.

6. D. M. Buss, *Evolutionary Psychology: The New Science of the Mind*, 5th ed. (New York: Routledge, 2015).

7. I. E. D. Restrepo Millan, http://www.redacademica.edu.co/webcolegios/18/IEDRestrepoMillanM/PAGINAWEBPRINCIPAL.htm.

8. SENA is a public institution and agency of the Ministry of Labor of Colombia. It was created in 1957 to develop and expand a technically skilled workforce in that country. See https://www.volunteerscolombia.org/sena.

9. A. Hunter et al., "Elements of Morphology: Standard Terminology for the Ear," *American Journal of Medical Genetics Part A* 149, no. 1 (2009): 40–60.

10. Y. Hur, T. J. Bouchard, Jr., and D. T. Lykken, "Genetic and Environmental Influences on Morningness-Eveningness," *Personality and Individual Differences* 25, no. 5 (1998): 917–25.

11. J. Kaufman, "Mom Always Said to Share," *New York Times*, March 3, 2013, RE-1, http://www.nytimes.com/2013/03/03/realestate/siblings-as-roommates-mom-always-said-to-share.html?mcubz=0.

12. P. E. Hyman et al., "Childhood Functional Gastrointestinal Disorders: Neonate/Toddler," *Gastroenterology* 130, no. 5 (2006): 1519–26.

13. *Entrada* literally means "entry." The term gets its name from the missing part of tickets torn upon admission to a show.

14. Recent research shows that other genetic factors also affect the expression of male baldness. A. M. Hillmer et al., "Genome-Wide Scan and Fine-Mapping Linkage Study of Androgenetic Alopecia Reveals a Locus on Chromosome 3q26." *The American Journal of Human Genetics* 82, no. 3 (2008): 737–43.

15. Segal, *Born Together—Reared Apart.*

16. N. van der As et al., "Genetic Influences on Individual Differences in Exercise Behavior During Adolescence," *International Journal of Pediatrics* (2010), doi:10.1155/2010/138345.

17. K. S. Kendler et al., "The Genetic Epidemiology of Irrational Fears and Phobias in Men," *Archives of General Psychiatry* 58, no. 3 (2001): 257–65; N. L. Segal, *Entwined Lives: Twins and What They Tell Us About Human Behavior* (New York: Plume, 2000).

18. H. Mead, "Colombia Celebrates Holy Week," *Colombia Reports*, March 25, 2013, http://colombiareports.com/colombians-celebrate-holy-week/; "Roman Catholic Church Holy Week in Colombia 2015," vercalendario.info, http://www.vercalendario.info/en/when/easter-week-colombia-2015.html.

19. F. Galton, "The History of Twins as a Criterion of the Relative Powers of Nature and Nurture," *Journal of the Anthropological Institute* 5 (1875): 391–406; E. Moriarty, "Just Alike: Twins Separated at Birth," *48 Hours*, CBS, February 5, 2017, https://www.cbsnews.com/news/just-alike-twins-separated-at-birth/.

Chapter 3: Miles of Memories

1. R. L. Williams and K. G. Guerrieri, *Culture and Customs of Colombia* (Westport, CT: Greenwood, 1999); J. McDermott, "20 Years After Pablo: The Evolution of Colombia's Drug Trade," *InSight Crime*, December 3, 2013, http://www.insightcrime.org/news-analysis/20-years-after-pablo-the-evolution-of-colombias-drug-trade; "The 31 Places to Go in 2010," *New York Times*, January 7, 2010, http://www.nytimes.com/2010/01/10/travel/10places.html?pagewanted=all&mcubz=0.

2. A. Newman, "An Attention-Getter, Irresistibly Interactive," City Room (blog), *New York Times*, October 21, 2010, https://cityroom.blogs.nytimes.com /2010/10/21/an-attention-getter-irresistibly-interactive/?_r=0; "International Sculpture Center Lifetime Achievement Award Gala Honoring Fernando Botero," International Sculpture Center, 2012, http://www.sculpture.org /botero/botero_postscript.shtml.

3. "Shakira," Biography.com, April 27, 2017, https://www.biography.com /people/shakira-189151; "Sofía Vergara," IMDb, http://www.imdb.com/name /nm0005527/#actress; Leslie Stahl, "The Alzheimer's Laboratory," *60 Minutes*, November 27, 2016, http://www.cbsnews.com/news/60-minutes -alzheimers-disease-medellin-colombia-lesley-stahl/; L. Kiniry, "Will the Real Juan Valdez Please Stand Up?" Smithsonian.com, September 1, 2011, http:// www.smithsonianmag.com/people-places/will-the-real-juan-valdez-please -stand-up-68594542/.

4. Washington Office on Latin America, "Social Leaders Face a Wave of Attacks in Colombia. The Peace Accord's Credibility Hinges on Immediate Action to Stop It," Colombia Peace, December 5, 2016, http://colombiapeace.org; "U.N. Observers Called 'A Joke,'" *Los Angeles Times*, January 4, 2017, A4.

5. Reuters, "Colombia's ELN Commander Orders Ceasefire Beginning Sunday," Nasdaq, September 29, 2017, http://www.nasdaq.com/article/colombias -eln-rebel-commander-orders-ceasefire-beginning-sunday-20170929-00976 /amp.

6. N. L. Segal, *Born Together—Reared Apart: The Landmark Minnesota Twin Study* (Cambridge, MA: Harvard University Press, 2012).

7. Ibid., 94.

8. N. G. Waller et al., "Genetic and Environmental Influences on Religious Interests, Attitudes and Values: A Study of Twins Reared Apart and Together," *Psychological Science* 1, no. 2 (1990): 138–42; Segal, *Born Together—Reared Apart*, 144.

9. T. J. Bouchard et al., "Intrinsic and Extrinsic Religiousness: Genetic and Environmental Influences and Personality Correlates," *Twin Research and Human Genetics* 2, no. 2 (1999): 88–98. See also the other papers in this edition of *Twin Research and Human Genetics*.

10. Segal, *Born Together—Reared Apart*, 146.

11. M. E. Holmes, *Being You* (London: Austin & Mcauley, 2008), 155–57.

12. N. L. Segal, *Indivisible by Two: Lives of Extraordinary Twins* (Cambridge, MA: Harvard University Press, 2005).

13. Segal, *Born Together—Reared Apart*, 286, 326–27.

14. Ray Williams, interview by author, October, 19, 2015, Riverside, California.

15. Javier B., review of Hoyo del Aire, tripadvisor, January 1, 2016, https://www .tripadvisor.com/ShowUserReviews-g4458586-d9802349-r336483401 -Hoyo_del_Aire-La_Paz_Cesar_Department.html.

16. "Leshmaniasis FAQs," US Centers for Disease Control and Prevention, January 10, 2013, https://www.cdc.gov/parasites/leishmaniasis/gen_info/faqs.html.

17. M. J. R. Garcia, "Colombian National Army Develops Methodology to Fight Leishmaniasis," *Díalogo*, March 4, 2016, https://dialogo-americas.com/en/articles/colombian-national-army-develops-methodology-fight-leishmaniasis/pdf_print.

18. A. Scheinfeld, *Twins and Supertwins* (New York: J. P. Lippincott, 1967); M. Joye, *He Was Not My Son* (New York: Rinehart, 1954); N. L. Segal, *Someone Else's Twin: The True Story of Babies Switched at Birth* (Amherst, NY: Prometheus, 2011).

19. Ibid.

20. D. Roos, "Skin Grafts," HowStuffWorks.com, November 4, 2009, http://health.howstuffworks.com/skin-care/information/anatomy/skin-graft2.htm.

21. M. F. A. Woodruff and B. Lennox, "Reciprocal Skin Grafts in a Pair of Twins Showing Blood Chimaerism," *The Lancet* 274, no. 7101 (1959): 476–78.

22. D. Klein, "Living History—Autobiography: Genetics and Environment from a Personal History," *American Journal of Medical Genetics* 37, no. 3 (1990): 323–35.

23. Joye, *He Was Not My Son*.

24. N.L. Segal, *Someone Else's Twin: The True Story of Babies Switched at Birth* (Amherst, NY: Prometheus, 2011).

25. Joye, *He Was Not My Son*.

26. Segal, *Indivisible by Two*.

27. Ibid.

28. Jan Batory, dir., *The Two Who Stole the Moon*, Syrena Film, 1962; C. Domonoske, "A Tale of Twin Brothers: Poland's Mourned Leader and Lonely Mastermind," *The Two-Way: Breaking News from NPR*, February 7, 2016, http://www.npr.org/sections/thetwo-way/2016/02/07/465926224/a-tale-of-twin-brothers-polands-mourned-leader-and-lonely-mastermind.

29. Johnathan Josephs, prod., "Twins Reunited After 70 Years Apart," *BBC News*, September 14, 2015, http://www.bbc.com/news/av/world-europe-34209018/twins-reunited-after-70-years-apart.; A. Harrold, "Twins Separated After WWII Are Reunited 70 Years Later," *Independent* (UK), September 15, 2015, http://www.independent.co.uk/life-style/health-and-families/twins-born-following-second-world-war-and-then-separated-are-reunited-after-70-years-apart-10500097.html.

30. Segal, *Indivisible by Two*.

31. Segal, *Someone Else's Twin*, 169–88.

32. *Convivencia* referred originally to the generally peaceful coexistence or cohabitation of Jews, Muslims, and Christians during the early years of medi-

eval Spain. While individuals from the different communities interacted and engaged in business together, there was competition and jealousy that sometimes devolved into hatred. However, this period, which lasted from 711 to 1492, was later marked by Jewish persecution, conversion, expulsion, and killings once the "Golden Age" began to dissolve. J. Rosenbaum, "Foreword," vii–ix; V. B. Mann, "Preface," xi–xiii; and B. R. Gampel, "Jews, Christians, and Muslims in Medieval Iberia: *Convivencia* Through the Eyes of Sephardic Jews," 11–37, in *Convivencia: Jews, Muslims, and Christians in Medieval Spain*, ed. V. B. Mann, T. F. Glick, and J. D. Dodds (New York: George Braziller, 1992); J. Ray, "Beyond Tolerance and Persecution: Reassessing Our Approach to Medieval *Convivencia*," *Jewish Social Studies* 11, no. 2 (2005): 1–18.

33. Segal, *Someone Else's Twin*.

Chapter 4: The Friends Investigate

1. Some material in this chapter is based upon information from *Séptimo Día*, the television program that featured the twins' story on October 26, 2014 (Part 1), and November 3, 2014 (Part 2), Paolo Rojas, prod., "Crossed Lives," *Séptimo Día*, Caracol Televisión. Caracol Televisión is a television network in Colombia, privately owned by the Santo Domingo Group.

2. Strycon is a multidisciplinary organization of consulting engineers.

3. Type A blood results when children inherit the dominant A gene from both parents, or the A gene from one parent and the recessive O gene from the other parent. Type O blood results when children inherit two O genes, one from each parent. The likelihood that fraternal twins and siblings would both be type A or type O depends upon the blood types of their parents. If, for example, both parents had two A genes or two O genes, then all their children would be type A or type O. If both parents had one A gene and one O gene, then an average of 75 percent of their children would be type A (25 percent would be AA and 50 percent would be AO; dominant genes overshadow the recessive genes) and an average of 25 percent would be type O. Unrelated individuals can have matching blood types, but not because of common descent. The positive or negative expression of each blood type stands for Rhesus, or Rh. The Rh factor is a protein on the surface of our red blood cells; positive refers to its presence and negative to its absence. Positive is the dominant form of the gene, and negative is the recessive form. Unrelated individuals can match on this factor, as well.

4. R. Plomin et al., *Behavioral Genetics*, 7th ed. (New York: Worth, 2016).

5. E. J. Yunis and J. J. Yunis, *El ADN en la identificación Humana* (Bogotá: Editorial Ternis, 2002).

6. S. J. Min et al., "Birth Weight References for Twins," *American Journal of Obstetrics and Gynecology* 182, no. 5 (2000): 1250–57.

7. These twins and other pairs from China were adopted by different families living in the United States and elsewhere, partly because of China's one-child policy and preference for male children, leading to the abandonment of thousands of baby girls, twins among them. I have been tracking the development of these pairs as it unfolds, in the only reared-apart twin project to do so. Also see N. L. Segal, *Indivisible by Two: Lives of Extraordinary Twins* (Cambridge, MA: Harvard University Press, 2005).

8. N. L. Segal, *Someone Else's Twin: The True Story of Babies Switched at Birth* (Amherst, NY: Prometheus, 2011).

Chapter 5: Revelations

1. N. L. Segal, "Twin, Adoption and Family Methods as Approaches to the Evolution of Individual Differences," in *The Evolution of Personality and Individual Differences*, ed. D. M. Buss and P. Hawley, 303–37 (New York: Oxford University Press, 2011). A small group of twins who had experienced the loss of both their twin and a spouse registered the same levels of high-intensity grief. Too few twins had lost children (fortunately) to permit a comparison of twin loss and child loss.

2. Comment from a surviving twin as part of an ongoing study of twin loss, conducted in my Twin Studies Center at California State University, Fullerton.

3. Sharon and Sita, "If I Had My Life to Live Again I'd Find You Sooner," FoundMySister, April 24, 2017, http://foundmysister.weebly.com/our-adventures.

4. C. Tomassini et al., "Risk of Suicide in Twins: 51-Year Follow-up Study," *British Medical Journal* 327, no. 7411 (2003): 373–74.

5. D. Lieberman, J. Tooby, and L. Cosmides, "The Architecture of Human Kin Detection," *Nature* 445, no. 7129 (2007): 727–31.

6. E. Burnstein, "Altruism and Genetic Relatedness," in *The Handbook of Evolutionary Psychology*, ed. D. M. Buss, 528–51 (Hoboken, NJ: John Wiley, 2005).

7. N. L. Segal, *Born Together—Reared Apart: The Landmark Minnesota Twin Study* (Cambridge, MA: Harvard University Press, 2012).

8. N. L. Segal, J. L. Graham, and U. Ettinger, "Unrelated Look-Alikes: A Replicated Study of Personality Similarity and New Qualitative Findings on Social Relatedness," *Personality and Individual Differences* 55 (2013): 169–76; N. L. Segal, *Entwined Lives: Twins and What They Tell Us About Human Behavior* (New York: Plume, 2000).

9. J. Ryall, "Japanese Man Born to Wealthy Parents Is Accidentally Switched at Birth and Endures Life of Poverty," *Telegraph* (Asia ed.), November 28, 2013, http://www.telegraph.co.uk/news/worldnews/asia/japan/10481091/Japanese-man-born-to-wealthy-parents-is-accidentally-switched-at-birth-and-endures-life-of-poverty.html.

10. "Switched at Birth Japanese Man Awarded Payout by Hospital," *Sydney Morning Herald*, November 28, 2013, http://www.smh.com.au/world

/switched-at-birth-japanese-man-awarded-payout-by-hospital-20131128
-2ye0i.html.

11. Y. S. Matsumoto, "Notes on Primogeniture in Postwar Japan," in *Japanese
Culture: Its Development and Characteristics*, ed. R. J. Smith and R. K.
Beardsley (London, UK: Routledge, 2004), 55–69.

12. J. Mann, "Nurturance or Negligence: Maternal Psychology and Behavioral
Preference Among Preterm Twins," in *The Adapted Mind: Evolutionary Psy-
chology and the Evolution of Culture*, ed. J. H. Barkow, L. Cosmides, and
J. Tooby (New York: Oxford University Press, 1992), 367–90.

13. G. Pison, C. Monden, and J. Smits, "Twinning Rates in Developed Countries:
Trends and Explanations," *Population and Development Review* 41, no. 4
(2015): 629–49; L. S. Forbes, "The Evolutionary Biology of Spontaneous
Abortion in Humans," *Trends in Ecology and Evolution* 12, no. 11 (1997):
446–50.

14. J. G. Hall, "Twinning," *The Lancet* 362, no. 9385 (2003): 735–43; K.
Kleinhaus et al., "Paternal Age and Twinning in the Jerusalem Perinatal
Study," *European Journal of Obstetrics & Gynecology and Reproductive Biol-
ogy* 141, no. 2 (2008): 119–22; E. L. Abel and M. L. Kruger, "Maternal and
Paternal Age and Twinning in the United States, 2004–2008," *Journal of
Perinatal Medicine* 40, no. 3 (2012): 237–39.

15. A. Campbell, "Aggression," in *Evolutionary Psychology: The New Science of
the Mind*, 5th ed., ed. D. M. Buss (New York: Routledge, 2015), 628–52.

16. Assisted reproductive technology (ART) has been largely responsible for the
dramatic rise in fraternal twinning, but it has also increased identical twinning, although to a lesser degree. Identical twinning rates are between two
and twelve times higher with ART, relative to the natural identical twinning
rate of .3–.4 percent. K. I. Aston et al., "Monozygotic Twinning Associated
with Assisted Reproductive Technologies: A Review," *Reproduction* 136,
no. 4 (2008): 377–86.

17. M. A. Joyce et al., "Births: Final Data for 2013," *National Vital Statistics Reports* 64, no. 1 (2015): 1–68; A. D. Kulkarni et al., "Fertility Treatments and
Multiple Births in the United States," *New England Journal of Medicine* 369,
no. 23 (2013): 2218–25.

18. Segal, *Entwined Lives*; P. Lichtenstein, P. O. Olaussen, and A. B. Källén,
"Twin Births to Mothers Who Are Twins: A Registry-Based Study," *British
Medical Journal* 312, no. 7035 (1996): 879–81.

19. N. L. Segal, *Indivisible by Two: Lives of Extraordinary Twins* (Cambridge,
MA: Harvard University Press, 2005); N. L. Segal and B. Marcheco-Teruel,
"'Street of Twins': Multiple Births in Cuba" and "The Cuban Twin Registry:
An Update," *Twin Research and Human Genetics* 17, no. 4 (2014): 347–53.

20. It is not uncommon for family members' impressions of twin type to conflict
with results provided by DNA tests. Most often, identical twins are incorrectly
classified as fraternal by their parents and other people who know them well

and are very sensitive to subtle behavioral and/or physical differences between the two.

21. A. Fetters, "The Origins of Gabriel Garcia Marquez's Magic Realism," *Atlantic Monthly*, April 17, 2014; O. Kaplan, "García Márquez' Magical Realism: It's Real," Political Violence @ a Glance, May 16, 2014, http://politicalviolenceataglance.org/2014/05/16/garcia-marquez-magical-realism-its-real/.

22. For the announcement of the branding campaign, see "Colombia, Magical Realism," http://www.procolombia.co/en/news/colombia-magical-realism.

23. N. L. Segal, *Born Together—Reared Apart: The Landmark Minnesota Twin Study* (Cambridge, MA: Harvard University Press, 2012); P. A. Vernon et al., "A Behavioral Genetic Investigation of Humor Styles and Their Correlations with the Big-5 Personality Dimensions," *Personality and Individual Differences* 44, no. 5 (2008): 1116–25; J. H. Stubbe et al., "Genetic Influences on Exercise Participation in 37,051 Twin Pairs from Seven Countries," *PloS ONE* 1, no. 1 (2006): e22, https://doi.org/10.1371/journal.pone.0000022; D. P. Moloney, T. J. Bouchard, and N. L. Segal, "A Genetic and Environmental Analysis of the Vocational Interests of Monozygotic and Dizygotic Twins Reared Apart," *Journal of Vocational Behavior* 39, no. 1 (1991): 76–109.

24. N. Eynon et al., "Genes and Elite Athletes: A Roadmap for Future Research," *Journal of Physiology* 589, no. 13 (2011): 3063–70; N. L. Segal, "A Tale of Two Sisters," *Psychology Today*, November–December 2015, 68–75, 88.

25. J. Shields, *Monozygotic Twins: Brought Up Apart and Together* (London: Oxford University Press, 1962); Segal, *Born Together—Reared Apart*.

26. M. F. MacDorman, T. J. Matthews, and E. Declercq, "Home Births in the United States, 1990–2009," *National Center for Health Statistics Data Brief* No. 84 (2012), https://www.cdc.gov/nchs/products/databriefs/db84.htm.

27. J. M. Snowden et al., "Planned Out-of-Hospital Birth and Birth Outcomes," *New England Journal of Medicine* 373, no. 27 (2015): 2642–53; American College of Obstetricians and Gynecologists, "Planned Home Birth," *Obstetrics and Gynecology* 128, no. 2 (2016): 420–21.

28. MacDorman et al., "Home Births in the United States, 1990–2009."

29. D. Boucher et al., "Staying Home to Give Birth: Why Women in the United States Choose Home Birth," *Journal of Midwifery & Women's Health* 54, no. 2 (2009): 119–26.

30. J. D. Davis et al., "Pregnancy Anxieties and Natural Recognition in Baby-Switching," *British Journal of Nursing* 10, no. 11 (2001): 718–26.

31. Boucher et al., "Staying Home to Give Birth"; R. R. Rusting, "Baby Switching: An Underreported Problem That Needs to Be Recognized," *Journal of Healthcare Protection Management: Publication of the International Association for Hospital Security* 17, no. 1 (2000): 89; "Identification Techniques for Preventing Infant Mix-Ups," DNA Diagnostic Center, May 3, 2016, https://dnacenter.com/science-technology/articles/infant-mix-up-3.html.

Chapter 6: Finding the Colombian Four

1. "Crossed Lives: Two Pairs of Twins Were Separated for 25 Years," Caracol TV (Colombia, South America), October 26, 2014, http://www.noticiascaracol .com/septimo-dia/vidas-cruzadas-dos-parejas-de-gemelos-estuvieron -separadas-25-anos. Caracol Internacional is also available in nearly eighty countries across five continents, but the twins' story was not widely distributed.
2. N. L. Segal, *Someone Else's Twin: The True Story of Babies Switched at Birth* (Amherst, NY: Prometheus, 2011).
3. "Separate Twins Shall Face Legal Battle to be Compensated: Lawyer," Caracol TV (Colombia, South America), October 26, 2014, http://www.noti ciascaracol.com/septimo-dia/gemelos-separados-deberan-librar-batalla -juridica-para-ser-indemnizados-abogado.
4. N. L. Segal and F. A. Cortez, "Born in Korea—Adopted Apart: Behavioral Development of Monozygotic Twins Raised in the United States and France," *Personality and Individual Differences* 70 (November 2014): 97–104; P. Pope-noe, "Twins Reared Apart," *Journal of Heredity* 13, no. 3 (1922): 142–44; N. L. Segal, J. H. Stohs, and K. Evans, "Chinese Twin Children Reared Apart and Reunited: First Prospective Study of Co-Twin Reunions," *Adoption Quarterly* 14, no. 1 (2011): 61–78.
5. Titus Maccius Plautus, *Menaechemi* (The Menaechmus Brothers), play, Archive of Performances of Greek and Roman Drama, http://www.apgrd.ox .ac.uk/productions/canonical-plays/menaechmi-the-menaechmus-brothers /500. The play was first performed in 1486 at the Palazzo del Corte (Ferrera, Emilia-Romana, Italy).
6. J. Weber-Lehman et al., "Finding the Needle in the Haystack: Differentiating 'Identical' Twins in Paternity Testing and Forensics by Ultra-Deep Next Generation Sequencing," *Forensic Sciences International* 9 (March 2014): 42–46. This technique could also distinguish identical twin mothers from identical twin aunts, but the need to do this would be rare since only one is likely to be pregnant at a given time. A hypothetical exceptional case in which this could be valuable might involve an unwed identical twin mother who secretly relinquished a baby for adoption and contested her relationship to the child when the child tried to find her.
7. N. L. Segal, *Twin Mythconceptions: False Beliefs, Fables, and Facts About Twins* (San Diego: Elsevier, 2017).
8. N. L. Segal, *Entwined Lives: Twins and What They Tell Us About Human Behavior* (New York: Plume, 2000).
9. N. L. Segal and W. D. Marelich, "Social Closeness and Gift Giving by MZ and DZ Twin Parents Toward Nieces and Nephews: An Update," *Personality and Individual Differences* 50 (2011): 101–5; D. M. Buss, *Evolutionary Psychology: The New Science of the Mind*, 4th ed. (Boston: Allyn & Bacon, 2012).
10. Segal, *Born Together—Reared Apart*.

11. Segal, *Born Together—Reared Apart*; K. S. Kendler, C. O. Gardner, and C. A. Prescott, "A Population-Based Twin Study of Self-Esteem and Gender," *Psychological Medicine* 28, no. 6 (1998): 1403–9; T. J. Bouchard, Jr., et al., "Sources of Human Psychological Differences: The Minnesota Study of Twins Reared Apart," *Science* 250, no. 4978 (1990): 223–28; M. McGue, J. W. Vaupel, N. Holm, and B. Harvald, "Longevity Is Moderately Heritable in a Sample of Danish Twins Born 1870–1880," *Journal of Gerontology* 48, no. 6 (1993): B237–44.

12. Segal, *Twin Mythconceptions.*

13. Segal, *Entwined Lives.*

14. N. L. Segal with A. Altowaiji and C. K. Ihara, "The Birth of Octuplets: A Research Puzzle," *Twin Research and Human Genetics* 12, no. 3 (2009): 328–31.

15. A. Tellegen et al., "Personality Similarity in Twins Reared Apart and Together," *Journal of Personality and Social Psychology* 54, no. 6 (1988): 1031–39.

16. N. L. Segal, *Indivisible by Two: Lives of Extraordinary Twins* (Cambridge, MA: Harvard University Press, 2005); N. L. Segal, "*Twinsters*, the Movie: Reared Apart Twins in Real Time," *Twin Research and Human Genetics* 19, no. 1 (2016): 80–85; Segal, *Born Together—Reared Apart*; N. L. Segal and M. Diamond, "Identical Reared Apart Twins Concordant for Transsexuality," *Journal of Experimental and Clinical Medicine* 6, no. 2 (2014): 74.

17. American Psychiatric Association, *The Diagnostic and Statistical Manual (DSM-5)*, 5th ed. (Arlington, VA: American Psychiatric Association, 2013); M. Diamond, "Transsexuality Among Twins: Identity Concordance, Transition, Rearing and Orientation," *International Journal of Transgenderism* 14, no. 1 (2013): 24–38.

18. T. J. Polderman et al., "Meta-Analysis of the Heritability of Human Traits Based on Fifty Years of Twin Studies," *Nature Genetics* 47, no. 7 (2015): 702–9; N. G. Waller and P. R. Shaver, "The Importance of Nongenetic Influences on Romantic Love Styles: A Twin-Family Study," *Psychological Science* 5, no. 5 (1994): 268–74.

19. H. Fisher, A. Aron, and L. L. Brown, "Romantic Love: An fMRI Study of a Neural Mechanism for Mate Choice," *Journal of Comparative Neurology* 493, no. 1 (2005): 58–62. The negotiator is intuitive and creative, and knows the thoughts and feelings of others; the director is devoted to personal and professional goals, with less interest in personal connections; the builder is people oriented, with loyalty to family, friends, and colleagues; and the explorer is energetic and fast paced, and may overlook the interests of others. H. Fisher, "What's Your Love Type?" reprinted from *O, the Oprah Magazine* at CNN .com, November 16, 2007, http://www.cnn.com/2007/LIVING/personal/11 /12/o.love.types/index.html?_s=PM:LIVING.

20. N G. Martin et al., "Transmission of Social Attitudes," *Proceedings of the National Academy of Sciences* 83, no. 12 (1986): 4364–68; R. Plomin et al., *Behavioral Genetics*, 7th ed. (New York: Worth, 2016); V. Jocklin, M. McGue, and D. T. Lykken, "Personality and Divorce: A Genetic Analysis," *Journal of Personality and Social Psychology* 71, no. 2 (1996): 288.

21. N. L. Segal, S. A. McGuire, and J. Hoven Stohs, "What Virtual Twins Reveal About General Intelligence and Other Behaviors," *Personality and Individual Differences* 53 (2012): 405–10.

22. Segal, *Entwined Lives*; Segal, Stohs, and Evans, "Chinese Twin Children Reared Apart and Reunited."

23. M. Herle et al., "Parental Reports of Infant and Child Eating Behaviors Are Not Affected by Their Beliefs About Their Twins' Zygosity," *Behavior Genetics* 46, no. 6 (2016): 763–71.

24. A. M. Burton and V. Bruce, "I Recognize Your Face but I Can't Remember Your Name: A Simple Explanation?" *British Journal of Psychology* 83, no. 1 (1992): 45–60; M. Calabria et al., "The Missing Link Between Faces and Names: Evidence from Alzheimer's Disease Patients," *Brain and Cognition* 80, no. 2 (2012): 250–56.

25. "The Difference Between Translating and Interpreting," Scientific Language, 2017, http://www.languagescientific.com/translation-services/multilingual-interpreting-services/interpreting-vs-translation-services.html.

26. Segal, *Born Together—Reared Apart*.

27. T. Spector, *Identically Different: Why We Can Change Our Genes* (New York: Overlook, 2012); A. H. Wong, I. I. Gottesman, and A. Petronis, "Phenotypic Differences in Genetically Identical Organisms: The Epigenetic Perspective," *Human Molecular Genetics* 14, suppl. 1 (2005): R11–R18; A. Petronis et al., "Monozygotic Twins Exhibit Numerous Epigenetic Differences: Clues to Twin Discordance?" *Schizophrenia Bulletin* 29, no. 1 (2003): 169; D. Mastroeni et al., "Epigenetic Differences in Cortical Neurons from a Pair of Monozygotic Twins Discordant for Alzheimer's Disease," *PloS ONE* 4, no. 8 (2009): e6617. A new twin study from Denmark that used a novel statistical technique estimated higher identical twin similarity for schizophrenia, but it still did not reach 100 percent; see R. Hilker et al., "Heritability of Schizophrenia and Schizophrenia Spectrum Based on the Nationwide Danish Twin Register," *Biological Psychiatry* (2017), DOI:10.1016/j.biopsych.2017.08.017.

28. G. Felsenfeld, "A Brief History of Epigenetics," *Cold Spring Harbor Perspectives in Biology* 6, no. 1 (2014): a018200; Plomin et al., *Behavioral Genetics*.

29. L. Hou et al., "Environmental Chemical Exposures and Human Epigenetics," *International Journal of Epidemiology* 41, no. 1 (2012): 79–105.

30. A number of molecular events can affect gene expression. A small chemical group, called a methyl group, can attach to a gene and silence it even though

the gene is still present. Histone acetylation, the addition of a DNA-packaging acetyl group to a histone protein, also affects how genes get expressed, but both processes are reversible. Spector, *Identically Different*; "Research Kits: Histone Acetylation/Deacetylation," Epigentek, 2017, https://www.epigentek .com/catalog/acetylation-deacetylation-c-75_24.html; D. Simmons, "Epigenetic Influences and Disease," *Nature Education* 1, no. 1 (2008): 6.

31. Current technology makes it possible to sequence every DNA methylation mark in the human genome.

32. E. L. Dempster et al., "Disease-Associated Epigenetic Changes in Monozygotic Twins Discordant for Schizophrenia and Bipolar Disorder," *Human Molecular Genetics* (2011): ddr416; G. C. Townsend et al., "Epigenetic Influences May Explain Dental Differences in Monozygotic Twin Pairs," *Australian Dental Journal* 50, no. 2 (2005): 95–100; C. Selmi, "Primary Biliary Cirrhosis in Monozygotic and Dizygotic Twins: Genetics, Epigenetics, and Environment," *Gastroenterology* 127, no. 2 (2004): 485–92.

33. H. Heyn, "DNA Methylation Profiling in Breast Cancer Discordant Identical Twins Identifies DOK7 as Novel Epigenetic Biomarker," *Carcinogenesis* 34, no. 1 (2012): 102–8; Segal, *Twin Mythconceptions*.

34. S. Robertson, "What Is DNA Methylation?" *Medical Life Sciences News*, September 17, 2015, https://www.news-medical.net/life-sciences/What-is-DNA -Methylation.aspx; B. T. Heijmans et al., "Persistent Epigenetic Differences Associated with Prenatal Exposure to Famine in Humans," *Proceedings of the National Academy of Sciences* 105, no. 44 (2008): 17046–49; M. Balter, "Can Epigenetics Explain Homosexuality Puzzle?" *Science* 350, no. 6257 (2015): 148.

35. D. Martino et al., "Longitudinal, Genome-Scale Analysis of DNA Methylation in Twins from Birth to 18 Months of Age Reveals Rapid Epigenetic Change in Early Life and Pair-Specific Effects of Discordance," *Genome Biology* 14, no. 5 (2013): R42; Y. J. Loke et al., "The Peri/Postnatal Epigenetic Twins Study (PETS)," *Twin Research and Human Genetics* 16, no. 1 (2013): 13–20. Dr. Jeffrey Craig was at the Murdoch Children's Research Institute, in Melbourne, at the time of our study.

36. R. Saffery et al., "Cohort Profile: The Peri/Post-Natal Epigenetic Twins Study," *International Journal of Epidemiology* 41, no. 1 (2012): 55–61; L. Gordon et al., "Neonatal DNA Methylation Profile in Human Twins Is Specified by a Complex Interplay Between Intrauterine Environmental and Genetic Factors, Subject to Tissue-Specific Influence," *Genome Research* 22, no. 8 (2012): 1395–1406.

Chapter 7: Discoveries

1. S. L. Farber, *Identical Twins Reared Apart: A Reanalysis* (New York: Basic Books, 1980), 65, 67. Identical female reared-together twins in Finland show average height and weight differences of .62 inches and 11.53 pounds, re-

spectively. See N. L. Segal, *Someone Else's Twin: The True Story of Babies Switched at Birth* (Amherst, NY: Prometheus, 2011), 245–46.

2. R. S. Hartley and J. Hitti, "Birth Order and Delivery Interval: Analysis of Twin Pair Perinatal Outcomes," *Journal of Maternal-Fetal and Neonatal Medicine* 17, no. 6 (2006): 375–80; B. A. Armson et al., "Determinants of Perinatal Mortality and Serious Neonatal Morbidity in the Second Twin," *Obstetrics & Gynecology* 108, no. 3, pt. 1 (2006): 556–64.

3. C. M. Ruitberg, D. J. Reeder, and J. M. Butler, "STRBase: A Short Tandem Repeat DNA Database for the Human Identity Testing Community," *Nucleic Acids Research* 29, no. 1 (2001): 320–22.

4. Although DNA can be easily extracted from saliva samples, Dr. Emilio J. Yunis used the twins' DNA from blood samples because blood contains more cells than saliva and therefore yields more DNA. When he compared twenty-one STRs (short tandem repeats) of the presumed identical partners, they matched exactly. E. J. Yunis and G.A.C. Pérez, Servicios Médicos Yunis Turbay y Cia S. En C. Instituto Genética (DNA Test Report, October 3, 2014). This finding proved beyond question that Jorge and William, and Carlos and Wilber were identical twins—and that the young men who had grown up together (Jorge and Carlos, and William and Wilber) were not fraternal twins as they and their families had believed; in fact, they were not even related.

5. N. L. Segal, "Psychological Features of Human Reproductive Cloning: A Twin-Based Perspective," *Psychiatric Times* 23, no. 20 (2006): 22.

6. N. L. Segal, *Twin Mythconceptions: False Beliefs, Fables, and Facts About Twins* (San Diego: Elsevier, 2017); H. C. McNamara et al., "A Review of the Mechanisms and Evidence for Typical and Atypical Twinning," *American Journal of Obstetrics and Gynecology* 214, no. 2 (2016): 172–91.

7. During the taping of the TV show *Séptimo Día*, Ana called Carlos "Wilber's little brother"—this may have been a term of endearment or a reference to birth size, rather than birth order.

8. M. R. Yalçin et al., "The Significance of Birth Weight Difference in Discordant Twins: A Level to Standardize?" *Acta Obstetricia et Gynecologica Scandinavica* 77, no. 1 (1998): 28–31; F. M. Breathnach et al. "Definition of Intertwin Birth Weight Discordance" *Obstetrics and Gynecology* 118, no. 1 (2011): 94–103; American College of Obstetricians and Gynecologists and Society for Maternal-Fetal Medicine, "Multifetal Gestations: Twin, Triplet, and Higher-Order Multifetal Pregnancies," *Obstetrics and Gynecology* (ACOG Practice Bulletin 169) 128, no. 4 (2016): e131–46.

9. Apgar scores give ratings of 0, 1, or 2 across five newborn physical characteristics; a score in the 7 to 10 range is considered to be good. See "Your Child's First Test: The APGAR," American Pregnancy Association, 2016, http://americanpregnancy.org/labor-and-birth/apgar-test/.

10. M. P. Umstad, personal communication with author, October 10, 2016.

11. L. Dubois et al., "Genetic and Environmental Contributions to Weight, Height, and BMI from Birth to 19 Years of Age: An International Study of over 12,000 Twin Pairs," *PLoS ONE* 7, no. 2 (2012): e30153.

12. J. Dineshshankar et al., "Lip Prints: Role in Forensic Odontology," *Journal of Pharmacy and Bioallied Sciences* 5, suppl. 1 (2013): S95–S97; J. Leibach, "What Your Lips Might Say About You," *Science Friday*, October 13, 2016, http://www.sciencefriday.com/articles/what-your-lips-might-say-about-you /?utm_source=Weekly+Newsletter+List&utm_campaign=76c1f716a5 -Newsletter_Oct_14_2016&utm_medium=email&utm_term=0_10d8eab927 -76c1f716a5-53948761; R. V. Prabhu et al., "Cheiloscopy: Revisited," *Journal of Forensic Dental Sciences* 4, no. 1 (2012): 47–52.

13. J. V. Peluchette, K. Karl, and K. Rust, "Dressing to Impress: Beliefs and Attitudes Regarding Workplace Attire," *Journal of Business and Psychology* 21, no. 1 (2006): 45–63; H. Wolf et al., "Self-monitoring and Personality: A Behavioural-Genetic Study," *Personality and Individual Differences* 47, no. 1 (2009): 25–29; K. Kendler, C. O. Gardner, and C. Prescott, "A Population-Based Twin Study of Self-esteem and Gender," *Psychological Medicine* 28, no. 6 (1998): 1403–9.

14. H. Alibeik and S. A. Angaji, "Developmental Aspects of Left-handedness," *Australian Journal of Basic and Applied Sciences* 4, no. 5 (2010): 877–81; C. E. Boklage, *How New Humans Are Made* (Singapore: World Scientific, 2010).

15. N. L. Segal, *Entwined Lives: Twins and What They Tell Us About Human Behavior* (New York: Plume, 2000); L. Mealey, R. Bridgstock, and G. C. Townsend, "Symmetry and Perceived Facial Attractiveness: A Monozygotic Co-Twin Comparison," *Journal of Personality and Social Psychology* 76, no. 1 (1999): 157–65; M. T. Liu et al., "Factors Contributing to Facial Asymmetry in Identical Twins," *Plastic and Reconstructive Surgery* 134, no. 4 (2014): 638–46.

16. Boklage, *How New Humans Are Made*; J. Levy, personal communication with author, October 20, 2016; L. Mastin, "An Investigation of Handedness—Some Facts, Myths, Truths, Opinions and Research," RightLeftRightWrong?, 2012, http://www.rightleftrightwrong.com/statistics.html.

17. Segal, *Twin Mythconceptions*; M. Roizen, "How Are Fingerprints Formed in the Womb?" sharecare, n.d., https://www.sharecare.com/health/fetal-development -basics-pregnancy/how-fingerprints-formed-in-womb; G. Steinman, "Mechanisms of Twinning: I. Effect of Environmental Diversity on Genetic Expression in Monozygotic Multifetal Pregnancies," *Journal of Reproductive Medicine* 46, no. 5 (2001): 467–72; A. K. Jain, S. Prabhakar, and S. Pankanti, "On the Similarity of Identical Twin Fingerprints," *Pattern Recognition* 35, no. 11 (2002): 2653–63; B. Karmakar, I. Malkin, and E. Kobyliansky, "Inheritance of 18 Quantitative Dermatoglyphic Traits Based on Factors in MZ and DZ Twins," *Anthropologischer Anzeiger* 68, no. 2 (2011): 185–93; T. Reed, R. J. Viken, and S. A. Rinehart, "High Heritability of Fingertip Arch

Patterns in Twin-Pairs," *American Journal of Medical Genetics Part A* 140, no. 3 (2006): 263–71.

18. W. J. Babler, "Quantitative Differences in Morphogenesis of Human Epidermal Ridges," *Birth Defects Original Article Series* 15, no. 6 (1979): 199–208; K. Wertheim and A. Maceo, "The Critical Stage of Friction Ridge and Pattern Formation," *Journal of Forensic Identification* 36/51, no. 1 (2002): 35–85.

19. H. S. Bracha et al. "Second-Trimester Markers of Fetal Size in Schizophrenia: A Study of Monozygotic Twins," *American Journal of Psychiatry* 149, no. 10 (1992): 1355–61.

20. K. Packard, "Deciphering Your Own Fingerprints—The Tented Arch," pt. 3, American Academy of Hand Analysis, August 30, 2010, http://academyofhand analysis.org/deciphering-your-fingerprints-the-tented-arch/.

21. D. T. Lykken, "The Diagnosis of Zygosity in Twins," *Behavior Genetics* 8, no. 5 (1978): 437–73.

22. A. Petronis, "Epigenetics as a Unifying Principle in the Aetiology of Complex Traits and Diseases," *Nature* 465, no. 7299 (2010): 721; N. L. Segal et al., "Identical Twins Doubly Exchanged at Birth—Genetic and Environmental Influences on the Adult Epigenome," *Epigenomics* 9, no. 1 (2017): 5–12.

23. M. Jolly et al., "The Risks Associated with Pregnancy in Women Aged 35 Years or Older," *Human Reproduction* 15, no. 11 (2000): 2433–37.

24. E. E. Birch and A. R. O'Connor, "Preterm Birth and Visual Development," *Seminars in Neonatology* 6, no. 6 (December 2001): 487–97; S. J. Woo et al., "A Co-Twin Study of the Relative Effect of Birth Weight and Gestational Age on Retinopathy of Prematurity," *Eye* 25, no. 11 (2011): 1478; H. L. Koch, *Twins and Twin Relations* (Chicago: University of Chicago Press, 1966); W. H. Knobloch et al., "Eye Findings in Twins Reared Apart," *Ophthalmic Paediatrics and Genetics* 5, no. 1–2 (1985): 59–66.

25. H. Hinrichsen et al., "Social Anxiety and Coping Strategies in the Eating Disorders," *Eating Behaviors* 4, no. 2 (2003): 117–26; I. Jáuregui-Lobera et al., "Psychometric Properties of Spanish Version of the Three-Factor Eating Questionnaire-R18 (Tfeq-Sp) and Its Relationship with Some Eating- and Body Image-Related Variables," *Nutrients* 6, no. 12 (2014): 5619–35; B. M. Neale, S. E. Mazzeo, and C. M. Bulik, "A Twin Study of Dietary Restraint, Disinhibition and Hunger: An Examination of the Eating Inventory (Three Factor Eating Questionnaire)," *Twin Research* 6, no. 6 (2003): 471–78; S. J. Elder et al., "Genetic and Environmental Influences on Eating Behavior—A Study of Twins Reared Apart," *The FASEB Journal* 23, no. 1 (2009): conf. ab. 545.7. The Elder at al. study has not been published.

26. H. H. Newman, F. N. Freeman, and K. J. Holzinger, *Twins: A Study of Heredity and Environment* (Chicago, IL: University of Chicago Press, 1937), 356.

27. N. L. Segal and J. H. Stohs, "Age at First Intercourse in Twins Reared Apart: Genetic Influence and Life History Events," *Personality and Individual Differences* 47, no. 2 (2009): 127–32.

28. A. Campo-Arias et al., "Factores asociados con el inicio temprano de relaciones sexuales en estudiantes adolescentes de un colegio de Bucaramanga, Colombia" ("Factors Associated with the Early Onset of Sexual Intercourse in Adolescent Students at a School in Bucaramanga, Colombia"), *Revista Colombiana de Psiquiatria* 33, no. 4 (2004): 367–77; G. A. Ceballos and A. Campo-Arias, "Sexual Intercourse Among Adolescent Students of Santa Marta, Colombia: A Cross-sectional Survey," *Colombia Médica* 38, no. 3 (2007): 191–96.

Chapter 8: Another World

1. K. T. Krizek, J. Horning, and A. El-Genedity, "Perceptions of Accessibility to Neighbourhood Retail and Other Public Services," in *Accessibility Analysis and Transport Planning: Challenges for Europe and North America*, ed. K. T. Geurs, K. J. Krizek, and A. Reggianai (Cheltenham, UK: Edward Elgar, 2012), 96–117.
2. N. L. Segal, *Born Together—Reared Apart: The Landmark Minnesota Twin Study* (Cambridge, MA: Harvard University Press, 2012).
3. J. H. Fowler, L. A. Baker, and C. T. Dawes, "Genetic Variation in Political Participation," *American Political Science Review* 102, no. 2 (2008): 233–48; R. D. Arvey et al., "The Determinants of Leadership Role Occupancy: Genetic and Personality Factors," *The Leadership Quarterly* 17, no. 1 (2006): 1–20; J. Scourfield et al., "The Development of Prosocial Behaviour in Children and Adolescents: A Twin Study," *Journal of Child Psychology and Psychiatry* 45, no. 5 (2006): 927–35.
4. Segal, *Born Together—Reared Apart*.
5. I. Morgan and K. Rose, "How Genetic Is School Myopia?" *Progress in Retinal and Eye Research* 24, no. 1 (2005): 1–38.
6. "Your Premature Baby's Appearance," Raising Children Network, May 13, 2016, http://raisingchildren.net.au/articles/premature_baby_appearance .html/context/1403.
7. K. Cathey, *Colombia* (London: Kuperard, 2014).
8. "Translocation Down Syndrome," *University of Rochester Medical Center Health Encyclopedia*, 2017, https://www.urmc.rochester.edu/encyclopedia /content.aspx?ContentTypeID=90&ContentID=P02153.
9. V. Prasher, "Comparison of Physical and Psychiatric Status in Individuals with Translocation and Trisomy 21 Down Syndrome," *Down Syndrome Research and Practice* 3, no. 1 (1995): 9–13.
10. N. L. Segal, "Laboratory Findings: Not Twin, Twins, Not Twins," *Twin Research & Human Genetics* 9, no. 2 (2006): 303–8.
11. N. L. Segal, *Someone Else's Twin: The True Story of Babies Switched at Birth* (Amherst, NY: Prometheus, 2011).
12. M. J. Russell, T. Mendelson, and H. V. Peeke, "Mothers' Identification of Their Infant's Odors," *Ethology and Sociobiology* 4, no. 1 (1983): 29–31.

13. B. Schaal, "Presumed Olfactory Exchanges Between Mother and Neonate in Humans," in *Ethology and Psychology*, ed. J. Le Camus and J. Cosnier (Toulouse, France: Privat-IEC, 1986), 101–10.

14. S. Nishitani et al., "Maternal Prefrontal Cortex Activation by Newborn Infant Odors," *Chemical Senses* 39, no. 3 (2014): 195–202; E. Hoekzema et al., "Pregnancy Leads to Long-Lasting Changes in Human Brain Structure," *Nature Neuroscience* 20 (2016): 287–96, doi: 10.1038/nn.4458.

15. J. Selwyn and S. Meakings, " 'She Just Didn't Smell Right!' Odour and Adoptive Family Life," *Adoption & Fostering* 39, no. 4 (2015): 294–302.

16. M. Kaitz, A. M. Rokem, and A. I. Eidelman, "Infants' Face-Recognition by Primiparous and Multiparous Women," *Perceptual and Motor Skills* 67, no. 2 (1988): 495–502.

17. D. Formby, "Maternal Recognition of Infant's Cry," *Developmental Medicine & Child Neurology* 9, no. 3 (1967): 293–98; M. Kaitz et al., "Parturient Women Can Recognize Their Infants by Touch," *Developmental Psychology* 28, no. 1 (1992): 35–39.

18. Segal, *Someone Else's Twin*.

19. Segal, *Someone Else's Twin*.

20. M. Santora, "Rolling DNA Labs Address the Ultimate Question: 'Who's Your Daddy?' " *New York Times*, November 8, 2016, A24.

Chapter 9: Different Versions of the Same Song

1. P. Watson, *Twins: An Uncanny Relationship?* (Chicago: Contemporary Books, 1981); T. J. Bouchard, Jr., et al., "Sources of Human Psychological Differences: The Minnesota Study of Twins Reared Apart," *Science* 250, no. 4978 (1990): 223–28.

2. P. Nugent, "Self-Esteem," *Psychology Dictionary*, April 13, 2013, http:// psychologydictionary.org/self-esteem/. The Rosenberg Self-Esteem Survey (RSES) was developed in 1989 by Professor Morris Rosenberg at the University of Maryland. Sample items are "I feel that I have a number of good qualities," and "I feel I do not have much to be proud of." People taking the survey either "strongly agree," "agree," "disagree," or "strongly disagree" with each statement.

3. R. F. Baumeister et al., "Does High Self-Esteem Cause Better Performance, Interpersonal Success, Happiness, or Healthier Lifestyles?" *Psychological Science in the Public Interest* 4, no. 1 (2003): 1–44; M. B. Donnellan et al., "Low Self-Esteem Is Related to Aggression, Antisocial Behavior, and Delinquency," *Psychological Science* 16, no. 4 (2005): 328–35; U. Orth, R. W. Robins, and B. W. Roberts, "Low Self-Esteem Prospectively Predicts Depression in Adolescence and Young Adulthood," *Journal of Personality and Social Psychology* 95, no. 3 (2008): 695–708.

4. N. L. Segal, "Personality Similarity in Unrelated Look-Alike Pairs: Addressing a Twin Study Challenge," *Personality and Individual Differences* 54, no. 1 (2013): 23–28.

5. D. P. Schmitt and J. Allik, "Simultaneous Administration of the Rosenberg Self-Esteem Scale in 53 Nations: Exploring the Universal and Culture-Specific Features of Global Self-Esteem. *Journal of Personality and Social Psychology* 89, no. 4 (2005): 623–42.

6. R. D. Arvey et al., "Job Satisfaction: Environmental and Genetic Components," *Journal of Applied Psychology* 74, no. 2 (1989): 187–92; R. D. Arvey and B. P. McCall et al., "Genetic Influences on Job Satisfaction and Work Values," *Personality and Individual Differences* 17, no. 1 (1994): 21–33.

7. J. S. Peper et al., "Genetic Influences on Human Brain Structure: A Review of Brain Imaging Studies in Twins," *Human Brain Mapping* 28, no. 6 (2007): 464–73; J. N. Giedd, J. E. Schmitt, and M. C. Neale, "Structural Brain Magnetic Resonance Imaging of Pediatric Twins," *Human Brain Mapping* 28, no. 6 (2007): 474–81; M. A. Lodato, M. B. Woodworth, L. Semin, G. D. Evrony, B. K. Mehta, A. Karger, S. Lee et al., "Somatic Mutation in Single Human Neurons Tracks Developmental and Transcriptional History." *Science* 350, no. 6256 (2015): 94–98; R. Plomin et al., *Behavioral Genetics*, 7th ed. (New York: Worth, 2017); R. Plomin and J. C. DeFries, "Genetics and Intelligence: Recent Data," *Intelligence* 4, no. 1 (1980): 15–24.

8. C. Cliffordson and J. E. Gustafsson, "Effects of Age and Schooling on Intellectual Performance: Estimates Obtained from Analysis of Continuous Variation in Age and Length of Schooling," *Intelligence* 36, no. 2 (2008): 143–52; H. H. Newman, F. N. Freeman, and K. J. Holzinger, *Twins: A Study of Heredity and Environment* (Chicago: University of Chicago Press, 1937).

9. C. N. Brinch and T. A. Galloway, "Schooling in Adolescence Raises IQ Scores," *Proceedings of the National Academy of Sciences* 109, no. 2 (2012): 425–30; I. J. Deary and W. Johnson, "Intelligence and Education: Causal Perceptions Drive Analytic Processes and Therefore Conclusions," *International Journal of Epidemiology* 39, no. 5 (2010): 1362–69.

10. N. L. Segal and S. L. Hershberger, "Virtual Twins and Intelligence: Updated and New Analyses of Within-Family Environmental Influences," *Personality and Individual Differences* 39 (2005): 1061–73.

11. G. P. Aylward, "Cognitive and Neuropsychological Outcomes: More Than IQ Scores," *Mental Retardation and Developmental Disabilities Research Reviews* 8, no. 4 (2002): 234–40; R. S. Wilson, "Twin Growth: Initial Deficit, Recovery and Trends in Concordance from Birth to Nine Years," *Human Biology* 6 (1979): 205–20; C. Amiel-Tison and L. Gluck, "Fetal Brain and Pulmonary Adaptation in Multiple Pregnancy," in *Multiple Pregnancy: Epidemiology, Gestation and Perinatal Outcome*, ed. L.G. Keith, E. Papiernik, D.M. Keith and B. Luke (New York: Parthenon, 1995), 585–97.

12. R. S. Witte and J. S. Witte, *Statistics*, 7th ed. (Danvers, MA: John Wiley, 2004).

13. E. Turkheimer et al, "Socioeconomic Status Modifies Heritability of IQ in Young Children," *Psychological Science* 14, no. 6 (2003): 623–28; E. Turkheimer and E. E. Horn, "Interactions Between Socioeconomic Status and

Components of Variation in Cognitive Ability," in *Behavior Genetics of Cognition Across the Lifespan (Advances in Behavior Genetics)*, ed. D. Finkel and C. A. Reynolds (New York: Springer, 2014), 41–68.

14. C. R. Reynolds and J. A. Hickman, *DAP:IQ: Draw-A-Person Intellectual Ability Test* (Dallas: Pro-Ed, 2004).

15. S. O. Lilienfeld, J. M. Wood, and H. N. Garb, "The Scientific Status of Projective Techniques," *Psychological Science in the Public Interest* 1, no. 2 (2000): 27–66.

16. R. Arden et al., "Genes Influence Young Children's Human Figure Drawings and Their Association with Intelligence a Decade Later," *Psychological Science* 25, no. 10 (2014): 1843–50; K. Imuta et al., "Drawing a Close to the Use of Human Figure Drawings as a Projective Measure of Intelligence," *PloS ONE* 8, no. 3 (2013): e58991; E. Willcock, K. Imuta, and H. Hayne, "Children's Human Figure Drawings Do Not Measure Intellectual Ability," *Journal of Experimental Child Psychology* 110, no. 3 (2011): 444–52.

Chapter 10: "Twin-Bred" Cultures

1. D. T. Lykken and A. Tellegen, "Is Human Mating Adventitious or the Result of Lawful Choice? A Twin Study of Mate Selection," *Journal of Personality and Social Psychology* 65, no. 1 (1993): 56–68; N. L. Segal, *Indivisible by Two: Lives of Extraordinary Twins* (Cambridge, MA: Harvard University Press, 2005). A few more recent studies have, however, found somewhat greater similarity in some behaviors and attitudes between identical twins' spouses than between fraternal twins' spouses, although the resemblance is small to moderate; see, for example, C. Kandler et al., "Left or Right? Sources of Political Orientation: The Roles of Genetic Factors, Cultural Transmission, Assortative Mating, and Personality," *Journal of Personality and Social Psychology* 102, no. 3 (2012): 633–45.

2. N. L. Segal, *Entwined Lives: Twins and What They Tell Us About Human Behavior* (New York: Plume, 2000).

3. Segal, *Indivisible by Two*.

4. M. C. Ashton and K. Lee, "A Theoretical Basis for the Major Dimensions of Personality," *European Journal of Personality* 15 (2001): 327–53; K. Lee and M. C. Ashton, "Psychometric Properties of the HEXACO-100," *Assessment* (July 13, 2016): DOI: 10.1177/1073191116659134. Emotionality shares some features with the Big Five trait of neuroticism (e.g., anxiety) but lacks its anger-related content. It also shares some sentimentality-related characteristics with the Big Five trait of agreeableness. M. C. Ashton, K. Lee, and R. E. De Vries, "The HEXACO Honesty-Humility, Agreeableness, and Emotionality Factors: A Review of Research and Theory," *Personality and Social Psychology Review* 18, no. 2 (2014): 139–52.

5. L. Veselka et al., "A Behavioral Genetic Study of Relationships Between Humor Styles and the Six HEXACO Personality Factors," *Europe's Journal of Psychology* 6, no. 3 (2010): 9–33.

Chapter 11: Twins, Pairs and Pedigrees

1. N. L. Segal, *Indivisible by Two: Lives of Extraordinary Twins* (Cambridge, MA: Harvard University Press, 2005); Dale S. Wright, *The Six Perfections: Buddhism and the Cultivation of Character* (Oxford: Oxford University Press, 2009).
2. N. L. Segal, *Born Together—Reared Apart: The Landmark Minnesota Twin Study* (Cambridge, MA: Harvard University Press, 2012); Reuters, "Candidate Admits Using Twin as Stand-In," *Banderas (Puerto Vallarta, Mexico) News*, July 6, 2005, http://www.banderasnews.com/0504/nw-twincastros .htm.
3. "Colombia—Military Personnel," Global Security, https://www.globalsecurity .org/military/world/colombia/personnel.htm.
4. N. G. Waller et al., "Genetic and Environmental Influences on Religious Interests, Attitudes, and Values: A Study of Twins Reared Apart and Together," *Psychological Science* 1, no. 2 (1990): 138–42; L. B. Koenig et al., "Genetic and Environmental Influences on Religiousness: Findings for Retrospective and Current Religiousness Ratings," *Journal of Personality* 73, no. 2 (2005): 471–88.
5. Segal, *Indivisible by Two.*
6. Segal, *Born Together—Reared Apart.*
7. N. Aghababaei et al., "Honesty-Humility and the HEXACO Structure of Religiosity and Well-Being," *Current Psychology* 35, no. 3 (2016): 421–26.
8. C. L. Park, "Religion as a Meaning-Making Framework in Coping with Life Stress," *Journal of Social Issues* 61, no. 4 (2005): 707–29.

Chapter 12: Band of Brothers

1. J. Mitchell, "Circle Game," *Ladies of the Canyon* (New York, NY: Siquomb Publishing Company, 1970).
2. Attorneys Carlos Medellín and his nephew, Pablo, during interviews conducted in their law offices, April 2015 and July 2016.

Index

OTHER BOOKS BY NANCY L. SEGAL

Entwined Lives:
Twins and What They Tell Us About Human Behavior

Indivisible by Two:
Lives of Extraordinary Twins

Someone Else's Twin:
The True Story of Babies Switched at Birth

Born Together-Reared Apart:
The Landmark Minnesota Twin Study

Twin Mythconceptions:
False Beliefs, Fables, and Fact About Twins

Please visit Nancy Segal's website for new reviews,
documents, photographs, and other information about
Accidental Brothers as these items become available:
http://drnancysegaltwins.org/accidental-brothers

Chapter 6: Finding the Colombian Four

1. "Crossed Lives: Two Pairs of Twins Were Separated for 25 Years," Caracol TV (Colombia, South America), October 26, 2014, http://www.noticiascaracol .com/septimo-dia/vidas-cruzadas-dos-parejas-de-gemelos-estuvieron -separadas-25-anos. Caracol Internacional is also available in nearly eighty countries across five continents, but the twins' story was not widely distributed.

2. N. L. Segal, *Someone Else's Twin: The True Story of Babies Switched at Birth* (Amherst, NY: Prometheus, 2011).

3. "Separate Twins Shall Face Legal Battle to be Compensated: Lawyer," Caracol TV (Colombia, South America), October 26, 2014, http://www.noti ciascaracol.com/septimo-dia/gemelos-separados-deberan-librar-batalla -juridica-para-ser-indemnizados-abogado.

4. N. L. Segal and F. A. Cortez, "Born in Korea—Adopted Apart: Behavioral Development of Monozygotic Twins Raised in the United States and France," *Personality and Individual Differences* 70 (November 2014): 97–104; P. Pope-noe, "Twins Reared Apart," *Journal of Heredity* 13, no. 3 (1922): 142–44; N. L. Segal, J. H. Stohs, and K. Evans, "Chinese Twin Children Reared Apart and Reunited: First Prospective Study of Co-Twin Reunions," *Adoption Quarterly* 14, no. 1 (2011): 61–78.

5. Titus Maccius Plautus, *Menaechemi* (The Menaechmus Brothers), play, Archive of Performances of Greek and Roman Drama, http://www.apgrd.ox .ac.uk/productions/canonical-plays/menaechmi-the-menaechmus-brothers /500. The play was first performed in 1486 at the Palazzo del Corte (Ferrera, Emilia-Romana, Italy).

6. J. Weber-Lehman et al., "Finding the Needle in the Haystack: Differentiating 'Identical' Twins in Paternity Testing and Forensics by Ultra-Deep Next Generation Sequencing," *Forensic Sciences International* 9 (March 2014): 42–46. This technique could also distinguish identical twin mothers from identical twin aunts, but the need to do this would be rare since only one is likely to be pregnant at a given time. A hypothetical exceptional case in which this could be valuable might involve an unwed identical twin mother who secretly relinquished a baby for adoption and contested her relationship to the child when the child tried to find her.

7. N. L. Segal, *Twin Mythconceptions: False Beliefs, Fables, and Facts About Twins* (San Diego: Elsevier, 2017).

8. N. L. Segal, *Entwined Lives: Twins and What They Tell Us About Human Behavior* (New York: Plume, 2000).

9. N. L. Segal and W. D. Marelich, "Social Closeness and Gift Giving by MZ and DZ Twin Parents Toward Nieces and Nephews: An Update," *Personality and Individual Differences* 50 (2011): 101–5; D. M. Buss, *Evolutionary Psychology: The New Science of the Mind*, 4th ed. (Boston: Allyn & Bacon, 2012).

10. Segal, *Born Together—Reared Apart*.

Chapter 6: Finding the Colombian Four

1. "Crossed Lives: Two Pairs of Twins Were Separated for 25 Years," Caracol TV (Colombia, South America), October 26, 2014, http://www.noticiascaracol .com/septimo-dia/vidas-cruzadas-dos-parejas-de-gemelos-estuvieron -separadas-25-anos. Caracol Internacional is also available in nearly eighty countries across five continents, but the twins' story was not widely distributed.

2. N. L. Segal, *Someone Else's Twin: The True Story of Babies Switched at Birth* (Amherst, NY: Prometheus, 2011).

3. "Separate Twins Shall Face Legal Battle to be Compensated: Lawyer," Caracol TV (Colombia, South America), October 26, 2014, http://www.noti ciascaracol.com/septimo-dia/gemelos-separados-deberan-librar-batalla -juridica-para-ser-indemnizados-abogado.

4. N. L. Segal and F. A. Cortez, "Born in Korea—Adopted Apart: Behavioral Development of Monozygotic Twins Raised in the United States and France," *Personality and Individual Differences* 70 (November 2014): 97–104; P. Popenoe, "Twins Reared Apart," *Journal of Heredity* 13, no. 3 (1922): 142–44; N. L. Segal, J. H. Stohs, and K. Evans, "Chinese Twin Children Reared Apart and Reunited: First Prospective Study of Co-Twin Reunions," *Adoption Quarterly* 14, no. 1 (2011): 61–78.

5. Titus Maccius Plautus, *Menaechemi* (The Menaechmus Brothers), play, Archive of Performances of Greek and Roman Drama, http://www.apgrd.ox .ac.uk/productions/canonical-plays/menaechmi-the-menaechmus-brothers /500. The play was first performed in 1486 at the Palazzo del Corte (Ferrera, Emilia-Romana, Italy).

6. J. Weber-Lehman et al., "Finding the Needle in the Haystack: Differentiating 'Identical' Twins in Paternity Testing and Forensics by Ultra-Deep Next Generation Sequencing," *Forensic Sciences International* 9 (March 2014): 42–46. This technique could also distinguish identical twin mothers from identical twin aunts, but the need to do this would be rare since only one is likely to be pregnant at a given time. A hypothetical exceptional case in which this could be valuable might involve an unwed identical twin mother who secretly relinquished a baby for adoption and contested her relationship to the child when the child tried to find her.

7. N. L. Segal, *Twin Mythconceptions: False Beliefs, Fables, and Facts About Twins* (San Diego: Elsevier, 2017).

8. N. L. Segal, *Entwined Lives: Twins and What They Tell Us About Human Behavior* (New York: Plume, 2000).

9. N. L. Segal and W. D. Marelich, "Social Closeness and Gift Giving by MZ and DZ Twin Parents Toward Nieces and Nephews: An Update," *Personality and Individual Differences* 50 (2011): 101–5; D. M. Buss, *Evolutionary Psychology: The New Science of the Mind*, 4th ed. (Boston: Allyn & Bacon, 2012).

10. Segal, *Born Together—Reared Apart*.